"As a father of young girls, I covet tl
into their lives. This book not only
so in such a relational way that y(
tored by a friend as you read it."
    – Pastor Roger Viksnes, Senior Pastor of Bethany Lutheran Church
    in East Hartland, CT

"I wish I could have had something similar to help me through my teen
years. Perhaps it would have prevented me having to learn some things
the hard way, especially when it comes to boyfriend/girlfriend relationships. I pray that it will make its way into the hearts of a multitude of young
ladies. Thank you for following the Lord's leading in taking on this project."
    – Rebecca (Becky) Swensen, NC Regional Coordinator of
    Student Exchange Program

It was a book filled with a myriad of emotions by the author which easily
was transferred to the reader. I found it easy to read and understand;
while at the same time, the author was able to convey deep thinking.
Clearly the target audience will grasp her teaching. While intended to
reach a younger reader than myself, it quickly became apparent that the
stories so well presented through great humor and tears, would tran-
scend all ages ... also both genders. The questions and scripture verses,
if answered honestly, were thought provoking.
In summation, this book will inspire those who read it to a better understanding of themselves in relationship to God our Father. In full disclosure,
I know and love the author and those written of in the book, so perhaps
I have an extra dimension of understanding with reference to the individuals written about. I laughed out loud and shed a tear or two. I found
myself in many of her situations. The author has uncovered her deepest
emotion to help better others who read this book."
    – Anne Marie Olsen, amazing mother and grandmother –
    and good friend with "skills"

As a teenager, I could connect to so many of the events and stories
in this devotional, in seeing how real life circumstances relate to what
God expects of us. Young girls like me will learn what it means to represent our Creator every day. This book is something I recommend to
any girl looking to grow closer to Christ or to simply learn how to live in
God's Light.
    – Emma Abrahamsen, sixteen-year-old high school student
    and guinea pig

Lessons Learned Climbing Trees

Sharon Joy Hansen

Xulon Press

Xulon Press
2301 Lucien Way #415
Maitland, FL 32751
407.339.4217
www.xulonpress.com

Unless otherwise indicated, Scripture quotations taken from the Holy Bible, New International Version (NIV). Copyright © 1973, 1978, 1984, 2011 by Biblica, Inc.™. Used by permission. All rights reserved.

Scripture quotations taken from the English Standard Version (ESV). Copyright © 2001 by Crossway, a publishing ministry of Good News Publishers. Used by permission. All rights reserved.

Scripture quotations taken from the King James Version (KJV)–*public domain.*

Printed in the United States of America.

ISBN-13: 978-1-5456-7253-2

Introduction

We are told today in so many subtle and not so subtle ways, that God didn't mean *exactly* what He said in the Bible, or worse – that the "theory" of God is irrelevant. Satan asked Adam and Eve at the very onset of time, "Did God *really* say…?" (*Genesis 3:1*) Commercials on TV, articles in magazines, friends and family tell us to look out for "number one" because we're "worth it." Movies and weekly television shows promote all kinds of behaviors that are not what God had in mind for us when He created us. The immediate gratification of healthy God-given urges become sin and remorse as they are distorted into something unhealthy or ugly that they were never meant to be. For a few fleeting moments of happiness we give up true peace, joy and love. Satan has a way of starting out with each of God's amazing gifts and twisting them into pathetic imitations of the real things. He is never original and he is "the father of lies." So, what are we thinking? Why do we keep falling for his schemes? We need to get into God's Word, discover truth, and apply it to our lives. We have drifted so far from the path that God created for us to walk, the one that leads to true joy! And like the proverbial frog in the pot of water on the stove who doesn't notice the slow increase in temperature, we are just as surely boiling to death.

Being one of three sisters and the mother of three daughters I wrote this book primarily for high school and college aged girls, though I welcome anyone to read it. I wrote a weekly devotional workbook because I thought this might be a good way to get together once a week daughter with mother – or friends in homes, youth group or Sunday school – to talk about important topics and to discuss what the Bible has to say about them. I am an authority only on my own story; God's Word covers the rest. This is a devotional study looking at His Word in relation to everyday life's struggles and concerns. I have used this twice with great results in my own high school girls' Sunday School classes. It took us through two years each time. It's not always easy to broach certain topics with a mom, a daughter, or a friend; so I've tried to touch on many of the more common sources of conflict in life in order to open doors of thought and discussion for you. And if reading through this with another person, I highly encourage you to share incidents in your own life that are similar to these in my life. Whether you read this alone, with Mom, or with your friends, one word answers to these questions will not be nearly as beneficial as really opening up and examining the issues. Don't be afraid to be honest with someone you can trust. And remember: there's no such thing as a dumb question. Okay, so maybe there are a couple of dumb ones out there but I'm sure that doesn't include any of yours!

Meanwhile, I really did learn a lot during my tree-climbing years – and much of it sitting in branches high above the world where I had a direct line to the Father! I consider those hours some of the best of my life and often wish I could spend as much time now atop a tree.

TREES

I think that I shall never see
A (book) as lovely as a tree

A tree whose hungry mouth is pressed
Against the earth's sweet flowing breast;

A tree that looks at God all day
And lifts her leafy arms to pray,

A tree that may in summer wear
A nest of robins in her hair

Upon whose bosom snow has lain;
Who intimately lives with rain.

(Books) are made by fools like me
But only God can make a tree.

Joyce Kilmer

In loving memory of

"Mimi"
my mother and my best friend
who loved me in spite of me

&

David
my cousin and friend
who listened to these stories
and encouraged me —
when I was supposed to be there
to encourage him.

Special thanks goes to Miles and Debra Muzio and Pastor Gary and Anne Kitchin, Debra Abrahamsen, Kristina Geraghty, and Beth Langlois, for encouragement in the early stages of this book; and to Pastor Roger Viksnes, Anne Marie Olsen, Becky Swensen, and Emma Abrahamsen for their editing advice and for their kind thoughts and input into how I could make this book better. Thank you to my high school girls' Sunday School classes (Melanie, Mariah, Ellie, Kyah, Ali, Avery, Ana, Emma, Juliana, Maggie and Emma-Leah) for letting me use them as guinea pigs. And special mention to Mary Beth Carlson for sweet encouragement and to Pastor Larry Burd for being used of God to give me and my husband the final push. Thank you to my husband for letting me zone out from time to time in the writing process and not feeling slighted.

Original Cover Design by Brita Skaret. Thank you so much for your talented design and for your patience.

The highest praise and thanks goes to my heavenly Father for being such a constant Presence in my life and for allowing me to share stories from my life along with stories from the Bible to inspire young women to learn to know Him better and to walk in His ways. God's blessings!

WEEK 1

"Get smart!"

"**W**arning, Will Robinson! Warning!" That frantic cry, along with mechanical arms flailing about wildly, was enough to get the adrenalin surging through my veins (or wherever it surges). The speaker was an absurdly cool robot who was trying to protect his young charge, a boy who all too frequently ignored those warnings. But would Will listen this time? I held my breath... It would have been the smart thing to do... But somewhere deep inside I didn't want Will Robinson to listen. The show would not have been nearly as exciting if he had. This was *Lost In Space*, one of the earlier science fiction shows to grace television in the 1960's. And once again Will did not listen, so my hopes were realized and we were off on another adventure!

I always loved a good adventure. My earliest memory of a real-life adventure was a devastating hurricane that ripped through Connecticut in the mid 1950's. I was four years old and was hidden behind the big comfy chair in the living room right below a window where I could watch the action without interruption. Rain was falling in hypnotic sheets that seemed to curl and uncurl like a giant wet flag slowly billowing right before my eyes. Lightning was flashing, followed by what seemed to be the poorly timed sound it made. The thunder with all its inherent authority charged my very insides to reverberate in time and to pulse with its power. I knew that something very powerful was behind it all, and I sensed an interested or at least a sentient Presence.

Then it happened, right outside my window! The streak of lightning and the sound of its arrival happened almost simultaneously! It was formidable! I watched as the big old tree in our back yard

1

gave off a sharp crack and a quick flash of fire. Then, in slow motion, half of the tree fell gracefully to the ground as if bowing in its ultimate respect for this unseen Power. The house rumbled in agreement. "Wow! How cool was that?" I asked myself. I pragmatically considered the chance of ever climbing that tree again. Chances were slim at best, but I'd check it out later.

So what is it about danger that attracts us? (granted, some more than others) I loved to go right to the edge and get a good look at it. I was smart enough to have a line that I wouldn't cross, but in retrospect I think that line should have been pulled in a bit because there were many times that Providence alone saved my skin. I should have many more scars to show for my adventures.

The hurricane left a big mess in its wake. My town was on high ground and pretty safe, but a nearby town had water up to the second floor of its downtown buildings! Roads below were washed out, and a helicopter was brought in to bring someone to the hospital. For just a moment I wished that I was the one in that helicopter. ... I was a kid and didn't really think that one through.

So, what are the typical reactions to something like this storm? Fear of physical danger, fear of loss, fear of loud noises, desire to warn or to help? In spite of the wide variety of possible reactions I think the intrigue of that enigma called *danger* is "in there" to some degree in each one, heightening these instincts and desires with the fear of the unknown. But why wasn't I afraid? I remember thinking it was all pretty cool. I had almost no fear, only a patient spectator's anticipation of what might happen next. I was thrilled beyond words with this display of what I had already recognized as a supernatural Power. What was it about the storm, about danger, that drew me in? Perhaps I was just too young (or too dumb) to think through the possible outcomes. Could it be that I felt indestructible, that nothing could hurt me? Or... maybe I just enjoyed the adrenalin rush I felt when I witnessed danger up close and personal.

Describe a time when you were frightened and felt you were in real danger.

What does God tell us to do when we are afraid?

> If you_make the Most High your dwelling–even the Lord, who is my refuge–then no harm will befall you, no disaster will come near your tent. Psalm 91:9-10
> So do not fear, for I am with you; do not be dismayed, for I am your God. I will strengthen you and help you; I will uphold you with my righteous right hand. Isaiah 41:10

Other than natural disasters, what are some real dangers facing young people today?

Have you ever intentionally done anything dangerous and maybe a little dumb? Discuss.

What was the attraction? the thrill of danger? peer pressure? something else?

What does God tell us to do when facing dangerous situations?

> The prudent see danger and take refuge, but the simple keep going and suffer for it. Proverbs 27:12
> Finally, be strong in the Lord and in his mighty power. Ephesians 6:10

What is this thing, this crazy, ever-present attraction between human beings and danger? Even at the very beginning of *Genesis*, Eve *must* have sensed the danger in her choice when Satan tempted her. Not only did she disobey, but she went on to lie about it! And this seems to have been passed on through the generations, because each of us displays evidence of this same genetic disorder to some degree when faced with danger, from a mildly elevated pulse in its earliest stages to a full-blown case of the disease complete with all of its symptoms. Even in the eyes of the most apprehensive young novice may be seen a gleam of excitement as she catches her breath vicariously participating while watching others play with danger. Or there's the seasoned expert whose appetite for danger never seems to be quenched. She is continually looking for the next extreme sport, adventure, or "high." How else can she continue to go to the very edge tempting God Himself to spoil her fun?

Why is it that the lower members of the animal kingdom, those not made in the image of God – those not endowed with the ability to thoughtfully reason, to artistically create or to hopefully

3

imagine – are so much smarter in this than we are? Animals are smart enough to avoid danger. We stay and watch and even choose to enter into the competition. Competition – is that what entices us so? And physical danger is not the only version of this game. There are so many emotional varieties of this game to be played with little or no concern for the danger that lies ahead for both self and others. Hearts can be broken as surely as bones. But what can we do?

We don't always think of the God of the Bible being in touch with our lives today. The stories in the Bible just don't seem to relate to us. They're about heroes and "dragons" and miracles – great stories of a time long ago. God doesn't talk out loud to many of us through a burning bush like He did to Moses; and what do we know about livestock or grain which are often mentioned in the law and in parables – unless we're from the Midwest? When is the last time any of us saw water turned into wine? And how many of us today have put our very lives on the line for our faith?

Still, it seems that God was very much aware of our future struggles, thoughts, desires and foibles when He had His prophets and disciples write down His words in the Bible. Think about Cain's *jealousy* toward his brother; the *verbal abuse* Noah probably took for building a giant ark on a dry earth that had yet to see rain; the *fear* Abraham showed when, just to protect himself, he had his wife (twice!) tell those *white lies* saying she was his sister; Sarah's *doubt* when she laughed at the angels' message of her giving birth in her old age; Joseph's *thoughtlessness* when he spoke to his big brothers about his dreams of ruling over them; Jacob's *deceitfulness* when he stole his brother's birthright and blessing; the *rumors* Mary and Joseph must have faced with her pregnancy; Thomas's *need for proof* when he saw the resurrected Jesus; Peter's *cowardice* when he denied Christ three times; and Paul's *remorse* over his past life before his conversion. Do you see yourself in any of these people? These stories could be happening right now! Each one of these men and women faced a type of danger related to the choices they made, most (not all) with self-interest as a big motivation.

4

I could add to the list above, but I think we can agree that there are some pretty typical shortcomings conspicuous in many of these otherwise heroic individuals or in those around them. Their stories were written down to help us as we face similar situations. Astoundingly average people can do some amazing things when they are smart enough to let God call the shots in their lives. Most of the men and women mentioned above were able to get past their own sins or the sins being directed at them to do some pretty significant things for God later on in spite of times of failure or trial.

The Bible is loaded with useful advice if we just look for it. God sometimes covers for us when we get mixed up with danger, but not always. Sometimes we get hurt … and sometimes we hurt others. He wants us to use His Word, the leading of the Holy Spirit, and the bright minds He has given to each of us to make wise decisions, especially as young people. And it's never too late to start! Be calm. Be cool. And be smart!

Bible Reading: *Genesis 3:1-13*
What was the real danger here?
How does Eve distort what God said to her?
How does Satan lie outright about God's warning?
What are the temptations that faced Eve?
Why do you think she invited her husband into the sin?
How did their relationship with God change?
Why did they pass blame?
What were the consequences? (verse 23)

Challenge: Think about some of the wisdom and warnings from the stories of these Bible heroes above when you next face danger or a tough decision. And be smart!

"For God hath not given us the spirit of fear, but of power, and of love and of a sound mind!"
2 Timothy 1:7 (KJV)

WEEK 2

"Skeletons in the closet"

I was three or four standing at the top of the stairs outside the upstairs bedrooms in our cape style house. The next minute I was belly-whomping head-first down those stairs. I reached the bottom with several slight bruises but not actually hurt that much considering. Did you ever notice how little kids seem to have a built-in "anti-what-really-ought–to-have-happened" mechanism that kicks in and keeps them unharmed in situations like this in which adults would wind up either dead or at least hospitalized for weeks?

This was the first time I can remember thinking that perhaps my older sister didn't fully appreciate me as much as she might have. Hey! What was not to like? Yet it was my big sister who had just pushed me down the stairs! Okay, it *was* out of character. Considering this was not a regularly occurring event, maybe it was not all that unheard of as far as the general population of siblings out there goes. Maybe it was temporary insanity, a scientific test, a juvenile lapse in judgment, or possibly even an accident? I probably deserved it. I was anything but perfect.

I'd like to be able to tell you that this had been an isolated sign of discord and that after discovering that an alien had taken over my sister's body forcing her against her will to commit this heinous crime, and that after subsequently managing to free her from its hold, we were the best of friends for the rest of our lives ... but that wouldn't exactly be true. Oh, we loved each other *for sure*, but we were the youngest of five siblings and we did not always get along that well.

There was the time that I locked myself in the bathroom while my angry sister determined how best to get the door open or off the hinges to get to me. I can't even remember what initiated this, but to be sure I had done something reprehensible. I'm not sure what I thought would happen, but fearing for body and limb (though we had never resorted to physical blows before, during, or after this event), I pretended to have taken a bottle of aspirin and lay on the bathroom floor with the open bottle next to me. You've got to admit – this was pretty creative, and yes, a little bit dumb too. When she gained entrance to the room, there I was apparently dying. I had counted on her heart of mush to see me through this one. And it worked! She entered in fierce anger, hesitated in momentary confusion, ran to my aid in genuine concern, and hugged me in sisterly love. After she got over the fact that I had duped her, we discussed how sorry we were and the two of us, arm in arm, walked about a mile to the grocery store where our mother was working to confess the whole sordid affair to her. We waited on a little bench outside in absolute contrition until she was able to listen to our tale. We assured her that we really did love each other.

As preteens while I was still smaller than my older sister, I was frequently the recipient of verbal zings and slights from her to which I couldn't yet adequately respond. After one particularly harsh episode I intentionally put a very slight cut with a pair of scissors in my sister's new pants, right at the knee. (If she's reading this, this might be news to her. Too late to apologize?) I was immediately sorry – I am *still* feeling guilty! However, "the die was cast." I hid in the laundry chute halfway between the first floor bathroom and the basement until I heard her give up looking for me. It was tough with my back against one side of the chute and my knees against the other, trying to keep from falling into the laundry basket below! But hide-and-seek was my forte.

For many years after that we were able to get along simply because we rarely crossed each others' paths. (I also grew taller than she was which may have helped.) Sure, we shared the same home, but my sister was the princess who was popular and pretty and I was the tomboy who was ... neither. Now don't get the wrong impression here. I would have hated sympathy because I truly never desired popularity or prettiness. I was unimpressed with the payoff. So I wasn't exactly struggling with this. Since my sister and I didn't have common ground upon which to compete, things were pretty quiet for a long time. I joined the debate team in high school and proved myself capable on later occasions of "nailing her to the wall" verbally. I hate to admit it, but I probably enjoyed it. Payback, I guess. Shame on me. So we each went our separate ways side by side.

> Describe something you've done that you immediately wished undone.
> Do you have siblings or friends with whom you have competed or struggled to get along?
> Have you ever been hurt by a sister, a brother, a friend? Have you hurt them?
> Were you able to forgive them? to ask for forgiveness?
> What do you think God's Word has to say about getting along?
> > *If it is possible, as far as it depends on you, live at peace with everyone. Romans 12:18*
> > *Make every effort to live in peace with all men and to be holy. Hebrews 12:14*
> What do you think He has to say about forgiveness?
> > *Be kind and compassionate to one another, forgiving each other, just as in Christ God forgave you. Ephesians 4:32*
> > *... If your brother sins, rebuke him, and if he repents, forgive him. If he sins against you seven times a day, and seven times comes back to you and says, "I repent," forgive him. Luke 17:3-4*

There are some people who are really good at letting things go, at forgiving and forgetting. Corrie Ten Boom who was a prisoner in a German concentration camp during World War II was one. She forgave the men who were responsible for the cruel deaths of both her family and friends! "You will find it is necessary to let things go simply for the reason that they are too heavy!" was her admonition against bitterness. But many of us choose to carry difficult memories into the rest of our lives, never dealing with them. Living side by side with someone you love and avoiding what's keeping you from enjoying each other's friendship and company is a colossal waste of time and energy and a serious loss to both in terms of love and mutual support. Confession really is good for the soul. And forgiving someone *even if he/she neither deserves nor requests it* is what Christ does for us every day! On the other hand, our attempts to fix bruised or broken relationships will not necessarily be successful leading to a BFF (best friends forever) scenario. The human element is a wild card that can change any anticipated outcome. We can never be sure how another person will respond to our efforts to restore friendship. People are full of surprises!

Are you carrying old sibling or friendship wounds?
Have you tried to deal with them?
If not, what's keeping you from trying?
Are you afraid that your siblings might not forgive you …
or that they don't think they need to ask for your forgiveness?

The people we love will likely forgive us if we are sincere, but we need to ask. Forgiveness should never be taken for granted. You may have already forgiven someone without a request from them for forgiveness. Excellent! You may be waiting patiently or not so patiently for an apology. But are you sure they're even aware that they've hurt you? Sometimes we get hurt a little too easily and we get frustrated when others don't see the pain they've caused. We get upset with them, and they may have no clue! How dare they? You need to either let it go or go talk to them. You may be the one who is trying to make peace but your brother, sister, or friend will have nothing to do with it. Then you need to rest in the Lord because you have done what you can. Or you may be the one holding out, knowing full well what the situation is but unable to forgive or to ask for forgiveness. Think about it. Isn't it pride that keeps you in that unhappy place? Get over it! It's time.

Meanwhile, God's patience with us is beyond human reason. He has paid the price for our mistakes – past, present and future. He is waiting, offering us His healing forgiveness. All we have to do is to receive that gift! I don't know about you, but I need forgiveness every day. And just as we hope in Christ's forgiveness, we need to forgive others. It's an amazing thing to be loved by the living God. As a teen-ager I remember being blown away by the love and forgiveness of God and finding expression for it in the words of a song:

For Me

I saw the Lord look down one day from heaven's throne above.
I wondered how in me this God found anything to love.
His eyes were filled with tears; He seemed so sad.
The tears He shed were meant for me… for me.

It grieved me so to see Him cry; I couldn't bear the shame.
To think that though I'd let Him down, He loved me just the same.
I cried, "Forgive me, Lord. I've been so blind!
I couldn't see Your love for me… for me."

A smile shone forth which made me know I'd nothing now to fear.
My task was just to share this Love with everyone who'd hear.
My life was so complete; He saw my joy.
The Lord looked down in love for me… for me.

Bible Reading: *Matthew 18:21-35*

How many times are we to forgive someone?
Do we stop after that?
The king did more than delay the due date for the debt.
What more did he do?
Does that remind you of anyone else?
Was the forgiven servant thankful? What did he do?
Had he learned anything from the gift? What about you?
Why did the king change his mind about punishing his servant?

Challenge: Call your sisters/brothers/friends this week and tell them that you love them. Don't forget to mean it!

"And forgive us our debts as we also have forgiven our debtors."

Matthew 6:12

WEEK 3

"Scratchy sheets"

My home may have had its moments, but there were times when I became gratefully aware of how fortunate I was to live there. Like one memorable night I spent at a friend's house. Well, I didn't exactly spend the night and she was more of an acquaintance than a friend... Let me start over: My sister was spending the night with *her* friend and she (or more likely my mom) decided it would be a good idea for me stay with her friend's sister who was just a year older than me. I was not really into this adventure, but I think my sister may have been trying to help me assimilate into polite society. My awkward lack of social ambition may have been a little embarrassing. Who knows, perhaps it was sheer beneficence toward me? Anyway, this house was way out in the woods, probably four miles from mine. There was a small party going on in the darkly lit kitchen with a handful of what I considered to be sketchy adults. (i.e., I didn't know them.) My sister had disappeared and I was left to hang out with a girl I barely knew. She was a very nice girl, but I don't think she was exactly thrilled with the arrangement either. Such fun!

The night crawled on until it was time for bed. My roommate quickly fell fast asleep. The first thing I noticed was that the sheets were kind of different – scratchy. Then I listened to the strange sounds of the people down the hall. I tried to find my sister but had no idea where to look. So I decided to go on home to my own bed and my own scratchy sheets and my own night-time sounds. I got dressed and quietly sneaked past the kitchen and out the door. I walked up the wooded path to the state road and from there headed home through the state forest. It was pretty dark, but I wasn't nearly as nervous as I probably should have been. When I saw the lights of a car coming from behind me I ducked into the woods, doing the same thing when the car returned. I finally came to the row of houses that signified the center of town. One more mile to go!

Eventually I reached the safety of my own home, a relieved mother, and a well-deserved lecture. It seems that I had worried her and caused a lot of fuss all around. When she realized that I had been truly uncomfortable staying where I was, she forgave me and never encouraged me to break out socially again. The car had been sent to look for me as I had feared, but a phone call and an apology were enough to call off the search. I guess I was not the sleep-over kind of kid, at least not when I was out of my comfort zone. As an adolescent I was not inclined to put up with any uncomfortable situation if it seemed of little essential importance and if I could get out of it easily. I wasn't overly concerned with what people thought of me, so that helped. On the other hand, that kind of attitude may have hurt a few people's feelings along the way, which I eventually came to consider. And I might have wound up being a chronic quitter if I hadn't reigned in that tendency. Sometimes we miss an opportunity to grow when we run away.

Describe an uncomfortable situation that you have been in. What did you do about it? What should you have done?
What could I have tried before sneaking out?
What if there's nothing that can be done?
Do you have a tendency to avoid all things uncomfortable? Explain.

I have a good friend who grew up in another home where things were different from mine. There was a shadow of abuse in her childhood that repeatedly derailed her emerging sense of worth as a new Christian. More than once she told me how jealous she was of my heritage and testimony. It's funny because I was actually a little jealous of her testimony! I considered mine boring. When we became friends I had been a Christian long enough to know that sin is sin and that God doesn't much categorize one from another. So when she would lament over her past life and the memories she struggled with, I would remind her, "The Bible says that when we come before God 'all of our righteous acts are like *filthy rags.*' (*Isaiah 64:6*). You and I will approach the throne of God some day dressed *exactly* the same – '*clothed ... with Christ.*' (*Galatians 3:27*) " So you see, the past is powerless to bring us down once the old self has been crucified with Christ. (*Romans 6:6*) God's grace is (among many more awesome attributes) a great equalizer! How cool is that?

Don't ever fall into the trap of thinking that you're worse *or better* than someone else because of your background. As the martyr John Bradford said, "There, but for the grace of God, go I!" It could have so easily been different. Besides, it's not our past that matters – it's today, and it's tomorrow. The teacher in *Anne of Green Gables* said, "Today is a new day with no mistakes in it." We all need to start over from time to time and leave the past in the past. We need to learn to forgive others and to forgive ourselves.

I'm not exactly quiet but I was always surprised by the decibel level of the conversation in my friend's home. Yet I am and was even then fully aware that God loves people of all volumes equally. Some people are simply more outwardly emotional than others! She was just beginning that heritage of faith that she had so often expressed a longing for when we talked. And who knows what plans God had in mind for her – or for me for that matter? Maybe she thought that because my home was quieter we had no problems to talk over. Not so. Or maybe she wondered why Norwegians so often kept things stoically locked up inside, never bringing them into the air for healing. (Do you know how a Norwegian says "Hallelujah!"? Take a short breath in while whispering "jah" (pronounced "yah"). That's it. Dramatic, right? Stoic.) God wasn't done with either of us yet!

> Think about your *home* – too loud, too quiet, crazy, unhappy, angry, sad, uncomfortable?
> Do you wish you could change it? How?
> What are some things that *you* might be able to do to make changes?
> What's your life like lately? Do you struggle with regrets?

If you are suffering from *any* kind of abuse, talk to an adult you can trust.

Some come from a home where everyone seems to be screaming or fighting all the time. Considering that "the fruit of the Spirit is *love, joy, peace, patience, kindness, goodness, faithfulness, gentleness and self-control*" (*Galatians 5:22*), I would suggest that this is probably not what God has in mind for us. On the other hand, He would not want us to use the silent treatment on each other either! A balance is needed – talk, but don't get angry. I am sure that not one of our homes consistently reflects all of the characteristics given above. So don't get too discouraged or too cocky. We all need to renovate from time to time.

The home with the "rock concert" type of environment has this going for it: People are less apt to hold things in, so individuals have a pretty good idea if and why someone else might be upset with them. Chances might be decent for issues being aired and consequently resolved, even if at eardrum-piercing decibel levels. If it's a newly Christian home there is probably still a fresh passion to reach out and share the Good News with others. The down-side is that this home is possibly just learning how to stop producing scars and is probably lacking a deep knowledge of the Bible and its basic building blocks for developing good decision-making skills. Role models may be scarce. The fruits of the Spirit are beginning to bud, but they need time to mature. And they will! Be patient.

The "string quartet" home is usually a pretty healthy place in which to flourish but is so good at being good that it is possible that no one is comfortable expressing anything negative, making it easy for unspoken hurts and concerns to go unattended and to fester. If this is a long-time Christian home, faith may be taken for granted; and in the *extreme case* the desire to share God's love with others might not even be considered. In the healthy Christian home there is a source of wisdom available to tap into, solid role models, and a plethora of opportunities for encouragement to grow spiritually and to serve the Lord. This home is filled and overflowing with Spirit-fruit.

Point is – there is no one correct formula here for "the" Christian home. Many of us feel uncomfortable even in Christian homes that are only slightly unlike our own, but we need to remember that all of our homes are unique with qualities that reflect different backgrounds, personalities, and paths chosen for us by God! And some of us stand alone in non-Christian homes. God deals with individuals. After all – He made us, each with our own special set of histories, idiosyncrasies, and dreams. And if we let Him, He will help us to develop lifestyles honoring to Him and healthy for us in whatever type of home. Meanwhile each of us has something we would like to rewrite in our lives. It's that "thorn in the flesh" that Paul talks of in *2 Corinthians 12:7-9.*

Bible Reading: Forget the Bible heroes they eventually became. *At this point in time,* would you be favorably impressed with these people given their actions? Why or why not?

Abraham?	*(Genesis 12:11-13)*	*...Say you are my sister..."*
Moses?	*(Exodus 2:11-12)*	*"...he killed the Egyptian..."*
Rahab?	*(Joshua 2:1)*	*"...a prostitute... Rahab..."*
Joseph?	*(Genesis 37:5-9*	*"...your sheaves... bowed down..."*
Matthew?	*(Matthew 9:9-11)*	*"...tax collector's booth..."*
Mary Magdalene?	*(Luke 8:1-2)*	*"...seven demons... out..."*
James + John?	*(Mark 10:35-37)*	*"...let one of us sit at your right..."*
Paul?	*(Acts 9:1-2)*	*"...against the... disciples..."*

Do you come from a Christian or a non-Christian home?

What are some of its greatest blessings? challenges?

How do you think these things affect your self-image?

If you are struggling to feel comfortable somewhere, ask yourself why.

Is it legitimate or are you unfairly judging someone for being different from you?

It doesn't really matter what you think of others or what others think of you – *it doesn't even matter what you think of you!* Did you get that? *It doesn't even matter what you think of you!* We can be overly critical of others and sometimes we are even our own worst critics, down on ourselves to the point of inaction. Then our self-imposed uselessness feeds our self-criticism and the vicious cycle begins. God takes people from all backgrounds with all types of personalities, and He uses them in amazing ways to further His kingdom here on earth. They are called "the body of Christ." They each have special gifts and experiences that will help them to fulfill their roles within the body. Remember this the next time you are tempted to judge your Christian brother or sister or the next time someone messes with your mind making you feel less valuable than you really are. Christ died for YOU! You can't get any more valuable than that!

Challenge: Examine your behavior with people different from you. "What would Jesus do?"

> *"Forget the former things; do not dwell on the past. See, I am doing a new thing! Now it springs up; do you not perceive it?"*
> *Isaiah 43:18 -19*

WEEK 4

"The goldfish bowl"

My husband and I both come from big families – we're talkin' BIG. Together we have over eighty first cousins! Yikes! My mother was one of seven kids, my father one of five. My husband's mother was one of only two, but his father was one of fourteen! And his grandparents lived with them in their very small house! He shared a room with three brothers in what is now a small walk-in closet in the family home in Norway! They had only five bedrooms altogether counting the walk-in closet and the present dining room – and no indoor bathroom! (And we think our homes are crowded!) Though most of my husband's relatives lived in Norway, most of *my* aunts and uncles and cousins (on my mother's side of our family) lived right next-door while I was growing up. I lived in a small town, half of which was probably related to me. The town was about 60% state forest, which meant that there were likely more deer, fox and other critters than people. My first home was between two small parallel roads, one named after my grandfather who owned most of the land accessed by them and the other named after the owner of much of the rest of the land. By the time I was born (one of the last cousins on both sides) the land had been divided amongst my mother's family. I lived in a house center stage. Talk about a goldfish bowl.

Here I was, right in the middle of a close-knit bunch of Scandinavians descended from a circuit riding preacher/singer/church-planter from Norway (via Canada, Montana, North Dakota and New York). And if that wasn't enough, many of the Norwegians in my small Connecticut town who were not related to me attended our little church and might just as well have been family. You could be sure that any indiscretion attempted anywhere within town limits would be reported promptly to the authorities (mom and dad) and that punishment would ensue. Being one of the youngest there were *so many* older people who all seemed to consider themselves somehow responsible for me! This could be a good or bad thing. One of my favorite cousins laughs now as she tells of baby-sitting for me and setting me in the bathtub to keep me out of trouble. (No water, so drowning was not a concern. Whew!) I remember being locked out of my own home when my oldest sister was "cleaning house," so that she and her friends, mostly cousins, could "twist and shout" to her Elvis records without me pestering them. I suppose I can thank her for my interest in nature and the woods. It was not easy being the youngest of five siblings *and* one of the youngest of over twenty actively involved cousins living nearby! Fortunately my father's family lived down in New York City and I did not have to add them to this number.

I thought things might change when my father built our new home almost a mile away from the epicenter of the family. Problem was – this house was only two doors down from our church which was an even bigger hub of activity! Everyone knew if you worked in your yard on Sunday (never to be considered), if you stayed home from church or school (better be having a near-death experience), or if you were dating anyone in particular (resulting in much input as to the quality of the match). I will never forget once when I was a teenager and a neighbor was walking behind me to church. This good-hearted older Norwegian woman had prayerfully decided years earlier that my mother could use her help in bringing up her last three kids and so decided to put her two cents (and then some) into my upbringing. I can't say that I was all that surprised when from behind me on the short walk I heard her thickly accented voice say with great authority, "You know, the devil makes you wear those short skirts!" Ah, life in the goldfish bowl ... but they do say that it takes a village to raise a child. At the time I could have gotten upset by her comment, but I didn't. I chuckled and tugged my skirt down a bit. Now it is a fond memory and I can see much humor in it.

On the positive side (the jury is still out on whether being the recipient of so much attention was positive or negative), I remember stopping by my aunt's house on my one mile walk home from school. My mother often worked until 8:00 pm and I hated to go home to an empty house, so I would stop. It was right on the way home and my aunt was always there. She would put a piece of cake or cookies and a glass of milk in front of me and hug me, weaving into my life's tapestry all kinds of warm feelings of visits with her. A little Italian woman who married into my big Norwegian family was another of my favorites. I liked her partly because she was so different from the rest of the family in her lively expressions of excitement and affection. As I mentioned, Scandinavians can keep their feelings so well-hidden that you might think they were state secrets! The little Italian was my godmother and took that position seriously, lavishing small gifts and exuberant attention on me for all of the special occasions in my life. As one of the lastborn I might sometimes have felt a little over-looked, but never with her. I actually felt loved by all of my mother's family when I was young. I have awesome memories of daily adventures with my amazing troupe of cousins. *Our Gang* (old TV show) had nothing over us! For Christmas we would gather at one of our homes and share gifts, songs, food and fun (mattress diving!). It seemed as if everyone in our family could sing or play an instrument. What good times! Cousins grew up more like siblings and my family expanded.

Do you come from a large or small family?
Do you ever wish the reverse? Why?
Think of your favorite aunt/uncle. What makes them so special?
Growing up, did you ever get tired of trying to be a good person?

Do you ever get the feeling that you live in a goldfish bowl, that everything you do is under a magnifying glass and that people are just waiting to criticize you? Well, it's true ... and they are. Does that surprise you? It's part of the price you pay for being part of a family, a church or of any group for that matter. People seem compelled to express their opinions on just about everything. And if you are a Christian, it's part of the price you pay for presuming to suggest to a broken world that they need to change if they want to find peace and joy. Immediately you will be scrutinized for flaws to find excuses to ignore what you're saying. But that's not a good reason to stop sharing your faith with them! It will ever be the most important decision they will make.

As I got older I often gave rides to college to a girl who lived in the next town. At one point in time I had to ask her not to swear so much on our hour-long ride. It was pretty bad and it was often the Lord's name that kept getting thrown around for no reason. It really bothered me so I asked her very nicely to stop. So she stopped! After several weeks she said, "You really don't swear do you? I've been trying to catch you at it." I had no idea she was watching me so closely. It's not that I was pretending to be perfect. I knew better. Pride tells the average person that she is as good as anyone else; and she can't seem to understand that Christians are not claiming to be perfect, just *forgiven*. And forgiveness, if appreciated fully, leads to an effort to deserve it.

> What does God's Word say about being examined as Christians?
> *In everything set them an example by doing what is good. In your teaching show integrity, seriousness and soundness of speech that cannot be condemned, so that those who oppose you may be ashamed because they have nothing bad to say about us. Titus 2:7 Don't let anyone look down on you because you are young, but set an example for the believers in speech, in life, in love, in faith and in purity. I Timothy 4:12*

> How can we help people to understand that we *don't* think that we're perfect, but that we *do* have something they desperately need?

> Do you know any Christians who are "holier than thou"? Are you?
> *Be careful not to do your 'acts of righteousness' before men, to be seen by them. If you do, you will have no reward from your Father in heaven." Matthew 6:1-2*

We all probably know a couple of Christians out there who pretend to be living the perfect life. They are very good at hiding their own shortcomings and equally good at pointing out others'. But God's Word tells us that it's not possible for anyone to be that good: "There is not a righteous man on earth who does what is right, and never sins." *(Ecclesiastes 7:20)* Meanwhile, the rest of us are all too aware of our shortcomings. That's why we find examination so unpleasant. We know, better than anyone, what is there to discover. But the worst thing we can do is to give up trying to do what's right. Considering the impossibility of success, why does God call us to live a perfect life? "Be perfect, therefore, as your heavenly Father is perfect." *(Matthew 5:48)* The second verse here sounds like a contradiction or at least an unattainable goal after the first one. Why would God require perfection knowing we could never achieve it? There must be an explanation.

And I believe there is. God brought His Son into the world to do for us what He knew we could never do ourselves. He knew that not one of us would be able to live a perfect life. Then why did He ask it of us? Maybe because it's good to set high goals? (Low goals never accomplished much.) Or maybe to show us just how badly we *need* a Savior. And the only Savior Who could intercede for us would have to be one who was able to meet that price – that "perfect life" price. C. S. Lewis writes that some people say that Christ had an unfair advantage in living a perfect life because He is God. But think about that carefully. It is only *because* He is God that He was *able* to live without sin and have victory over death and hell. And if He hadn't done that, death and hell would be our lot for eternity. That's a long time.

It's not that hard to live in a goldfish bowl if you actually are a fish and are not just *pretending* to be one. Are you serious about following the Lord? Be humble. Be honest. And ask the Lord for strength and wisdom. Remember that He is the only One whose opinion of us really matters. And that opinion is evident in His death on the cross! He will help you to be the kind of Christian who will be salt and light in this darkening world. Just keep pointing people to Christ and taking the spotlight off yourself. And think of life in a goldfish bowl as free advertizing for the Lord!

Bible Reading: *Matthew 5:13-16*
>How many uses of salt can you think of??
>How can we be like salt?
>How many uses of light can you think of??
>How can we be like light?
>What danger is there in trying to obey God's command to be good?

Challenge: Try to live the kind of life that will show Jesus to the world, and stop complaining that they're critical. That's only to be expected.

>*"...since we are surrounded by such a great cloud of witnesses, ...let us run with perseverance the race marked out for us."*
>
>*Hebrews 12:1*

WEEK 5

"Hand-me-downs"

For some surely well-intentioned yet unfortunate reason – from my perspective – mothers like to dress little kids in matching outfits, especially girls. My mother was no exception. I remember a particularly pretty white dress with red embossed flowers that was fit for a princess! Dressing alike wasn't such a big deal when we were very small, but come on moms, give the youngest ones a break! Don't you realize that clothes are handed down? I would get a beautiful new dress that I really loved and it would fit me for maybe two years – long enough even for a beautiful dress. Then I would get my sister's hand-me-down! Two more years of the same dress. Sheesh. This happened often enough to warrant me gathering courage and going to my mother and asking her *please* not to dress us the same anymore. She seemed to understand but I could tell she was disappointed.

I've already mentioned that I was the baby in my family. My older siblings, by the way, enjoyed using that term with a certain flourish that would drive me crazy! I grew up with two older brothers and two older sisters. (I also had an older brother who was the third-born who died as a baby. I'll meet him one day.) We were kind of like two separate families when we were young. The oldest brother and sister were all grown up by the time I remember interacting with them. The next brother and sister, along with me, were a little sub-family within the larger one.

There were times when I felt not quite as special as the rest of the family. Before I was born my parents had studio portraits taken of the entire family along with separate ones of each child. Awesome pictures! There is *exactly one* picture of me under the age of two and it is so poorly exposed that it could be anyone! My mother promised me that it is a picture of me but I think she had her fingers crossed behind her back at the time. Then there are maybe five more pictures of me under the age of ten or twelve. In contrast there is an entire album for my two eldest siblings and probably half that for the next two. I had no photo of me as a baby to submit to my yearbook. In some ways it stinks to be the youngest. When people ask me what I looked like when I was little I have to tell them that I really don't know. My brother and sister even had me convinced at one point that I had been adopted! It seemed to explain a lot.

Have you ever been the victim of the dreaded hand-me-down?
How did you feel about them?
What place do you hold in your family?
Do you believe it makes a difference? How?

Read *Genesis 49:1-28.*
Which of the sons' blessings would you most like to get? Why?
There are two that stand out in length and in positive promise.
Which two?
Does birth order seem to matter here?
Does it ever matter in the Bible?

> *He must acknowledge…the firstborn by giving him a double share*
> *of all he has…."Deuteronomy 21:17*
> *"There is still the youngest, …he is the one." I Samuel 16:11-12*

I was the kid who had learned not to need much attention because there simply wasn't much left to give. My seat in the family car was the exceptionally deep back window where I could curl up in the sun and fall asleep – just like a cat. I guess we would be arrested for that today! My sister, the next in age, was up front between Mom and Dad, and the three oldest had the back seat. Memories of special times spent with my father loom large in my oldest sister's stories, but I remember so little. Don't get me wrong – I always felt loved by my parents, but I'm not sure I ever felt as …

noticed I guess. Perhaps like many men my father just related better to the older kids. And Mom was just too busy by the time I arrived. Years later when I was able to talk to my mother about it she said that I had never seemed to need much attention. Parents mess up sometimes too.

I remember my oldest brother singling me out when I was very young and treating me kind of special there for a while. (Note to brother: If this has been wishful thinking on my part, I would rather remain blind to it. Thank you.) When he was living at home with us – only until I was about five – he would come home from work and I would run to the door to meet him. Then he would swing me up onto his shoulders and give me a ride through the house. Not long after that he moved out on his own and he would just come home for visits. (Note to self: I may actually be imagining more from this memory than is deserved. It may only have happened once and I have wished it into a reoccurring event. Pretty sad, huh?) One year at Christmas time he brought gifts for us all – he loved to give gifts. He gave my sister a transistor radio and he gave me a record player! That had to be the first time in my then short life that I had ever gotten the better end of any deal that included her. I remember thinking that there must have been some kind of mistake with the tags. But there wasn't! My sister eventually wound up getting the same thing I had but it didn't matter at all because I would never forget that day. I had been favored! Catch that sinful nature in there? I also got to be the flower girl in my brother's wedding; though I remember his fiancée insisting that a relative of hers also share that honor. I wasn't sure that she wanted me at all, but he did.

Describe a time you felt unloved or overlooked by your parents or siblings.

Did you ever try to talk to them about it?

Have you ever felt as if a parent or sibling was favoring you?

How did that make you feel?

I think that what got me through some of the hard times as a kid was finally figuring out that I was *very* special to God and that He loved me and always had time for me. I was fortunate to get a handle on that early on, albeit through some tough times. Even as a child I think I knew that I could become a victim of my circumstances or I could choose to rise above them like Joseph in *Genesis 37-41*. Joseph had reason to be down: He was thrown into a well, sold as a slave (by his brothers!), falsely accused by his master's wife, and thrown into jail for years. But he chose to move on and to rise above it all! It's as Abraham Lincoln once said: "Folks are usually about as happy as they make up their minds to be." I always wanted to be able to fly so the choice was easy – rise!

Tim Keller has a great little book called *The Prodigal God* that brings this out. Jesus was speaking to the Pharisees in the Parable of the Prodigal Son. While most focus on the younger brother's redemption in this story, Keller focuses on the older brother's selfish attitude. He had a victim mentality and couldn't be happy for his brother. I knew my parents loved me and that they had their hands full trying to make ends meet and trying to resolve the day-to-day challenges that plague most people's lives. They were doing their best. I forgave them and moved on.

Bible Reading: What does God's Word have to say about YOU? Discuss the importance of each one of these verses:

So God created man in his own image, in the image of God he created him; male and female he created them. Genesis 1:27

I praise you because I am fearfully and wonderfully made; your works are wonderful, I know that full well. Psalm 139:14

Consider the ravens: They do not sow or reap, they have no storeroom or barn; yet God feeds them. And how much more valuable you are than birds! Luke 12:24

But God demonstrates his own love for us in this: while we were still sinners, Christ died for us. Romans 5:8

How great is the love the Father has lavished on us, that we should be called the children of God! And that is what we are! I John 3:1

I no longer call you servants ... I have called you friends, for everything that I learned from my Father I have made known to you. John 15:15

...and surely I will be with you always, to the very end of the age.
Matthew 28:20
...I have loved you with an everlasting love. I have drawn you with
loving kindness. Jeremiah 31:3
In my Father's house are many rooms; if it were not so, I would have
told you. I am going there to prepare a place for you. ... I will come
back and take you to be with me that you also may be where I am.
John 14:2-3

Which one of these facts/promises is especially important
to you? Why?

I don't think there will be any hand-me-downs in heaven. I
think we'll get one incredible, heavenly robe or gown that never
wears out and it will be so beautiful that we'll never get tired of it.
According to the Bible God has prepared a special place for each
one of His children. In that place we will never feel neglected or
abandoned. And we will be happy for the honors given to others.
Just read the verses above to know how much you are loved. And
there are many more like them in the Bible. Life here on earth
isn't always perfect, but God has us here for a reason and we are
to be "very careful" how we live, and to "make the most of every
opportunity" because "the days are evil." *(Ephesians 5:15-17)* The
time is short to tell others of His great love and of the hope for an
awesome eternity. But that's our job. And *nothing* should keep
us from it.

Challenge: Don't get hung up on some real or perhaps just per-
ceived wrong that your parents or other family members or friends have perpetrated against you. So often
we don't see the whole picture, and even more often,
it's simply smarter just to let it go and to get on with
your life.

"For God so loved the world that He gave his one and
only Son, that whoever believes in Him shall not perish
but have eternal life."
John 3:16

WEEK 6

"City People"

One of my favorite memories of my father is his snoring, yes his snoring. I would lie awake at night and listen to this impossibly loud sound coming from the next room and wonder how anyone could sleep through it — especially without a wall between. How, oh how could my mother take it? Then again, this was my safety barometer, the sound that told me, "All is well." If dad was sleeping in the next room, my protection and thereby my peace was assured. Any bogeymen in the vicinity had better run because my dad was tough. And he was home. I could tell.

My dad worked hard during the week and took his weekends seriously as well. Often the weekend meant an unplanned trip into the city. New York City was simply "the city" to us. This was where my father was born and raised (the Bronx) and where my parents met (Manhatten). There was no other city of note in our lives. On any Saturday or Sunday he might decide at a moment's notice to bring my oldest brother and sister to a Yankee game, or to pack up the entire family and go down to the Bronx Zoo or to visit one of his sisters and their families living in that magical city. I would come into school on Mondays with stories of adventures in the city. The other kids' eyes would light up as I told them my stories – and thus my skill (or lack thereof) as a story-teller was born. At times I'm sure they doubted me because people didn't travel as much then; and at other times they may have been a little jealous. But this was my edge, the one thing I had that the other kids who had fancier homes, or clothes, or toys, or whatever, didn't have. I had my adventures!

My father's family was different from my mother's. They were city people and talked and acted differently. They were louder, talked faster with an interesting accent, and usually said *exactly* what they were thinking. It was all very exciting. Spiritually I think there were several fence-sitters. One sister, the one we visited the most, lived in the Bronx in the basement of an apartment building where she was the superintendent ("super"). She and her husband had four kids, fish tanks, and were lots of fun. They had a cement backyard. Can you believe it? Cement! Another sister and her husband lived in "the village" in Manhattan. We never stayed overnight with them. They had no children and could only take so much of our fun. The third sister we usually visited in upstate New York. Their son and daughter (who later became a nun) were much older than me. I never even remember meeting the nun until my wedding when she happily showed up unexpectedly. I learned to play poker (practically a felony in my home), got introduced to a Venus Flytrap plant, and ate chocolate covered ants at this home – pretty neat stuff for a kid. The last member of my dad's family was his oldest brother whose wife was an invalid due to a fire she had survived. This made visiting them difficult.

Two of my Dad's sisters had cottages out in Putnam County in upstate New York where we would often visit. Down the hill from their cottages under the trees was a great swimming hole formed by damming up a pretty little stream. All of the cousins would pile into the crystal clear water, balance-beam walk over the little dam and back again, and picnic on the shore. It was a little scary to go out on the dam because the water there was over my head, and though I would have denied it then, I wasn't able to swim well enough for the turbulent water spilling over its rim. But occasionally I would resolutely pull together the courage in order to keep up with my older cousins and cross the dam. Otherwise I stayed pretty close to the shore while the others swam out into the deeper water. I loved to visit my Dad's family.

My dad was smart. His whole family was into learning. His niece (the nun) taught at a prestigious New York university. As a little girl I guess I thought he must have been the smartest man in the world. He could answer all of my constant, innumerable questions. Even though he quit school after the eighth grade to help out his family during the Great Depression, he was self-educated well beyond high school. He did the *New York Times* crossword puzzle most Sunday afternoons – and often finished it! He built our house in his spare time. Later in life he worked in a large defense plant in nearby Hartford. But I mostly remember him reading his Bible or the newspaper and singing in church. He had a great voice. We have a couple of records (78's) of him and another man singing duets.

Are your parents' families alike or very different?
With which family are you most comfortable? Why?
Are either of your parents impulsive? Are you?
Do you have any examples?

I don't ever remember a time when my dad was not a Christian, but my mom told me about their early days of marriage. My mother eloped with my father against her father's wishes while her family was living in New York City. Meanwhile, back home in the Midwest, a nice young man was expecting to marry her. If you knew my mother this would shock you. My father was ten years older than she was, and though he played the mandolin and sang in the string-band of an evangelical Norwegian church, he was not a Christian. Mom had just turned nineteen and he was nearly twenty-nine. After they were married and later moved to northwestern Connecticut, they hung out with a group of friends whose main interest was playing cards and socializing. My mother, who was a Christian all this time, convinced my dad to rent out an empty room in their house to an interim pastor at church, and he agreed because they needed the money. This man quickly became a great friend and soon afterward led my father to the Lord. He sang on those records with my dad. Years later I was told by that same pastor that my dad's conversion started a little revival in the church.

Very cool. Life changed in my home after that. This is when my parents' aversion to playing cards developed. Since I was born last in the family, I only remember the "after that" years.

What things do you admire most about your father?
Is/was he a Christian?
Does/did your father snore?
Is there something that bugs you about your dad?
Have you talked to him about it?
> *Honor your father and your mother, as the Lord your God has commanded you, so that you may live long and that it may go well with you ... Deuteronomy 5:16*
> *Do nothing out of selfish ambition or vain conceit, but in humility consider others better than yourself. Philippians 2:3*

It's tough to know what to do when someone you love isn't a Christian, especially a parent. You can't share some of the most important things in life – prayer concerns, spiritual joys, and *eternity*. You try so many things to reach them: direct confrontation, sneaky set-ups, gifts with a message, and humongous amounts of prayer, among other things. I'm not suggesting that any of this is wrong. I guess I'm saying that you never know what is going to work because whatever gets that person to finally open up to the Holy Spirit can be so completely random that it often surprises us. There is no one set formula for sharing God's Love. All too often our loved ones know the truth already, but are unwilling to surrender their own plans to follow the Lord's. Is it pride or something else? My Italian aunt said that it was pride that kept her from accepting the Lord until she was sixty years old. She thought she was a pretty good person and couldn't understand why that wasn't enough. I have other relatives and friends struggling with that same thought. They don't get it. We can *never be* good enough. Understanding that is the first step to believing. Setting down our pride and accepting God's free gift is the next.

Have you ever had the joy of seeing someone you love come to the Lord?

What was it that worked for him or her?

What do you think is the best way to witness to a family member?

What does the Bible say we should do?

> Live such good lives among the pagans that, though they accuse you of doing wrong, they may see your good deeds and glorify God on the day he visits us. I Peter 2:12
>
> Do not cause anyone to stumble... I try to please everybody in every way. For I am not seeking my own good but the good of many so that they may be saved. I Corinthians 10:32-33

What makes us so afraid to witness to those we love the most? My oldest brother has yet to give his heart to the Lord. I've tried talking straight to him but all he seems to hear is criticism. He completely misses the love in there. It's hard to know what to do. I need to remember that God loves him more than I do. I know I've made mistakes trying to encourage him to see his need, but I *really* want to see him in heaven! I can't undo mistakes I've made. I don't know what else to do except to keep loving him and praying for him. I know it's between him and the Holy Spirit.

Bible Reading: *Hebrews 3:12-19*

What does it mean to "harden one's heart"?

What are some reasons people ignore the Holy Spirit?

What is the penalty for not obeying God's call?

How does this Scripture say that we can help others to receive the Lord?

Challenge: Get more serious in your prayer time. Pray *every day* for specific people you care about to find the Lord. Pray now.

Since, then, we know what it is to fear the Lord, we try to persuade men... Christ's love compels us, because we are convinced that One died for all..."
2 Corinthians 5:11-14

WEEK 7

"Go out there and sing!"

I was a singer from birth I think. I may have sung in the womb. As a little girl I sang riding in the car, hanging upside-down from the front of our comfy chair, anywhere, anytime, all the time. I've been told that my tendency to break out in song was quite remarkable. I must have driven more than a few people nuts. It was partly genetic with both parents musically gifted but also environmental since I was surrounded by music all the time. My church helped to develop talents in a children's meeting every Friday night where a few of the older kids took turns organizing the service and getting the other kids to share in several ways including reading missionary stories, memorizing Bible verses, and singing. My very first big-time solo developed from that service when I was about eight. The couple who gave years of their time to the children were Uncle George and "Tante" ("aunt" in Norwegian). I don't know how many careers in music were initiated by these two, but the church was overflowing with talent. After I had sung at the children's meetings a few times, Tante decided that I should sing a solo at a regular church service, and I foolishly agreed. On the night of the service I realized what I had done, ran downstairs and threw up. Sure that this would get me off the hook I went to Tante to tell her the bad news. To my surprise she said something like: "Very good. Now go out there and sing!" … and so I did.

I'm a great admirer of true Godly humility, but I am not impressed with false modesty. It keeps many people secure in their cocoons never actively involved in God's work. You can't get hurt as often there, but it's a cop-out. You're on the sidelines watching. You're not even the main character in your own life! (I heard something like that in a movie once. It's a good line.) You probably have an idea where your talents lie. And if you are good at something, it's not a sin to admit it. It's simply a fact. As long as you remember that your talent is a gift from God given both to you and to many others and not something for which you somehow deserve credit, you will remember to place that credit where it belongs and not let it go to your head. You should also realize that there is always someone out there who is better at this talent than you are. (Ouch!) Sometimes that's hard to swallow. And it can be even harder to cheer for them when they outdo you. All of our talents are *from God,* and we need to use them *for God.* There was a tune we would sing at our Friday night meetings that promoted that "use-your-gifts" attitude and I firmly believe the warning to be true:

> "If you have a talent, use it for the Lord.
> If you have a talent, use it for the Lord.
> If you do not use it, you will surely lose it.
> If you have a talent, use it for the Lord."

When I was older we tried an experiment at our teen youth group one night. We talked about the difference between *talents* (which might include athletics, music, etc.) and *spiritual gifts.* Sometimes the two words get interchanged. After studying about spiritual gifts (some God-given spiritual ability or tendency that is innately or naturally strong in a person) and looking at those listed in the Bible (including teaching, helping, encouraging, leading) we handed out forms that we had put together listing each spiritual gift along the top and each person's name down on the left. Each teen was to list his/her choices for their friends' top three gifts. Three of the spaces after each name where the columns and rows crossed were to be filled in with a number from one to three, three being the strongest. The leaders collected the forms to determine what everyone's best friends thought his/her three strongest gifts were. Interestingly most of the forms agreed. It was an eye-opener for everyone who took part, and very encouraging. Our spiritual gifts tied in closely with what we considered our talents which was cool too. If you're not sure what your gifts are, ask your best friends or your family. They can probably tell you.

What are your *talents*? (Come on, *everyone's* got them...)
Do you use them for the Lord? If so, how? If not, why not?
What are your *spiritual gifts*? (Everyone's got these too.)
What does the Bible say are spiritual gifts?

> Now about spiritual gifts, ... <u>there are different kinds of gifts, but the same Spirit</u>... to one there is given ...wisdom, ...knowledge, ... faith, ...healing, ...miraculous powers, ...prophecy, ...ability to distinguish between spirits, ...tongues, ...interpretation of tongues. All these are the work of one Spirit, and he gives them to each one, just as he determines. I Corinthians 12:1-11
> <u>It was he who gave</u> some to be apostles, ...prophets, ... evangelists, ...pastors and teachers. Ephesians 4:11
> <u>We have different gifts according to the grace given us.</u> ... prophesying, ...serving, ...teaching, encouraging, ...contributing to the needs of others, ...leadership, ...showing mercy. Romans 12:6-8

Well, not only did I launch a singing career in church as a child, but I also started singing in school. My small elementary school had a program at the end of the year in which each class participated in a short play or musical number. I remember some of the parts I played – I had so much fun! I was the middle goat in *The Three Billy Goats Gruff*, Gretel in *Hansel and Gretel* (I still remember one of the songs.), the wife in *The Shoemaker and His Wife*; and in eighth grade I was in a shortened version of *Annie, Get Your Gun*. This was where my faith was tested a bit. This was a longer play than the others mentioned and there were a couple of times when I was supposed to use four-letter words (relatively tame) that were not a part of my approved vocabulary. I approached the teacher when I got the script and said that I would have to withdraw from the musical with regrets. Surprised, she asked me why and I told her about my problem with the four letter words. She laughed and said, "So, we'll change the words." Nice lady. I got to stay in the play.

I rarely got nervous performing in elementary school. I'm not sure why. It wasn't because I thought I was that great – because

I knew better. It wasn't because I didn't care if I messed up -- because I did ... both. I think it was because it was just so much fun. I loved acting and singing. And it was great training for my role in later life -- teaching teenagers. No fear.

> Do you use your talents in school or otherwise outside of church?
>
> If your answer to the last question was "yes" but "no" to the second question in this week, I have to ask, "Why?"
>
> *(Go ahead and check it out – we'll wait...)*
>
> Have you ever been faced with taking a stand against what someone was asking you to do with your talents?
>
> What does the Bible have to say about that?
>> *Whatever you do, work at it with all your heart, as working for the Lord, not men. Colossians 3:23-24*
>> *...what does the Lord your God ask of you but to fear the Lord your God, to walk in all his ways, to love him, and to serve the Lord your God with all your heart and with all your soul, and to observe the Lord's commands and decrees... Deuteronomy 10:12-13*
>> *Stand firm then... Ephesians 6:14-17*

"Whatever you do, work at it with all your heart..." It goes on to say that we should be doing everything for the Lord, not for men's praise. That verse has always been a motto of mine, which is why my mistakes can be quite dramatic (BIG ones!). Somewhere along the way in my life I decided that if I was going to sing or do anything else well I should just "let it rip." I can remember a couple of times when I may have regretted that motto. Not that long ago while singing with a few friends I came in on a song quite alone and with a great deal of gusto and volume. A big smile and a deep bow were enough to get the audience (not sure about my friends) smiling and forgiving, and on we went with our songs. Mistakes can break the ice, especially if you know how to laugh at yourself. I have discovered through numerous goofs that people almost like you better when you show that you're human and can laugh at yourself ... not that I'm encouraging mistakes. But, don't be afraid to make them or you will never try anything.

Are you afraid of making mistakes? Why?
Have you ever made a big mistake publicly?
How did you handle it?
Do you work at things "with your whole heart"?
Why/why not?

It's not easy to risk losing a big chance to use your talents, but God will give you a greater win when you stand for Him. Remember Erik Liddell in the movie, *Chariots of Fire*? Okay, it's a pretty old movie, but well worth watching. It's a true story of a British athlete who bowed out of running in an Olympic race that he had trained for for years because it had been scheduled on a Sunday. He felt that this would not honor God. Sunday was God's day. He did this in spite of pressure from his team, his coaches, and his country's royalty. God allowed him later in the same Olympics, to run in and win another race for which he was not scheduled and for which he had not trained. Erik Liddell has been honored for years as a great athlete and a missionary who took a tough stand for his faith. The verse at the end of this "week" was handed to him prior to the start by the American athlete running in that same race that Erik went on to win.

Our talents can put us into a spot where we have to make a tough choice and take a stand risking loss, and our desire to honor God may put us in the same situation for other reasons as well.. I had to take a stand as a teenager on at least two more occasions that I can remember. When I applied for jobs waitressing I had to explain to my potential bosses that I couldn't work on Sundays – scary for a young teen. In both cases my future employers must have decided that any teenager brave enough to admit that she either wanted to be or had to be in church Sunday mornings would probably be a responsible worker and an honest employee. In both cases I got the job. And I made a statement for my faith too! Yet we often fail to take a stand simply for fear of embarrassment. How weak we sometimes are. Esther in the Old Testament used her position *at risk of death* to take a stand for her people. And there was a man named Joseph in the New Testament who took a stand for his faith using the opportunity due to his position. He was definitely stepping out on a limb. It's easy to "go with the flow," but taking a stand requires courage and strength of character, and sometimes sacrifice. *You have to be willing to suffer the possible consequences.*

Bible Reading: *Luke 23:50-54, John 19:38-42*
    Who was Joseph of Arimathea?
    Why do you think he started out a secret disciple of Jesus?
    What is he famous for?
    Was it difficult for him to do this? What was at stake?
    Why was what he did for Jesus important?

Challenge: Take a stand for the Lord in whatever way you know
          you should, even though you might be afraid or embar-
          rassed, face criticism or lose out on something.

    "...Those who honor me, I will honor, but those who despise me will be distained."
                                                    I Samuel 2:30b

WEEK 8

"Picked last again"

B eing the "runt of the litter," I was quite used to being picked last in sports. It was always humiliating, waiting and hoping that maybe this time I wouldn't be dead last. I was unimpressive in sports, not completely hopeless, but unimpressive. For that reason I only got interested in team sports when I was in high school and had grown a little. Meanwhile, the mortification of constantly being one of the last two picked in sports was mine day after day at home and in school. My teachers hadn't grasped the fact that letting *kids* pick their own teams in our loose version of physical education might be a difficult experience for some.

But I did have heart. I remember playing football once in the neighborhood. I was playing my little heart out when I got tackled by a big kid and went down. This kid was *really* big. It was the first time I had ever had the breath knocked out of me and I wasn't sure if I was dead or only "mostly dead " (*Princess Bride*). Turns out I lived – if you were wondering. I don't think I ever played football with the big kids again. In high school, my 5'10" frame began to be appreciated. Basketball and track coaches were interested in what I could do – not that much as it turned out. Though I remember enjoying sports, I hadn't really developed my skills much as a kid, nor had I grown to love sports enough to do so at this point, especially with the pathetic lack of importance placed on girls' athletics at that time.

I enjoyed playing field hockey, but we played only two or three games. Total. In basketball we still used the old girls' rules where the court was divided into sections with two or three players in each who couldn't leave their designated areas. I think my position was called "roving forward" and I could cross the lines. We could hold the ball for only three seconds and dribble it only three times before we *had* to pass it, even if we had a clear run to the basket! – which never made sense to me. Not sure we had *any* scheduled outside games. I was also on the track team. We had one or two meets all season. I did the running and standing long jumps and the 50-yard dash. None of these sports required a lot of time or effort given the situation. I liked the rings and uneven bars in P.E. gymnastics, but my height was not helpful there. In my junior year the girls' basketball team started using the boys' rules, but by then I was done with school sports and had moved on to other things, including a new school.

Are (were) you involved in sports? Explain.

Are (were) you a superstar, the last one picked, or somewhere in between?

Is (was) being involved in sports a good experience for you? Explain.

Do you prefer team sports or individual sports? Why?

The Bible talks about sports as illustrations often:

...and let us run with perseverance the race marked out for us... *Hebrews 12:1-3*
Do you not know that in a race all the runners run, but only one gets the prize. Run in such a way as to get the prize. Everyone who competes .... goes into strict training. They do it to get a crown that will not last, but we do it to get a crown that will last forever. I Corinthians 9:24-25
I have fought the good fight, I have finished the race, I have kept the faith. 2 Timothy 4:7-8
The race is not to the swift or the battle to the strong, ...but time and chance happen to them all. Ecclesiastes 9:11

God is comparing our lives here on earth with a race that we should strive to win even though winning isn't really our goal. Confusing, right? Let me explain: We need patience and perseverance because *finishing* the race to the best of our ability for His honor *is* our goal. Striving to win will bring out our best, but ironically, it's not really a contest. Huh? Christ has already won this race and the prize is awaiting us. Weird race, right? It's already won *for* us! But that doesn't mean that we are exempt from taking part in the race. We are called to do our best. Again – confusing. You see, it's not just the end of a journey that is our goal; it's the journey itself. What we do along our paths is what prepares us for Heaven and what helps others to see the Way.

Participating in sports can be valuable to bring discipline, responsibility and teamwork into our lives – and it can keep us out of trouble; but it can also be a problem if too much time is given to it at the expense of learning or doing other things that are possibly more valuable. I've seen many people look back at their lives and wish they had spent more time on something that would have helped them more later in life. How many will actually turn professional and make a living out of sports? I'm not trying to discourage you if this is what God is leading you to do, but be sure to ask Him first. Way too many wanna-be sports stars are wondering how the "nerds" who did their homework and aced their exams passed them out along the way. Keeping balance is important.

Do you have balance in your life?
Is there anything that you spend too much time on? Explain.

There was one sport I loved and never really outgrew - skiing. I learned to ski on a sweet little hill across from my church in old wooden hand-me-down skis with bear-trap bindings where they kind of strapped the skis to your feet with no release mechanism – very dangerous. Much of my later experience in skiing was with my expert older cousins. We would go to the top of the mountain and choose our route down – usually a black diamond (i.e., most difficult trail). They would quickly descend to a point on the hill where they would stop and take a look around. After a few minutes I would catch up and we'd be off – only I never got those little breaks because I was always in catch-up mode! I loved being with them and I'm sure it helped me to become a better skier in the long run. (No pun intended.)

My cousins skied all over North America and Europe and made several short home-grown ski movies which were pretty creative; some of their scenes looked like ballet on snow. I even got to star in one of them. One of my best friends and I were the comic relief portion. We were coming down an *incredibly* steep narrow slope covered in *sheer ice*. Get the picture? It was really scary. The guys were waiting for us below. As we carefully descended the near-vertical cliff (which looked much less steep and icy in the movie from the full front view of the video), we looked absolutely inept snowplowing for our very lives down the icy *precipice* barren of any real snow — and all to the chaotic sounds of "Tijuana Taxi." Ouch! I learned to laugh at myself at a very young age.

Have you ever noticed how hanging out with people who are better than you are at something can sometimes draw you up to a higher level of skill? Not sure how that works, but it often does. (It *could* do the opposite too I suppose…) When I ski with good skiers, I ski better. When I golf with good golfers, I take fewer strokes. When I sing with gifted singers, I sing like an angel. (I wish.) My vocabulary even improves when I talk to a friend of mine who is a writer. There's a lesson in this: we are highly influenced by our friends. So it is very important to surround yourself with people who are good at making wise choices. You might find yourself making wise choices as well. Be careful though not to become a snob and leave out your non-athletic or non-musical friends who just might turn out to be those with the greatest wisdom.

Getting picked last for all of those years never really hurt me that much. I can't remember struggling with it except maybe when it was happening. And I haven't had any kind of anxious thoughts recalling it now. I haven't spent time on a counselor's couch over it; it just never seemed that important. We let too many trivial things in our lives steal our peace and joy. Pretty dumb. Did you ever think that we may fail at certain things because God has something better for us?

You may have been disappointed in your sports career or in some other endeavor in life and wished for more. There may have been many times God called you to do something you really didn't want to do. Maybe you were picked last once too often or were simply afraid to try. Pride or a fear of failure can cripple us. Then again, it could be a basic lack of self-confidence or even sheer laziness keeping us in our seats. The verses above make it pretty clear that God wants us in the race and doing our best even if we are not superstars. And the race might not involve sports; it's anything God sets before us to do. God wants to use each of us in mighty ways.

Bible Reading: *I Corinthians 1:27-31, 2 Corinthians 12:7-10*
>Why do you think God chose the foolish, the weak and the lowly?
>Paul had a "thorn" in his flesh. What do you think it was?
>When he pleaded for relief, what did God say?
>What does "My power is made perfect in weakness." mean?
>Do you delight in weakness, insults, persecution and difficulty? Discuss.

Challenge: Is there any disappointment in sports/life bugging you? Think it through. Compared to eternal things, how important is it? Is it time to let it go?

>*"...for when I am weak, then I am strong."*
>*2 Corinthians 12:10b*

WEEK 9

"The truth is out there"

Teachers have a big impact on kids, many for good, a few for bad. My elementary school teachers were very good. None scarred me for life, even though I may not have considered each of them a gift. Kindergarten had not arrived yet in my town. I had my first grade teacher, Miss P., for second grade as well, and I'm pretty sure I was teacher's pet. Go figure. That's a great way to begin the days of formal education, and since it never happened again, I should have appreciated it more! I needed help to remember my third grade teacher, Mrs. H., but I loved my fourth grade teacher. She was tough but fair, and taught me all kinds of interesting stuff. I remember part of a poem I wrote for her in which we were to use the many poetic devices we were learning:

"I sat at my window one wintery night–
The falling of snow was a beautiful sight!
Feathery flakes from the darkness on high,
And the night itself seemed to gently sigh,
Like the baying of sheep on a mountainside."

There was more to it, but I can't remember the rest. Not bad for a fourth grader, I guess... (Maybe starts to make up for the sports' ineptitude?) I see alliteration, personification and simile. Anything else? Yes, Mrs. B. was a good teacher. But she also had me sitting out in the hall on occasion for disciplinary reasons. I deserved being sent into the hall, and I knew it. In fifth grade I met the first of three men I had as elementary teachers. Mr. B. was the closest I came to "not a gift" in my thinking. I don't remember learning much in his class, but I definitely remember ducking as he chucked chalk across the room at anyone who did something he didn't like.

Sixth grade brought another man who was a good teacher but who tried to no avail to teach us evolution. Poor guy. He had no idea what he was up against! We had been taught well in Sunday School. *Micro-evolution* is everywhere – that is, evolution *within* a species. Changes can happen within a species. It's *macro-evolution* that is the problem. There is simply no hard evidence to support one species morphing into another over time, and "the scientific process" (which requires a *repeatable* process with the *same results every time*) is impossible to use to prove the so-called scientific "facts" being taught on this subject. Has anyone *ever* seen it happen? *It's a theory!* Unless I see evidence to the contrary, I'll go with the Bible's account in *Genesis 1:20-25* where it *repeatedly* says that animals were all created "according to their kinds." *It makes more sense.* It actually requires more faith to believe in evolution.

Why do we presume to hold God to human limitations? If He is powerful enough to create at all, why challenge His Word with no evidence? On the other hand, not having a God out there to Whom we are accountable is a good escape from the tough parts of the Bible. There is something emotionally comfortable in not having to account for the way we live. Blaise Pascal (well known mathematician) put forth a famous wager: "Either God is or He is not. You *must* choose." Not choosing *is* a choice. It's like stopping to think about helping someone who is drowning. A point comes when it is too late to help and you have firmly chosen not to. If there is no God out there, your thoughts about Him are irrelevant. If there is a God out there, this is the most important wager you will ever make! You will either win or lose *everything* based upon your decision.

Seventh and eighth grades brought a woman and a man, Mrs. M. to emphasize language arts and Mr. P. to send us soaring in math, both excellent teachers for a student like me who needed to be challenged and then set free to try it for herself. Mr. P. doubled as principal and was loved by everyone. He was famous for practicing his golf swing in class with a yardstick – which could get

45

a little dangerous. He must have been at the school longer than any other teacher because everyone in town over a certain age seems to have had him as a teacher.

Who were some of your favorite teachers?
What made them good?
Were they tough? Did they challenge you to think and achieve?
If you could say something to them right now, what would it be?
Have you ever considered writing one of them a thank you note?

To keep me busy they assigned me stockrooms to clean. I became quite good at organizing reams of paper and the supplies needed to help teachers do what they do. I guess I was just in the way when I finished up my work. Advanced placement at my school meant me and two or three boys in grade eight being handed a "new math" book and being told to work our way through it. It was fun. We learned to do math in different base systems, including the very latest – the binary system! I filled my fine arts' "requirement" with singing and by making elaborate pictures for either my school projects or for the monthly hotdog/hamburger sales which passed as the hot lunch program of our small school. I cherish those easy days of adventure and creativity. It was a good time to be a kid in our town.

I must have been a *little* bit of trouble from time to time though, because I remember sitting in the principal's office more than once in the early years, mainly for talking too much or for cracking one too many jokes. I was somewhat impulsive and didn't always think things through – like the time I put a tack on the chair of my good friend. Well, he sat on it and howled – in spite of the fact that he was in some pretty heavy snow pants. (I was a little disappointed in him.) I got in trouble … deservedly I suppose, so I took it pretty well. But after that there seemed to be a rash of tacks winding up on chairs and I caught the heat for every one of them even though I was innocent. I didn't take it as well when I was blamed for something I didn't do. You see, even though I was mischievous, I was also very honest, and all a teacher ever had to do was to ask for me to spill out the truth. It's amazing to me how many of them failed to try *that* "tack." (Pun intended.) Lots of people will tell you the truth if you simply ask.

Did you ever *deservedly* get into trouble in school?
Did you take it well? Explain.
Did you ever *undeservedly* get into trouble?
Did you take that well? Explain.
Are you a truthful person? How important is that to you?
What does the Bible say about truthfulness?
> The Lord detests lying lips, but *he delights in men who are truthful.* Proverbs 12:22
> Therefore each of you must *put off falsehood and speak truthfully* to his neighbor, for we are all members of one body. Ephesians 4:25

Many people think that lying is a pretty minor offense in relation to other sins, but it is actually listed second of the seven things the Lord *detests* in *Proverbs 6:16-19:* "There are six things the Lord hates, seven that are detestable to him: haughty eyes, a lying tongue, hands that shed innocent blood, a heart that devises wicked schemes, feet that are quick to rush into evil, a false witness who pours out lies, and a man who stirs up dissension among brothers." If you think about it, lying is probably a big part of most of these. And remember what happened to Ananias and Sapphira in *Acts 5* for lying? They died on the spot.

As much of a rascal as I was, truthfulness was important to me. But I had yet to deal with the issue of exaggeration. I remember a time when, because of my tendency to enhance the truth in stories, friends started to doubt them. That was frustrating – especially if I was not exaggerating. I decided that I had to clean up my act. I recognized the fact that I did have a tendency to see the glass as either half full or half empty as it suited my case, but that seemed fair. And I was more often optimistic than pessimistic about things without any intentional exaggeration. Again, fair. Admittedly, I did know how to exaggerate to make a story more interesting; but I told the truth about the important things. Here's where I started to squirm a bit. I justified myself by arguing that when I did exaggerate, it was obvious – like saying there must have been "a million people" at a concert. People had to know that was a stretch, right? So that didn't really count. On the other hand, the facts about who went with me and what happened while we were there were safely in that "important things" category that I wouldn't mess with. Perhaps I should have stuck to the facts even in the little things. I determined to do better.

Can you think of anyone who constantly exaggerates?
Do you see any harm in it? Explain.
Do you have a hard time believing that person?
Is exaggerating the same as lying? Discuss.

I hope that I am a person whose word is considered trustworthy. Even then, we all need to choose *when* to speak the truth and when to be silent. It's not easy. We shouldn't tell hurtful things to people with no good reason. (e.g.; You don't *need* to tell your friend how bad her new haircut is. She knows.)

There's another type of misinformation that comes to mind in relation to education. Some people don't realize that they are presenting theories as fact because they have come to honestly believe what they have been taught over the years. I watched a television show where college students were being interviewed and were asked why they believed certain scientific "facts." It was amazing how many admitted that it was solely because that is what they were taught in school. Options were never even suggested in their classes. They had never really thoughtfully considered the fact that much of what they were taught was just theory.

Textbooks have actually been rewritten intentionally to take out God and anything relating to Him (see below*) – even though our nation was founded upon biblical truth. And if it's in a textbook, it must be true, right? Wrong! Those who don't know the Lord are often in the dark when it comes to the Bible. There are many well-intentioned teachers out there who share what they've learned with students without even considering possible error. But science itself is not the enemy of truth. Science just keeps confirming the Bible and will continue to do so as science learns more and more. I recently read that the problem is that "Men put the brakes on when science heads for God." For some sad reason biblical truth has been outlawed from our schools. On the other hand, humanism, (i.e., atheism), a religion according to the US Supreme Court, is taught every day in our schools. Humanism says that the only one you can ever count on and that you need to please is yourself. Sound familiar? What about God? *Check out the *Humanist Manifesto II* signed by many prominent Americans – politicians, bankers, CEO's, etc.(*including textbook company officials*) – to see their agenda for removing the "myth" of God from education. The 1973 version is especially eye-opening. We have come a long way from our roots. Never hesitate to question the "facts" given out in school. They break their own rules of scientific process. To quote a popular sci-fi show: "The truth is out there." Evidence for God's truth is all around us. Open your eyes!

Bible Reading: *Psalm 25:4-5, 143:10, Malachi 2:6-7, Proverbs 8:6-12*
Who *alone* should be your teacher?
What is *the* most important quality in a teacher?
What does *Malachi* say are the qualities of a teacher?
Who or what is the master teacher in *Proverbs*?

Challenge: Most of us are at times tempted to stretch the truth either for fun or profit. Join me as I hold myself accountable to truth by not stretching my facts.

"Teach me to do Your will, for You are my God; May Your Good Spirit lead me on level ground."
Psalm 143:10

WEEK 10

"When the almond tree blossoms"

D o you like to hang out with old people? You know, grandpas with no teeth and grandmas who like to pinch your cheeks (the higher ones). Sometimes they smell a little funny, like an overdose of aftershave or perfume, or yummy baking ingredients, or strange medicines. They come in all sizes and shapes and personalities just like younger people. Many have filled out, thinned down or softened up over the years. They may have short hair, long hair, no hair, gray hair, white hair, dark hair, and even cutting edge blue hair. Many of the oldest of them have one very important thing in common – they *love* to tell you stories about the past and are usually pretty good at listening to yours. Maybe it's because they would love to have their favorite stories live on through you after they're gone. The best thing that we can do for them is to listen.

By the time I was born my mother's parents had already passed away, and only my father's father was living. That last remaining grandfather died when I was pretty small because I only have one memory of him in which he scared me. So much for warm, fuzzy memories of grandparents … I always felt a little cheated and surprised at my friends who weren't camped out at their grandparents' homes all the time listening to stories and learning cool stuff. So I adopted a couple of grandparents. My neighbor (the friend who sat on the tack) had a grandfather who was one of my choices. I would help him to pick wild concord grapes in the field behind my house and then we'd go to his house where he lived with his two unmarried daughters, and I would help him to make grape jelly. I suppose I helped more with the picking than the jelly-making. "Pop" was very cool. The other one I adopted was a lady who lived down behind my home off of a dirt road. She might not have been quite old enough to be my grandmother, but she definitely fit my *idea* of "grandmother." I would pick wildflowers for her and leave them on her doorstep. I'd ring the bell and run and hide where I could watch her find them. In retrospect, I just may have been a nuisance.

Are your grandparents living? healthy? nearby?
Do you go out of your way to visit them and help them out?

Some people are very fortunate with grandparents their best dreams couldn't improve upon. I wonder if they realize just how lucky they are? But many may not have grandparents who fit the idyllic image of love and care they might wish for. Some may be bitter over life's disappointments, and it may be difficult to love them. Some simply may not be healthy enough to do "grandma/grandpa" very well, and may even need the care of a nursing home. But many today are healthy. With people living so much longer, some grandparents have moved on to a second life of retirement and busyness that may not allow for the time and love their children and grandchildren long for. Maybe it's because they don't feel needed or wanted? Maybe they're not. Three seniors just recently shared with me their feelings of being pushed aside as if they had nothing valuable to offer.

Having lived in and loved the multi-generational home, I would have to say that we miss out on a lot today with the growing dispersion of our elderly into the warmer states or simply into retirement communities where they begin to lose touch with family and wind up very much alone. Most difficult is when we see even healthy loved ones hopelessly stored away in the closets of the health care system because we don't have time for them. The answer is simple — make time. What's more important?

Would you miss your grandparents if they weren't around?
What are some good ways to spend quality time with grandparents/elderly people?

What does God expect of us with regard to the older people in our lives?

Rise in the presence of the aged, <u>show respect for the elderly</u> and revere your God. I am the Lord. Leviticus 19:32

<u>Is not wisdom found among the aged</u>? Does not long life bring understanding? Job 12:12

<u>If anyone does not provide for his relatives</u>, especially for his immediate family, he has denied the faith and is worse than an unbeliever. I Timothy 5:8

There's a wide variety of ways in which societies have dealt with their elderly throughout the world and time. Some Asians revere their elderly to the point of worshipping them after they're gone. While alive the elders rule the family, and in death they are still looked to for the wisdom that only comes from a long, full life. Some early American Indian tribes out of cruel necessity would leave the aged and infirm along the trail to fend for themselves as these tribal nomads traveled long, hard days on end to find food. Some American movies (*The Giver, Logan's Run, Wild In The Streets*) have sanctioned euthanasia (murder) and internment for the "elderly" who had reached their twenties and thirties! Surprisingly, these plots weren't completely unbelievable.

I recently read about a "death with dignity initiative" for anyone near death (primarily the elderly) in a New England state. It lost by a thin margin (51%/49%) in the general election. Just imagine how that could have been abused! I know of two cases personally where the life of an elderly person would have been "generously" and legally cut short by professional caregivers if the family had not intervened on their behalf. In both cases the elderly person revived to be able to enjoy their lives and to take care of things that they would not have been able to do otherwise.

There are some seniors who may *choose* to live in the growing number of modern senior complexes that offer different levels of activities and care, but this is often too expensive for the average person. And health issues may of necessity force some families to seek outside care. But when societies deposit their oldest members who are lucid and relatively healthy into institutional nursing homes for strangers to care for, never even considering alternatives, they rob them of the joy of living their lives surrounded by everyone and everything that they are familiar with and that they love. I am so encouraged by the recent trend in keeping seniors at home with in-home caregivers. And there will always be families who choose to integrate their elders into their own lives forming multi-generational homes that thrive and abound with love and respect.

When confronted with choices like these in life, don't forget that "what goes around, comes around." God tells us to take care of our families, every member. If we treat our grandparents and parents poorly, leaving them feeling unloved and alone in the last years of their lives, then we should expect no less ourselves when we reach our final years. I have a special affinity for the elderly. I don't expect everyone to enjoy them as much as I do. We're all different. But I wouldn't hesitate to say that we have a sacred duty (yes, sacred) to be there for our grandparents and parents to the best of our abilities when they grow older and infirm. I'm talking about being there in the real sense with love and compassion and a regular physical presence.

A while back I discovered the part music can play in bringing joy to the elderly. I visited an older gentleman in a nursing home with no real response from him. The second time I visited, I sang a song to him and he brightened up with such joy! It was as if I had turned the key in a car. He suddenly came alive. Music is therapeutic, especially songs they love. Sometimes it's not easy to physically be there for an elderly person, especially if he/she is a bit persnickety, but it's important to try.

How have families you know resolved elderly issues?
Has the solution surrounded them with love and respect in their old age?
How do you think you would want to be treated when you're old?

There are a lot of people afraid to get old. They use a thousand skin treatments, energy boosters, and "what-not" to make themselves look and feel younger. Some of them dress as if they were still teenagers. It's tough to accept aging without fighting back at least a little. Though I am still most comfortable in jeans and a sweatshirt, I think I'd like to grow old gracefully. Of course I've never been graceful before in my life, but I might be able to pull it off if I really put my mind to it. What does "graceful" really mean anyway? *Can* a person be graceful in jeans? ...Okay, maybe graceful is out for me.

I know that I definitely want my family to be a big part of my old age, as long as I'm not such a burden that I need professional care. There are some who obviously need the constant medical care that a nursing home can offer. I have no desire to move to Boca (city in Florida with many retirees) and watch my grandchildren grow up via Facetime. I just hope they feel the same way. Meanwhile, remember that many older people around you are frightened by what's happening to them both physically and mentally. You probably all know someone with Alzheimer's or some form of dementia. That's got to be scary for the victim. On some level, especially in the beginning, they are probably aware of their diminishing capacities. Maybe that's why they often seem unhappy. Try to imagine being them. Fear can make people do odd things. And speaking of odd – I have the potential for being quite a handful for my kids when I'm older. I'm trying really hard to start changing now so that when that day comes, they won't stick me in "Happy Acres" (as they sometimes threaten already) and lose the address. I would like so much to be a cool old lady who my daughters, sons-in-law and grandchildren might enjoy hanging out with once in a while even if they have heard my stories a million times before. We could even read this book together.

Bible Reading: *Ecclesiastes 12:1-8, Exodus 20:12,*
I Timothy 5:1-2

Ecclesiastes talks of old age, of the senses fading, of fears rising, and of death. Discuss this verse by verse.

Do you think this is a good description of aging? Explain.

What do you think these changes mean to the elderly?

This topic is important enough to be included in what important list in *Exodus 20*?

In what way are we to treat the elderly? (*I Timothy 5:1-2*)

What is King David's concern in *Psalm 71:9* (below)?

Challenge: Find ways to show love to an older person in your life. Step one is to simply be there in their lives.

"Do not cast me away when I am old; do not forsake me when my strength is gone."
                                                                    Psalm 71:9

WEEK 11

"Get lost!"

"Get lost!" I heard that fairly often. My oldest sister wanted me out of the way when she had her parties. My older brother wanted me to stop following him all of the time. The younger of my two sisters was tired of me being there when she brought her boyfriends home. (One boyfriend slipped me a dollar, not realizing I would have left for free.) "Get lost!" they cried. I can't imagine, writing this now, how I managed to get through all of this without deep emotional scars. (A moment for self-pity, please...) Maybe it's because I never thought they actually expected me to listen. They just wanted me to give them space and not spoil their plans by getting in the way.

Have you ever been told to get lost? By whom?
How did that make you feel?
> "... _no one is concerned for me_ ... no one cares for my life."
> Psalm 142:4

Will God ever tell you to get lost?
> _Though my father and mother forsake me_, the Lord will receive me. Psalm 27:10
> "Though the mountains be shaken and the hills be removed, yet _my unfailing love for you will not be shaken_ nor my covenant of peace be removed," ... Isaiah 54:10

There were a couple of times in my life when my family may have feared that I had listened to them. At least I hope that that would have been their reaction. The first time was when I had gone to a nearby lake in Massachusetts with my family. We had all been down at the water having a wonderful time when I decided that I was tired and would go back to the car and take a little nap. I never liked the sun and heat that much. When you're just a little kid (six or seven ?), it's a good idea to check these things out with your parents before you put them into action. I didn't always think things through. I was tired and the beach was noisy. So I had a great nap in the back of our station wagon under the trees in the parking lot with a slight breeze blowing through the open windows. (This was before we had to worry so much about twisted people and missing kids.) Suddenly someone woke me up rudely: "What on earth were you thinking? Don't you know that everyone is looking for you, including the lifeguards? Boy, are you in trouble!" Okay, I blew it, but I didn't mean to. I had simply gotten lost.

The next time I remember getting lost was when my sister and my cousin, visiting from Long Island, kindly decided to teach me how to ride a two-wheel bicycle. Their idea of teaching was to put me on the seat, get me balanced, and start me down the big hill next to our house. I proved to be a pretty good balancer, but the hill proved to be a pretty good hill. I started to gain a lot of speed and found it difficult to reach the pedals on the boy's bike that was way too big for me. The brakes were in the pedals! The hill didn't end for over a mile as it continued past the dead end sign onto an unused road which literally ended in a huge reservoir. I was smart enough not to take this ride to the end of the track. I turned into a field long before the lake, was stopped abruptly by a stone wall, went headlong over the stones into the field, and lay bruised and embarrassed on the other side until I got my bearings. Rather than confronting the ridicule of my teachers, I returned to my home through the back fields, hurried down into my basement, and climbed up a big pipe that led to a little shelf (unnoticed due to inaccessibility) at the top of a closet. There I fell asleep once again. (What's with me napping all the time?) Remember what was said after the lake incident above? Except for the lifeguard part – ditto: "What on earth was I thinking? Didn't I know that everyone was looking for me? Boy, was I in trouble!"

One more story about getting lost, but this time *I* did not get into trouble. My family decided to go to an amusement park nearby in Massachusetts. When we got there I decided to hang out with my brother and so informed my mom. Trouble was that my brother hadn't agreed to this and I hadn't shared that part with her. Very quickly he raced away through the crowd to lose the little shadow behind him. I'm sure he expected me to return to my mother after he succeeded, but I kept trying to find him until my return was thwarted by the fact that I had indeed become lost. I was smart enough to know that moving from place to place was only going to make things worse. I got to the gate we had entered and considered waiting there, but some sketchy people ruled that out. I decided to return to the car thereby ensuring the fact that they couldn't leave without me and would eventually find me. I thought I had a great plan.

The parking lot was dark, so I sat down by the back wheel of the car where no bad guys could find me. I have to admit – it was kind of scary. I was there for quite some time before my brother came looking for me. A few moments later I heard a lot of noise coming through the now half-empty lot. Everything being said sounded familiar except that it was being directed toward my brother: "What on earth had *he* been thinking? Didn't *he* know that *she* would get lost? Boy, was *he* in trouble!" It turns out that park security was involved in the somewhat lengthy hunt, but it was my brother who finally found me. And I was not asleep this time.

If you have ever seen the movie, *Taken,* you will realize that going off on your own is not an option in our world today. Young girls, but much older than I was in this story, have disappeared never to be seen again. It's cliché to say, but "You *really* can't be too careful!" Kids do dumb things and I was the queen of dumb when it came to getting lost at beaches and parks. I got lost because I was tired and thoughtless, because I was embarrassed, and because I tried to keep up with my older brother who I knew full well didn't want me tagging along. But only in the last story was I actually in a situation where I was at all afraid. Once again God had His angels looking out for me. (*Psalm 91:11, Matthew 18:10, Psalm 34:7*) Things could have turned out so much worse.

What's the difference between "Get lost!" and getting lost?
Have you ever actually been lost? Explain.
How did that make you feel?
> *You have taken my companions and loved ones from me;* the
> darkness is my closest friend. Psalm 88:18
> *You will live in constant suspense,* filled with dread both day and
> night, never sure of your life. Deuteronomy 28:66

Have you ever considered the fact that there are angels looking
out for you?

Being truly lost must be a terrible thing. You may have some
harrowing tales of getting lost in your life, but I guarantee you that
there's a worse place to be lost. To be lost in the spiritual realm
is the *ultimate* "lost" because it may be an eternal state of being.
Hopefully if you are lost spiritually, you know how to find the Way
and how to get back to your Father. Jesus says, *"I am the way and
the truth and the life. No one comes to the Father except through
me." (John 14:6)* And hopefully if someone you know is lost, you
can direct him/her to the Way. First we have to admit that we are
sinners and then commit our lives to the One who can save us
from sin's penalty of death.

The Romans' Road might help:
> *(Write these on an index card and keep it in your Bible.)*
>
> *Romans 3:10, 23: As it is written, "There is no one righteous, not even
> one." ...for all have sinned and fall short of the glory of God.*
>
> *Romans 6:23: For the wages of sin is death, but the gift of God is
> eternal life in Jesus Christ our Lord.*
>
> *Romans 5:8: But God demonstrates his own love for us in this: while
> we were still sinners, Christ died for us.*
>
> *Romans 10:9-10, 13: ...if you confess with your mouth, "Jesus Christ
> is Lord," and believe in your heart that God raised him from the dead,
> you will be saved. For it is with your heart that you believe and are
> justified, and it is with your mouth that you confess and are saved. ...
> "Everyone who calls on the name of the Lord will be saved."*

Romans 1:17: For in the Gospel a righteousness from God is revealed, a righteousness that is by faith from first to last, just as it is written: "The righteous will live by faith."

Romans 8:1, 37: Therefore there is now no condemnation for those who are in Christ Jesus....No, in all these things we are more than conquerors through him who loved us.

It is said that women, unlike men, are more apt to ask for directions when they're lost. If this is the case, then we should find it easier to follow the directions given above and elsewhere in the Bible. If you have ever been lost and you remember how you felt when you were found, you will understand the special thrill the verse at the end of this week gives to so many.

Bible Reading: *Acts 7:59-8:3, 9:1-22*

Saul (Paul) was certainly lost when we first see him in *Acts*.

What was he doing when we first see him?

What happened on the Damascus Road? (chapter 9)

How did Ananias (not the one married to Sapphira) feel about Saul?

Can you think of anyone else in the Bible who felt this way about someone God told him to speak to?

(Hint: A book in the Old Testament is named after him.)

What did God tell Ananias?

What did Paul do after meeting with Ananias? (especially verses 9:20 and 9:22)

Challenge: Help someone, spiritually, to find the way back home.

"For the Son of Man came to seek and to save what was lost."

Luke 19:10

WEEK 12

"My brother, my hero"

absolutely adored my brother who was five and a half years older than me. He knew how to make great tree forts high up in the best trees – which I often moved into after he had abandoned them. He was pretty good with a B-B gun – which I got to try a couple of times. And I learned so much just tagging along after him. There was that time he tried to lose me (and succeeded) in the amusement park; but he *was* the one to find me in the end. Then there was the time in the snow ... Being so much younger my legs were a lot shorter than his. We had just had a huge snowstorm and the snow was nearly up to my waist. My brother headed out into the drifts of snow and I began to follow. It was a lot of work following in his footsteps (no pun intended). He began to take larger and larger strides and I'm sure he must have noticed how much more difficult that made it for me to lift my little legs up and over the waist deep snow to make it to the next footprint made by his longer legs. I couldn't see his face but can imagine there was a hint of a smile on it. It wasn't long before I was stuck solid in that snow. He kept going and I struggled for quite a while to eventually turn around and get back to the house. But I don't remember feeling discouraged.

Probably the worst thing my brother ever did to me aside from decapitating Susie, my favorite doll, at the center of a dart board in a knife-throwing act, was to actually *let* me play with him one day. He said that I could play "Cowboys and Indians" with him and that he would tie me to a tree like the Indians did in the movies. I was thrilled! So, he tied me securely to a tree in the state forest across the street from our home and walked off. I've been pretty patient throughout my life and perhaps it all started here. I waited. I watched a caterpillar crawl up right next to me on the tree, watched him crawl from the bottom of the tree to a spot above my head as I waited. I listened to the birds and the wind and waited some more. I waited *a very long time*. Finally, I heard someone coming toward me through the woods. It turned out to be my brother with my dad. I could hear my father's anger as my brother led him to the spot where I was "one with the tree." It seems that my family had sat down to eat supper and my parents asked if anyone knew where I was. The truth came out. My brother had tied me to a tree and then went off and forgot all about me. Big trouble. I wasn't mad at him at all and hated to hear him being punished that night. In spite of everything, he was still my hero.

Do you have a brother or sister you look up to? Explain.
Has your admiration ever been shaken? Lost? Why?
What (if anything) helped to restore It?

I don't want you to get the wrong impression about my brother. He could definitely screw up from time to time, but he did find me in the park that day and he did show me how to use a BB gun. He was also the one who made sure I didn't get into a car with some strangers one day. I was walking home alone when a car pulled up with two or three men in it. They held out a toy and asked me if it was mine. Something inside me said to back off and I refused to come nearer the car telling them that the toy wasn't mine. Just then my brother came up the road behind me and told me to go into the house, which we did together as the car sped away. I'm not sure what happened that night, but I heard that a few men including my dad, had had "a talk" with two or three strangers they had discovered in a car in town, men who had approached more than one child that day. It seemed that the men would never be returning. Our little town had been shaken and parents were telling children all over the neighborhood that night to watch out for these strangers and to run home if they saw them. You see, my brother really did love me, just as I always knew.

Take some time on these:
If you could pick one person, who would you just love to meet? Why?
If you could talk to him/her, what would you want to ask him/her?
What makes your heroes truly worth your admiration?

We don't always admire the right people. We revere athletes and movie stars, musicians and politicians. Usually for the wrong reasons. And don't forget that they are paid a lot of money to play with a ball, to act or to entertain – not exactly motives that should inspire confidence. And yes, I'm afraid that politicians today need to act and entertain just to get elected. Sure our heroes work hard at their trades, but we pay them ridiculous amounts of money for the throw of a football, or for acting in a movie or singing a song that leads us where we are not always comfortable going. And why should we give *their* opinions so much attention? We have good cause to question their wisdom when we take a look at their life decisions. We vote for them because they are good-looking or because they tickle our ears with sweet words. Why? It's ridiculous and a little scary that we have allowed it to go so far. Can't we come up with better heroes than we've got out there today?

As I grew up I learned to love my brother more and more and for better reasons, but I've got new heroes. C. S. Lewis is a hero of mine; he has taught me so much. And this humble guy I know in a low-income job – I am so impressed with his quiet wisdom. My mother is maybe my greatest hero, and she's a tough act to follow. My brother regained some footing when he called me from Billy Graham's porch a few years ago to tell me that he was doing some work for the Grahams enclosing their pool. Anyone who hung out with Billy and Ruth deserves *some* respect. Right?

What types of heroes does our society emulate?

They rejected his decrees and the covenants he had made with their fathers and the warnings he had given them. They followed worthless idols... they imitated the nations around them... they did the things the Lord had forbidden them to do. 2 Kings 17:15

What does the Bible have to say about what's really important?

... be on your guard so that you may not be carried away by the error of lawless men ... But grow in the grace and knowledge of our Lord and Savior, Jesus Christ. 2 Peter 3:17-18

Finally, brothers, whatsoever is true, ...noble, ...right, ...pure, ... lovely, ...admirable – if anything is excellent or praiseworthy – think about such things. whatever you have learned or received or heard from me – or seen in me – put it into practice... Philippians 4:8-9

Do not love the world or anything in the world... I John 2:15

But if serving the Lord seems undesirable to you, then choose for yourselves this day whom you will serve... Joshua 24:15

The world really hasn't changed that much from the Old and New Testament days. Nor was it all that different after 500 years of Christianity having its influence on the world. In St. Augustine's *Confessions* he describes a society that sounds surprisingly like ours today. He was even into clubbing. Then and now people have chosen to reject God, follow worthless idols, and imitate the nations around them. We listen to songs and watch movies that we know are not God-honoring. The progression goes something like this: "There are only a couple of bad words in this song." Then: "I don't really listen to all of the words." Next comes: "Except for one or two scenes, it's a good movie." Finally: "I fast forward through half of the movie anyway." We justify everything we do that is contrary to what that still small voice is trying to tell us. *Luke 16:15* says, "You are the ones who justify yourselves in the eyes of men, but God knows your heart. *What is highly valued among men is detestable in God's eyes.*" Stop making excuses for your sinful nature and do something about it! If Christians stopped paying to see bad movies, the industry would start cleaning them up. There are too many of us to ignore.

What else could Christians do or stop doing that could make a difference?

What character traits should our heroes have?

Think about the qualities listed above in *Philippians* that the Bible says are worth admiring: true, noble, right, pure, lovely, admirable, excellent and praiseworthy...

Examine the true meaning of these words.

Who, when you look around at your world, exhibits these qualities?

Do you love the world or anything in the world?

Do you need new heroes?

Bible Reading: *Romans 1:18-2:1*

How do people suppress the truth?

Why are they (and we) without excuse?

Who or what are our idols (heroes) today?

Are they a part of our world today as described in verses 26-32?

Are your heroes really worthy of praise?

Though we may need new heroes, why are we not to judge?

Challenge: Research a little and find a couple of heroes who are really worth emulating.

"Be imitators of God, therefore, as dearly loved children."
Ephesians 5:1

WEEK 13

"Why *should* the sun be shining?"

When I was young, we didn't have a private phone line; it was a party line. This meant that we might pick up the phone and hear someone else talking. So then we would have to wait to make our call. Sometimes it could be a long wait. And the worst part for us was – the other party. We shared our line with a couple who had an older single son who was (sorry to say) a little bit sketchy. His mail included magazines covered in brown paper (porn) and he listened in on our phone conversations regularly, especially my sister talking to her boyfriend. He was relentless and we could easily hear his heavy breathing on the phone. We would tell him to get off the phone and then we'd hear the "click" when he hung up.

Have you ever had a difficult neighbor?
Did you handle it well? (It's not easy.)
How should we deal with people like our eavesdropper?
"...*Love your neighbor as yourself.*" Matthew 22:39b
"Be completely humble and gentle; *be patient*, bearing with one another in love." Ephesians 4:2

One night my father wasn't feeling well, so my mother and my sister took him in to see the doctor. An hour or so later the phone rang and someone answered it. I don't remember who. It didn't seem important. Shortly after that the front doorbell rang and I went to answer it. It was the other party on our phone line. He pretended to be selling magazines when suddenly he asked, "Did your father just die?" Shocked at this ridiculously rude question I said, "No!" and slammed the door. I was ten years old at the time. Then things started to happen fast. My uncle showed up; and I think a couple of other relatives came over. My uncle called us into the living room to tell us the unimaginable. My father *had* just died. I wasn't surprised because somewhere inside I struggled with the fear that the eavesdropper knew something I didn't. The party listening in on us had heard the bad news before I had and had come over to confirm it. I liked him even less now.

Everything after that happened so fast that I hardly remember it. My worst memory is of my father in a casket made up in a way that made him look like a whitewashed, mime-like caricature of the father I loved. That image is seared into my memory. I would rather have remembered him alive and healthy. He was buried in the cemetery next to my mother's parents and the infant son that my parents had lost. It was raining during the burial which somehow seemed to suit the situation. I remember thinking, "Why *should* the sun be shining today?" I just did whatever they told me to do. Sit. Stand. Walk. Whatever... Everyone was crying. I guess I did too. I don't remember.

My father was a young man, a friend to many, and his death was unexpected. He had been a heavy smoker before they knew how bad it was for your health. But he had quit! It seemed so unfair. There was no town ambulance and no car emergency flashers back then. My sister told me how difficult it was to get people to let them pass their cars on the way to the hospital. (To this day, I move over for people trying to pass. Maybe it's an emergency.) My father had had a massive coronary and had died quickly before the people at the hospital could respond. He hadn't gone to the doctor after all, but to the hospital. I guess they thought it was better for us not to know how serious it was when they left that day.

Have you ever had a parent or grandparent die?

How were you able to get through it (or maybe you weren't)?

What does God's Word have to say about this kind of loss?
Blessed are those who mourn, for they will be comforted.
Matthew 5:4

Where, Oh death, is your victory? Where, Oh death, is your sting? …
thanks be to God! He gives us the victory through our Lord, Jesus
Christ. I Corinthians 15:55-57
He will wipe every tear from their eyes. There will be no more death
or mourning or crying or pain, for the old order of things has passed
away. Revelation 21:4

Each of us kids from my perspective responded differently to my father's death. The sister closest to me in age did a lot of crying. She was a daddy's girl and she spent a great deal of time with our mother over the next few weeks. She seemed to be burdened with a fear of death after that for many years. My "hero" brother seemed to be trying to hold everything inside, growing more and more angry with each passing week. He had to work through some issues with anger when he was a young adult, but God brought him the perfect wife to help him with that. My oldest sister was in the car with my mother when she drove my dad to the hospital. When they arrived at the emergency room there was no one around, so my mother ran in to get help. While she was gone, my dad died in my twenty-one year old sister's arms. His last request was that she help our mom with the younger kids. So my sister's method for dealing with the death of my father was to honor that request, taking responsibility for all kinds of things, things for which she basically gave up her own life. It was years before I understood just how much she gave up for us. My oldest brother seemed shaken, but he was married and not around much, so I didn't get to see his response – unless it was avoidance.

Of course the one I am best able to speak for is me. I looked around and saw all of the crying shoulders taken and all of the listening ears engaged, so I went off alone into the woods. I had it out with God. I wrote arcane poetry sitting in the branches at the tops of the trees. I talked to Him about my sadness, my anger, my confusion, and my fears. And He listened. He really did! I so totally felt His presence and His love that I don't think I've ever felt as close to Him in my life as I did during those next few months. I think it was here that my overly strong lifelong independent streak began (independence from other people, not from God). My desire to be without the emotional need for others was so extreme that I have been struggling to keep it restrained for many years since. I also made peace with death, no slight thing as I later discovered. Good thing too because in the next couple of years death seemed to become a frequent visitor to my life. Not long afterward two of my dad's sisters also passed away.

How do different people respond to a loved one's death? How about you?

What advice does God give us?

When calamity comes, ... even in death the righteous have a refuge. Proverbs 14:32

...weeping may remain for a night, but rejoicing comes in the morning. Psalm 30:5b

Precious in the sight of the Lord, is the death of his saints. Psalm 116:15

Rejoice in the Lord always ... Do not be anxious about anything, but in everything, by prayer and petition, with thanksgiving, present your requests to God. And the peace of God, which transcends all understanding, will guard your hearts and your minds in Christ Jesus. Philippians 4:4-7

If our loved ones have accepted Jesus as Lord of their lives, we have no reason to be anxious for them. I know that may seem trite to say that, but it's true. My cousin, David, who was more like a brother to me, was very sick a few years ago and was nearing death, but he had lived for the Lord all of his life and he and his wife had a special peace "which transcends all understanding." (*Philippians 4:7*) One of his doctors was so bewildered by his peace that he asked David if he truly understood his prognosis. He had no fear, only concern for those he left behind. He and I talked about heaven and how awesome it would be. We talked about how God loved his family even more than he did and how they would be left in the very best care possible – God's. We asked for God's healing, but God chose to take him home (the ultimate healing). Why is it that we only begin to truly understand what's important in life when we come face-to-face with eternity? My father's death prepared me for so much in life. I came to understand, even as a child, that I would see my father again "in the twinkling of an eye" (*I Corinthians 15:52*). The Lord chose to take my cousin to heaven, but I know I will see him again, along with all of those who have gone on before me. How awesome is that?

I remember a short film I saw once at camp. It was a court-room scene with four teenagers who had just died in a car crash who were now in front of a judge. The first three all made cases for their personal goodness and pled for a positive verdict, but were each in turn sentenced to hell. Good deeds were not enough. The fourth one came forward and was exonerated through the perfect goodness of his Savior, Jesus Christ. He was headed for heaven. The thing that really struck me and stays with me to this day is the look that was on each of the other three teens' faces as they looked at their friend and asked him why he had never shared his faith with them. That movie should be seen by all of us. It might help us to focus on what's really important. I'm sure we all want to see our friends in heaven some day, but who will tell them about Jesus if we don't? According to the Barna Group's research, over 80% of the unchurched people polled would go to church if invited, but only 2% of church-goers ever ask.

We live in a broken world beset with sin and its consequences, one of which is death. It was not something that God wanted for us, but something that we brought upon ourselves when we chose disobedience. Losing someone we love to death stinks. However, we do not grieve "like the rest of men who have no hope." (*I Thessalonians 4:13*) Is that a great verse or what? "Hope" in the Bible is not the weak uncertainty we talk of today when we say "I hope I get a new i-phone for Christmas." The hope that God promises has an assurance attached to it that gives us full confidence in the fruition of that for which we hope.

Are you comfortable with the thought of eternity and Heaven?
What's the most important thing we should be focused on here on Earth?
Is that your focus? (Whew! Tough question for anyone.)

"Why should the sun be shining?"

Why does a good God tolerate death? (*Romans 5:12*)

Bible Reading: *John 11:32-44*

Were Martha and Mary both disappointed with Jesus for His delay?

Do you sometimes feel that way? Explain.

Why do you think Jesus cried?

Did Martha think removing the stone from the grave was a good idea? Why not?

What do verses 25 and 26 of this chapter tell us?

What insight into the character of Jesus do we get from this story?

Challenge: Refocus on things of eternal value, and find ways to do so regularly.

"...What is your life? You are a mist that appears for a little while and then vanishes."

James 4:14

WEEK 14

"Never alone"

My father's death was obviously not over and done with in my life by writing a few strange poems and having it out with God. The scab kept getting pulled off over and over again. Like the day I returned to school and curious friends bluntly asked me once again, "Did your father die?" None of them knew what it felt like to lose a parent or how much it hurt to be asked that question repeatedly. It would never have occurred to their parents to coach them on this issue. But at least this time they were kids and they had that excuse for their unintentional insensitivity. It was at times a real challenge to hold my tongue. I lived in a single-parent home long before that phrase had become a category of interest on forms and in studies.

Life changed abruptly and dramatically. Right away money became an issue. My parents had never bothered with life insurance, so my mother suddenly joined the work force full-time. She had grown up in Wolf Point, Montana, and had graduated from high school in Grand Forks, North Dakota with a major in music. I bet you didn't know that was ever even possible. …surprised me. She was a very talented lady. She was a great pianist; she could sew up a storm; she pulled off many do-it-yourself projects around the house; and she was artistic and creative beyond the norm. The trouble was that no one in our small town needed an employee with those qualifications. So she worked at the local grocery store for little pay and long hours. The owners were old friends from "back in the day" before my dad had turned his life around. I'm not sure the wife had ever forgiven my mom for pulling away from their former friendship, but the husband was kind, sneaking mom a bonus ham or a roast for special occasions. This was the reason we had little supervision at home in the afternoons. My sister and I began to be responsible for much of the cleaning and cooking since my oldest brother was married and my oldest sister had a full-time job. Meals definitely went downhill when mom started to work eight to ten hours a day. I could do spaghetti, hotdogs, and a couple of other things – not that different from today, now that I think of it.

Life also changed slowly and subtly. At first, people were kind and attentive because we had had a death in the family, but I began to notice them drifting away and dropping us (mom) off of the invitation lists for certain events. I guess people don't like to be reminded of sadness. Or maybe they didn't think she would want to be included with a bunch of couples. Either way, my mother was now "odd man out" and rarely got invited to the things she and my father had always enjoyed going to together. I would sometimes catch her crying in her bedroom when she didn't think we could hear her. She would recover quickly and rejoin the regimen of life barely missing a beat, but it was a lonely time for her. We now had many more homemade clothes because she could make them for much less money than she could buy them. Had my mother not been so talented that might have become a difficult memory, but she was gifted so it is actually a memory of joy and pride – except when I think of how long she sometimes worked into the night finishing something special for one of us. I guess we were kind of poor, but it's funny how I never really felt poor. We always had enough to eat, though we rarely had steak, and most of our food was from scratch – no pre-packaged stuff. But that was actually better for us. And we had nice clothes to wear, though our closets were not exactly hard to find things in. Life was surprisingly good in spite of the sadness. I attribute that to my mom and to God's grace.

Has anyone ever said or done something unintentionally that hurt you?
The tongue has the power of life and death, and those who love it will eat its fruit. Proverbs 18:21

How did you handle that?
Were you raised in a single-parent home?
What was the hardest part?
Were you rich? poor? or somewhere in between?
How did that affect you?
Did/do you rise above your struggles or fall into trouble?

He who walks with the wise grows wise, but a companion of fools suffers harm. Proverbs 13:20
If any of you lacks wisdom, let him ask God... James 1:5

Sure, I was raised in a single-parent home for half of my youth, but my father died. He didn't walk out on me. I don't pretend to know how it feels in that case. I do, however, understand the struggles, financial and otherwise, that follow the separation. I had to struggle with the issues of death; you may have struggled or still be struggling with the issues of divorce or desertion. I had no warning of my father's impending death; you may have seen the signs coming and have additional scars from that. Either way we both would have dealt with the tears and the loneliness and the scramble for stability, financial and emotional. Or ... you may have been one of the lucky ones never to have had crisis or hardship in all of your life. Do you know what a blessing that is? But you must have a friend who has experienced the loss of a loved one in some way. The statistics are too high for anyone to remain totally untouched by them. Be a good friend. Listen, and love them. Talking often doesn't help that much, especially if you've never gone through anything similar. Just listen.

I said and did some pretty dumb things myself after divorce became a part of a good friend's life. I started quoting Scripture and giving all kinds of wonderful advice. I guess I expected a couple of Bible verses might do the trick. Naïve. Now I'm certainly not minimizing the Bible verses and the power of God's Word, but my friend knew the same verses I did and they were not helping! Not because there was no power behind the verses, but because this relationship had raced so far down the road toward divorce, that one or both parties had given up hope. We can only pretend to understand the hurt, anger, sense of betrayal, and blow to self-worth that arise in the midst of most divorces unless we've been through one ourselves. And the loneliness can be so deep. I had to apologize several years later for being such a poor friend. I really had no idea what I was doing.

> If death, desertion or divorce is a part of your life, you may be bitter, angry, or depressed over it. What does the Bible say about dealing with all of these things?
> *I will strengthen you and help you; I will uphold you with my righteous right hand. Isaiah 41:10*
> *I have told you these things, so that in me you might have peace. In this world, you will have trouble. But take heart! I have overcome the world. John 16:33*
> *Peace I leave with you; my peace I give to you. I do not give to you as the world gives. Do not let your hearts be troubled and do not be afraid. John 14:27*

> What does the Bible say about being a good friend?
> *A friend loves at all times, and a brother is born for adversity. Proverbs 17:17*
> *… Jonathan became one in the spirit with David, and he loved him as himself. I Samuel 18:1*

I know that God hates divorce and that we should do all we can to avoid it, but sometimes it's out of our control. Especially if we're one of the children in a broken relationship. Our only option is in how we choose to handle it afterwards. We can grow bitter, angry and depressed, or we can rise above it. The sad thing is that the bitterness, the anger, and the depression often can hurt those who allow these strong emotions to rule or to undermine their lives for many years later, sometimes throughout adulthood. These cancerous feelings will cripple us and steal the joy and peace that God has planned for us, and they will actually make it harder for others to love us. And as difficult as this might sound, it is often through our response in loving a family member or friend, in spite of hating his/her actions, that *we* begin to heal and that that person begins to soften to the Holy Spirit. That should be our ultimate desire, not necessarily a restored relationship, and certainly not revenge or self-righteous judgment. We can love them and pray for them from a distance if that's all they'll allow, even if they have not yet shown any remorse for the hurts they have caused. It may take a little while to get there because most people don't just bounce back from these kinds of hurt quickly. Time really does help to heal. But it won't unless you let it. You have to *choose* to forgive.

There are so many people hurting from the scars of divorce in this self-centered world. Its newborn perfection is broken. And we broke it. God loves the victims of divorce just as much as He loves the rest of us. We are not somehow better because we have never experienced divorce. We are all sinners. But we can find healing and forgiveness at the foot of the Cross. And repentance can open the door to a forgiving heart. One thing I do know is this: forgiveness for others and for yourself is a big step toward healing. Talk to someone who can help you if you're struggling with this. Don't wait. And remember that with God, you are *never* alone.

Bible Reading: *Job 1:9-22, 13:15a*
What happened to Job?
Why did it happen? because of sin?
Why does God allow bad things to happen to good people?
What was Job's response?
Job 13:15a is one of my favorite Bible verses.
Think about it. Can you claim that verse?

Job took some big hits in his life. I'm always amazed at how he challenges God (respectfully) and how God honors Job's questions by answering them. Of course His answer does come with a significant disciplinary reminder of His omniscience and omnipotence. It was hard for me at first to understand why it was permissible for Job in relating to the sovereign God to be so fearless as to question Him at all. In *The Lion, the Witch, and The Wardrobe* by C.S. Lewis, Susan asks a question of Mr. Beaver concerning Aslan, the lion (and type of Christ): "Is He – quite safe?" ... "Safe?" said Mr. Beaver. ... "Who said anything about safe? ... but He's good. He's the King I tell you." There is something a bit scary about God, about boldly going before His throne and really talking to Him, the Creator God. But then I grew to understand better His deep love for us. He actually wants to hear our questions and to help us to know Him better. At the end of the book of *Job*, God does call Job out and basically asks him "Do you know who I am? Do you remember who you're talking to?" He reminds Job of his place in relation to God – something we all need to think of more often. In chapter 40 God asks Job, "Would you discredit my justice? Would you condemn me to justify yourself?" Would *you*?

Challenge: Forgive God for allowing other people to make choices that hurt you. Forgive your parent(s) or spouse for choosing divorce instead of honoring their vows. Forgive yourself for not dealing with your hurt sooner.

"The Lord gave and the Lord has taken away; may the name of the Lord be praised."
                                                                                                    Job 1:21b

WEEK 15

"The party's at my house!"

I'm not sure if my house became the party house *because* my father wasn't there or *in spite of* it. Fathers can be scary and a definite cooling agent for fun at times. All I know is that we had way more than our share of parties. Keep in mind that these parties never involved alcohol, drugs or sex, and you might be surprised at just how popular they were. I'm not sure kids know how to throw a party that is as much fun today. There seem to be expectations today in society that are way too grown-up and not half as entertaining. I was blessed to be a part of a group of Christian teens who knew how to have fun, who really lived their faith, and who understood that alcohol, drugs and sex could ruin lives even if only dabbling in them. We weren't perfect (far from it), but we had some pretty smart boundaries and lots of fun.

When I was young it was my oldest sister who had the parties. We had a semi-finished basement in our ranch style house that my father and mother had built a few years before he passed away. The floor was tiled with a few throw rugs here and there, and the walls were either painted cement (on the outer walls) or sheetrock (on the partitioning walls). This was the house near the church. All of my sister's friends would pile into the basement with their guitars and their autoharps (miniature harps that could be played on the lap – very cool). We had a big old upright piano and a cozy fireplace on the finished side of the basement, so in the cold weather a fire was usually blazing to warm the heart of these parties. I would sneak downstairs from time to time and my sister would chase me right back upstairs, banishing me from the festivities below. Her best friend would take compassion on me and get me all charged up to help her make popcorn. It worked every time. I would come upstairs dejected and disappointed and be happily involved in making popcorn for the gang downstairs minutes later. She was good. The music coming from downstairs was a mix of choruses from the church string-band and the pop music of the Elvis generation. He was my sister's favorite. It sounded like so much fun! I got to know the music of her generation before I was ten.

Do you have older siblings?
Did they like having you around?
Did you learn much from them? Good or bad? Explain.

Years later it was my turn. Only this time, you would hear the Beach Boys, Simon and Garfunkel, the Beatles, and even some of the older Everly Brothers and Elvis, all mixed in with the newer choruses being sung in church at that time. We had guitars (including a bass), plus a piano, and, ready for this? Drums. (Drums had *never* been a part of our music prior to this. This was a very big deal.) My brother was our drummer. He was and still is a very good drummer. But his practice sessions were a source of concern for my mother. One young boy who lived next door to us complained to his mom that he couldn't get up for school because of the drums the night before. She was laughing as she told us this, so she didn't seem to have a problem with it. He went to school. Besides, my brother never practiced that late at night. And practice is important for a musician. How else can skills be improved?

Well, time changes things, but not always in the fundamentals. There was still a fire blazing in the fireplace and lots of creative games that made us all laugh. Good clean fun was being enjoyed to the background of good music. I'm not sure if we should have been mixing the church songs in with the secular, but we did *a lot* to clean up any words we didn't like in the popular songs, though I'm not sure that the artists would have approved of us messin' with their lyrics. (e.g., In the Beachboys' song, *Sloop John B.*, the first mate got "in a funk," not "drunk.")

In addition to music, my cousins and their friends were into cars, fast cars. We had GTO's, Corvettes, Mustangs, Camaros, Roadrunners, an older Jaguar XKE, all kinds of cars parked out in front of our house and on the lawn. Our house became the youth extension of the church. There were of course those who did not approve, and my mother took some unwarranted blows to her good name; but if anyone knew what was going on at our house, it was me; and I can tell you for sure that it really was just good clean fun. Most of the gang who hung out in those days are still active Christians, and I wouldn't be surprised if my mother's warm, open home had contributed to that.

Is there a safe house that you can go to and have fun?
What is it that makes that house fun? safe?
What do you think about secular music? Christian music?
    Mixing them together?
Who are some of your favorite popular artists? Why?
What are some of your favorite popular songs? Why?
How would their lyrics stand up to God's standards?
    May the words of my mouth and the meditation of my heart
    be pleasing in your sight, O Lord, my Rock and my Redeemer
    Psalm 19:14
    Put to death, therefore, whatever belongs to your earthly nature:
    sexual immorality, impurity, lust, evil desires and greed, which is
    idolatry. ... rid yourselves of such things as these: anger, rage,
    malice, slander, and filthy language from your lips. Colossians 3:5, 8b
Would you want to have Jesus attend one of your parties?

For a long time ours was the last house on our street. We would get all the people who would get stuck or lost down at the dead end past our house. And I think it made the guys in the fast cars feel safer "peeling out" right in front of the house to know that most likely no one was coming up the hill. There was so much tire rubber on the road out front that we would joke that the road would never need repaving. And eventually, my cousins taught *me* how to drive – *in their cool cars*! Can you believe it? One of my favorite cousins took me in his '65 mustang round and round in the elementary school parking lot one rainy night patiently waiting for me to come to terms with the whole clutch thing. Another one told me that I wasn't done learning until I could "catch rubber" in all four gears. If you don't know what catching rubber means, it's when you pop the clutch on a standard car just enough to get a little "chirp" from the tires on the road. First and second gears were easy. Third wasn't too difficult, but fourth? Whew! That took a while to master. Today, most people drive automatic cars and never get to have the thrill of deciding for themselves when and how to change gears, or if they want to go for that little chirp.

Sometimes I would feel bad for my mother. She really did put up with a lot of youthful shenanigans. And though she never encouraged them, I don't remember her ever getting angry. She would sit in the living room while our parties were going on (never went to sleep) and she would talk to the kids who wandered upstairs to take a break from the noise, or maybe just to find her. I have a feeling she was often praying up there too. There were many kids who got counsel from her. Good thing she was a woman of God with wise advice. There was a short time when I got a little jealous of her attention toward other kids, but I remembered that not all parents were as easy to talk to as she was. I would share. I knew I was fortunate, and I was even a little proud of my mother.

Can you "catch rubber in all four gears"? (just curious...)
Can you talk to one or both of your parents? Discuss.
What adult, besides them, can you talk to openly?
Can you trust their wisdom? How do you know?
From whom does the Bible say we should seek counsel?
> *Show me your ways, O Lord, teach me your paths; guide me in your truth and teach me, for you are God, my Savior, and my hope is in you all day long. Psalm 25:4-5*
> *Blessed is the man who does not walk in the counsel of the wicked or stand in the way of sinners or sit in the seat of mockers. But his delight is in the law of the Lord, and on his law he meditates day and night. He is like a tree planted by the streams of water, which*

*yields its fruit in season and whose leaf does not wither. Whatever
he does prospers. Psalm 1:1-3*
*The way of a fool seems right to him, but <u>a wise man listens to advice</u>.
Proverbs 12:15*

We all need a safe place to hang out in once in a while and we need a good person to talk to whose advice we can count on. I was fortunate to have both right at home when I was growing up, but others have had to look outside of their homes. Sometimes it can feel pretty risky to trust another person, especially if you've been hurt. God wants the best for you and He will bring another person into your life to come alongside you. Just make sure that the person you trust is following God's Word and not his/her own opinions or the teachings of anyone other than Jesus Christ. And remember that as much as you respect your friends' advice, they probably do not yet have the experience and wisdom that an adult might have. Pray about it and God will help you. And don't ever forget that the Bible is the best source for wisdom. Read it regularly and memorize helpful verses. Even Christ Himself quoted Scripture when he was tempted by Satan in the desert.

Bible Reading: *Proverbs 4:18-27*

How are light and dark contrasted? Explain.

Why is it important to listen to good advice? (verse 22)

What is the most important thing to guard? Explain.

How would you advise someone to keep on "the straight and narrow"?

Challenge: Find a parent or another adult with whom you can communicate well and whom you can trust for wisdom, someone who obviously spends time in God's Word. Talk with that person regularly.

"Whether you turn to the right or to the left, your ears will hear a voice behind you, saying, 'This is the way, walk in it.'"

Isaiah 30:21

WEEK 16

"In over my head"

After I discovered God in the woods, I became more and more of a loner. I don't mean to suggest that I never hung out with other kids, because I did, but I developed an appreciation for spending time alone too. I did a little of both. Originally there was no one in the neighborhood at the new house my age. If I wanted to see my cousins in the old neighborhood, I would have to walk about a half mile or so, and though this was only a short hike, I made the trip less and less often.

After a few years I was delighted to discover a new friend in my neighborhood. We had gotten a new young pastor, Pastor B., who had preceded his family to town to perform my father's funeral, his first service at our church. He had a daughter who was only a couple of years younger than me. They lived two houses away, right next to the church. We started to hang out either in the woods or playing *Barbie* dolls together at her house. Can you imagine? Me, playing with Barbie dolls? She is a great lifelong friend, but probably looked up to me back then more than I deserved. Her dad kind of adopted me, inviting me along with his family to go swimming and to do other fun stuff. They opened their door to me day after day (amazing!) as I showed up to get my "father fix." I learned goofy songs (two about hotdogs) and even goofier catch phrases from him that I remember to this day. (e.g., "What a meatball!" and "Sad deal!") He gave me away at my wedding. Awesome guy.

The state forest around my house and the long reservoir within it were a growing attraction for me. There were actually two parts to the reservoir; the upper one near me supplied water to the city of Hartford and was completely restricted from public use of any kind;

the lower one was open to the public on a limited basis with two or three swimming beaches and boat access for rowboats, small sailboats, and eventually the very smallest powerboats for fishing. I spent many carefree hours exploring the woods around the upper reservoir, usually alone, but occasionally with a friend. When I was young the lower reservoir's beaches were all populated by families from the area, and we went there often to swim with our friends; but over the years the attraction diminished as they drew more and more strangers from the bigger cities, becoming crowded, losing that safe, familiar feeling –and no longer free. I'm glad that others get to share the beauty of the reservoir, but I do miss the small-town familiarity of the old days too. Why do things have to change?

Has anything in your life changed dramatically over the years? Explain.

What is it that you (would) really miss? Why?

Do you think times are getting worse or just different? Explain.

There was a family with four younger boys, followed by a sister and a fifth brother who moved in next door to us. The older boys were way beyond mischievous and had long rap sheets (not actually – only in the minds of the neighbors) before they reached their teen years. Among other things, they had set fire to the little hill across from the church. I remember hearing their cries many a night as their father dispensed physical punishment with language that made me thankful not to be on the receiving end. Though I loved my solitude, I spent two summers babysitting for them at the pleading of my mother who was trying to help their mother to be able to work at a much needed job while she and her husband tried to work through some problems. Those were two of the most difficult summers of my young life as I tried to manage this gang of lovable ruffians, make lunch, clean the house, and do the laundry, all for $25 a week. I was too young (13-14) to handle them all and did a terrible job of it. I would clean up the house and they would demolish it in minutes. I wish I could have been more tenderhearted, but I was in way over my head and functioning on a level of desperation as I gained control over them and my frustration by keeping them outdoors except when absolutely necessary. I wasn't babysitting; I was engaged in mob control ... without the stun gun! I would make a terrible nurse – low on compassion. It's not that I don't care. I'm just a "pick-yourself-up-by-your-bootstraps" kind of gal. I'm not sure exactly what that means, but try lifting yourself up by your shoelaces and you'll get the idea. I had high expectations. I just wish there had been an adult available who could have given these kids more of what they really needed.

How do you feel about rough language?
Do you hear it much? Where?
What do you do about it (if anything)?
Have you ever felt in over your head?
See how David felt in *Psalm 57* and *61*, among others.

> *Have mercy on me, O God, have mercy on me, for in you my soul takes refuge. I will take refuge in the shadow of your wings until the disaster has passed... My heart is steadfast, O God, my heart is steadfast... Psalm 57*
> *Hear my cry, O God; listen to my prayer... I call as my heart grows faint; lead me to the rock that is higher than I. ... I long to...take refuge in the shelter of your wings... Psalm 61*

What did you do when/if you were in over your head?
Describe a situation where you failed at something.
Have you come to peace about it?

I should have gone to my mother and told her how overwhelmed I felt with the babysitting job. I guess I didn't think that that was an option. After all, she thought I was responsible enough to do this and I didn't want to let her down. Besides, it was just one more challenge to meet. After the second summer of babysitting, I found other jobs with less frustration, a greater chance of feeling successful, and better pay.

The neighborhood had two older couples move into new houses, one on either side of us. Then a third house went in just next to ours on the street. A family moved in with kids several years younger than me, three boys and a little girl. This held little interest for me unless I wanted to reconsider babysitting after swearing it off forever. I didn't. The neighborhood was small and quiet, just like the town. Everyone knew their neighbors, and most of the town for that matter. I could ride my bike around the three and a half mile "block" and stop in at any house for help if I needed it. It was a great place to grow up. I found myself needing my father fix less and less often.

What is your relationship to your father?

If your biological father is not a part of your life, do you have a father figure?

What made you choose him?

Have you ever really considered God, the Father, as *your* father?

> *I will be a Father to you, and you will be my sons/daughters, says the Lord Almighty. 2 Corinthians 6:18*
> *...you received the Spirit of sonship. And by him we cry, "Abba, Father." Romans 8:15-16*
> *He defends the cause of the fatherless... Deuteronomy 10:18*
> *...Our Father in heaven, hallowed be your name, Matthew 6:9*

What kind of feelings do you have toward God?

Many people struggle with their feelings toward God, the Father. They think of Him as a law enforcement officer looking for someone to catch and punish in a crime. They think of Him as an impersonal "force," totally uninterested in them or anyone else (e.g., "Luke, use the force." from *Star Wars*). They think of Him as a powerful CEO, interested, but just too busy to get involved. Some choose to think of Him as non-existent, thereby rarely thinking of Him at all. The sad thing is that even some Christians don't have a very good relationship with their Father God. They can relate to Jesus, the Son, and to the Holy Spirit, but the Father scares them for some reason. I wonder if it's because they never had a strong relationship with their own fathers in some cases? For me, God the Father was the One I always felt closest to. I guess that developed when my earthly father died. God the Father is the One I pray to when I feel overwhelmed with life's burdens. He is the One who assures my peace.

Do you need to mend some bridges with your father?
(You will regret it someday if you don't.)
What part of that is your responsibility?
How can you help that to happen?
Do you need to get closer to your Father God?
How can you do that?

The boys I babysat for probably did not have good relationships with their father. He even scared me. And the marriage did not last in spite of everything. I felt so sorry for these kids because I knew that I was not able to meet their rising emotional needs. I was just maintaining some semblance of order with meals and supervision. I can only pray that God filled in where I failed. I was too young to really understand how to help. I was in way over my head babysitting for them. My hope is that they too learned to appreciate and embrace the love of God, our Father. I pray for them even today.

Bible Reading: *Psalm 23*
What is the role of a shepherd?
What are the promises of God in this psalm?
Read it through carefully and talk about each verse.
Which one is the most important to you? Why?

Challenge: Are you in over your head in something? Ask for help.

"...My grace is sufficient for you, for my power is made perfect in weakness..."
2 Corinthians 12:9

WEEK 17

"Brother, where art thou?"

Talk about dysfunctional relationships... My oldest brother is a study in relationships gone awry. I'm not sure what went down prior to my birth, but my mother and oldest sister told me stories over the years about his escapades in and out of trouble when he was young. I know he was loved dearly, but perhaps too dearly. Is that possible? My mother at times blamed herself for giving him too much too easily. As the firstborn and with the benefit of my father's income, he was the one who got the new bike and the new car and so much that the rest of us were not able to have. Yet he was the one who seemed to have the biggest issues throughout life. My mother prayed for him non-stop. His salvation was her greatest concern.

Enough said of that which happened before I was born; and I've already told you how much I enjoyed this brother's special attentions toward me as a little girl. He was my big brother and I loved him. Still do. At the age of seven I was even one of the two flower girls in his wedding, very exciting for a little girl. His marriage, however, didn't last long, though long enough to bring a handsome little boy and a gorgeous little girl into the world. All the stories about interfering mothers-in-law come into mind here, but responsibility falls mainly at his feet. He bailed on his family, left his kids fatherless. I don't understand ... never did. He was in and out of our lives during this time, mostly out after the divorce. I found it difficult to accept the absence of my nephew and niece from my life. It was particularly hard on my mother who lost touch with them completely for a while after my sister-in-law remarried.

Was there a difference in the way the oldest and youngest
were treated in your family?
Was there a good reason for it?
Do you think it made a difference?

Against my better judgment I continued to grow up, but my
brother seemed to get stuck at eighteen. He showed up every once
in a while, often needing money, and I would hear him making his
case to my mother who would usually help him out. We visited him
at his apartment in West Hartford once only to discover later that
he had remarried and had made his new wife hide out while we
were there to avoid telling us about her. What could he have been
thinking? That marriage lasted long enough to bring three more
beautiful children into the world, an older boy and twins, a boy and
a girl. He reneged on that relationship when the twins were infants.
It was getting easier. My mother wound up taking in the struggling
mom and kids until they could get on their feet and into a house of
their own. It was actually a joy to have them with us. The next time
my brother came around mom finally cut him off. She had younger
children to think of. It was about fourteen years before we saw him
again and it nearly broke her heart. She did what she could to find
out how he was doing or if he was even alive. A couple of rumors
served to keep her hopes alive.

Do you know anyone like my brother?
How responsible are you?
How does the Bible say we should react to the irresponsibility
of others?
We who are strong ought to bear with the failings of the weak...
Romans 15:1-2
Make every effort to live in peace with all men and to be holy;
without holiness no one will see the Lord. See to it that ... no bitter
root grows up to cause trouble... Hebrews 12:14-15

My brother came back into the lives of his youngest children
again briefly and thus into ours. When he was told that he couldn't
keep doing some of the thoughtless things he was doing, he

disappeared once again. He had trouble hearing the truth. It was impossible to be honest with him and yet have him in our lives no matter how much love we tried to offer him along with the truth. I say "tried" because once he heard the difficult words bearing the truth, he seemed to become deaf to the love behind them. Years later he moved south, not far from my other brother who had recently moved to the mountains of western North Carolina. Then, after over twenty years of separation, he remarried his second wife. She had loved him all that time.

Not long afterwards I called to tell my brothers that our mother was dying. They flew up to Connecticut together in time to see her one last time. While visiting, my oldest brother had his turn to go into mom's bedroom to talk to her alone. Almost the minute he entered the room a violent thunderstorm broke out that shook all of the windows in the house. I've never heard one louder. It shook our very insides. When he finished, it subsided. Those waiting in the living room looked at one another in amazement. Someone said: "You think God is trying to tell him something?" and another: "I hope he's listening." Upon exiting the room white as a ghost, he leaned on my shoulder and whispered, "I'm scared. I don't know what to do." I answered gently, "Yes, you do." Immediately he stiffened and left my embrace. I was beyond disappointed. I thought maybe this would be the moment he would turn to the Lord. But he fought it. What is holding him back? What will it take?

He began to be a part of his youngest children's lives through the influence of his wife. The kids were cautious but open. When he remarried their mother they were protective of her, justly so, but I think he thought them spiteful. Physical abuse was not their fear, but they did not want to see their mother hurt again. Through his youngest children and their recent introduction to his oldest children from his first marriage, he began to reconnect with the oldest two as well. If our mother had still been alive she would have loved to have seen the reunion with him and all five of his children. Granted, it was a bit awkward, but it was a start. Ironically the church-going children were the toughest on him. I guess they expected more. But one thing I've learned over the years is that it's hard enough for Christians to live according to the standards set in the Bible; expecting others to do so is unrealistic.

The movie, *As Good As It Gets,* in which Jack Nicholson plays a man with no idea how to interact politely or successfully with others, was mentioned by one of his kids when expressing their expectations of him. However, I refuse to believe that it is even now "as good as it gets." I still believe that God will have His way in my brother's life. If he could just get past his pride and tell his children that he's sorry, sorry for abandoning them, sorry for not being a father to them for all of those years, I think he might be able to move forward in a relationship with them. Of course of greatest concern is that he give his heart to the Lord and heal that relationship. But both of these take repentance and I don't know if he knows how to do that. I guess it would take a miracle. Then again, our God is "the God who performs miracles." *(Psalm 77:14)*

How difficult is it for you to hear the truth about yourself?
Has God ever tried to get your attention? How?
How difficult is it for you to say you're sorry?
What does God's Word have to say on this subject?
> *Repent, then, and turn to God, so that your sins may be wiped out, that times of refreshing may come from the Lord. Acts 3:19*
> *Rid yourselves of all the offenses you have committed, and get a new heart and a new spirit. Why will you die...? For I take no pleasure in the death of anyone, declares the Sovereign Lord. Repent and live! Ezekiel 18:31-32*

Do you *really* believe that God can perform miracles? If not, why not?

I can't help but think of the proverbial guy on the city street corner dressed in a white robe holding up a big sign on a stick saying, "Repent! The end is near!" Though that guy is often mocked in movies and cartoons, he's right! The end of our lives could come at any time and the only way to enjoy those "times of refreshing ... from the Lord," *for eternity*, is to repent. First we ask for God's forgiveness and then for forgiveness from those we've hurt. Then we allow Him to work in our lives. Before taking communion we are told to repent of sin and to let go of any grudges that may be persisting. This is a poignant reminder of the forgiveness and love of Jesus towards us even before we accepted Him as Lord of our lives. He is the Initiator of our faith and our hope for eternity.

Sadly, the sins of the father are often repeated in the next generation. My nephew has also left his faithful wife and three children in pursuit of happiness. It breaks my heart because I love him … and fear for him. People can really mess up their lives with poor decisions. But the good news is that God can take the results of our selfish choices and still make something beautiful of our lives if we ask Him to in humility and sincerity. There's a story in the Bible of a couple of brothers who screw up their lives in two very different ways. One way is obvious; the other is often overlooked in this parable:

Bible Reading: *Luke 15:11-32*
>What did the younger son do wrong?
>What did he later do right?
>What did the older son do right?
>What did he later do wrong?
>Which son was better off at the end? Explain.
>What was the father's reaction to each?

Challenge: Just say you're sorry, humbly and sincerely. It's time.

>*"The sacrifices of God are a broken spirit, a broken and contrite heart, O God, you will not despise." Psalm 51:17*

WEEK 18

"Dating scandals"

The sister closest to me in age was, as mentioned before, a "princess." For some reason guys always wanted to take care of her. Sure, she was cute and smart and fun, but come on... What is it with guys and their need to be macho protector/providers? (Although, that's probably not as much the case today since women have become liberated. – not sure if that helped us or hurt us.) Well. I was not impressed. For a long time I wasn't even interested in dating, but eventually time has a way of bringing even many of the toughest of cases to the realization that boys *can* be kind of cute at times. (and another tomboy bites the dust.) I began to notice them. On the other hand, I wasn't about to let one "take care" of me. Just let one try, and I'd "take care" of him.

My sister started dating early in high school. She started out with a couple of guys from church, one a little older who seemed interested in something long-term. He taught her to ski and lavished attention on her. She was too young to realize how she was about to hurt him. She moved on. I remember once when my sister had two separate dates with two different guys on the same night, one early and one late. I couldn't believe she would do anything so dumb. (Sorry sis.) Against all odds it worked out. She went away her junior year of high school to the Christian boarding school in the Midwest that our mother had graduated from, but didn't last for more than a year due partly to a special scholarship she hoped to get at her old school. Was there possibly a bit of homesickness as well? While at the boarding school in Minnesota she fell for a guy a couple of years older who was in the Bible college associated with the high school. I guess he was a pretty amazing guy from what

I heard. When I arrived at the school three years later, everyone who knew him was impressed that it had been my sister who had dated him. ...whatever.

Absence did not make the heart grow fonder; it made the heart wander. Not long after returning to Connecticut my sister started to date a guy from the public high school she was attending, a catholic guy and one of ten or twelve children. He was one of the more popular kids at our high school. Along with him came a whole bunch of seniors (scholars, athletes, fun-filled guys) who all started to hang out at our house along with the church kids. Though only a lowly freshman, I got to be friends with several of them on a "little sister" basis. I think I knew more of my sisters' classmates than my own. However, while dating this guy she also got interested in another guy from a rival high school. Trouble was afoot. Of course she was totally setting up the next event in her dating career. At a party nearby, these two guys nearly came to blows over her in the front yard of the home hosting the party. Guys can be pretty juvenile.

Are you a princess, a tomboy, or something else?
Did you ever date more than one guy at a time?
What does the Bible say about dating?
(*Was* there dating in the Bible?)
What is a good age to start dating? Why?
What would a perfect date be like?

My sister's dating life came to an abrupt end after she graduated from her three-years' nursing training. She got a job as an RN in New York and got engaged to a "wonderful Christian guy." So she thought. It turns out that Christian guys are not always that wonderful. The engagement was on and off a couple of times (first she broke it off and then he did) until she finally got smart and let it stay off. Meanwhile I was out in Minnesota struggling with this whole thing. I had actually known her fiancée before she did and was having a great deal of difficulty trying to decide if, when, and how to tell her what I thought of him. I was not his biggest fan. I was so glad when it ended for good. But that sent her back home and back into the dating game. Providentially, one of the two guys who had been fighting over her on the lawn years before had grown up by now and had come back into her life. They started to date once again. The problem was that he was not *yet* a Christian …

Have you ever been hurt dating? Explain.

Have you ever done the hurting? Explain.

Have you ever dated a non-Christian?

What does the Bible have to say about *that*?

> *Do not be yoked together with unbelievers. For what do righteousness and wickedness have In common? Or what fellowship can light have with darkness? … What does a believer have in common with an unbeliever? … "Therefore come out from them and be separate". says the Lord. 2 Corinthians 6:14-18*
>
> *Do not love the world or anything in the world. If anyone loves the world, the love of the Father is not in him. For everything in the world-the cravings of sinful man, the lust of his eyes and the boasting of what he has and does-comes not from the Father but from the world. The world and its desires pass away, but the man who does the will of God lives forever. I John 2:15-17*

The Bible has some pretty tough warnings about getting mixed up with unbelievers in any situation – dating, marriage, business, or any other way. How is it that so many Christians can just ignore these verses and somehow fool themselves into believing that it doesn't apply in their cases? They claim blindly and in all sincerity that the unbeliever is actually a believer. After all, he or she is not a heathen. Or they argue that the unbeliever will surely come to the Lord soon because he/she is so close. Sometimes the unbeliever claims to be a believer just to win over the believer. It is important to be sure because it matters so much in a relationship that the two people share the same set of values and the same hope of eternity. That's why we are so often advised to wait. Time has a way of bringing the truth to light. These decisions are too important to take lightly. But waiting is not often considered as an option by young people. It's not a word in their vocabulary.

In retrospect, I think I should have told my sister what I knew about her fiancée. She could have wound up in a miserable marriage. But it probably wouldn't have made a difference –it usually doesn't. Most people do not want to hear the difficult truth when it comes to this type of situation. It's as was said in the movie *A Few Good Men*: "You can't handle the truth!" Sometimes we just do not want our plans derailed by the impertinent truth. Oftentimes we already know the truth deep within but are ignoring the "still small voice" warning us of the danger ahead. My sister's ex-fiancée was engaged again in no time to another unsuspecting girl. Meanwhile, God graciously took care of that big problem with my sister's new "old" boyfriend. (Confusing, isn't it?) At a young adults' event in our church he made a decision to follow Jesus. And it turned out that he really meant it – it wasn't just a ploy to get approval. I have to emphasize here that this is *definitely the exception* to the rule in these relationships. One thing led to another and they were eventually married. I'm sure she appreciates now what a huge gift that was from God.

As I've told many young people, "You really shouldn't even date someone you couldn't consider possibly marrying some day." Missionary dating (when a Christian dates a non-Christian hoping he or she will come to the Lord) rarely works out, so don't assume it will. Don't even start down that road because it's hard to back-up on a twisted road. Most of the time the Christian winds up in a relationship that pulls him or her away from the Lord, or in a marriage that is filled with despair. More often than not the relationship brings only heartache and remorse. This may sound cliché, but that very fact implies that it is widely understood to be true. My sister was fortunate – my mother must have been praying overtime.

The rules have changed dramatically in this game over the years. It used to be that dating, being engaged, and getting married were the three stages toward a family of your own. A fourth category has arisen since the sixties: "living together." Somewhere along the way people have convinced themselves that this is a good way to find out if you're compatible with another person. It has all the perks of marriage without the commitment. You can walk out at any time. Even many Christians have come to accept this as a given step towards marriage. Most don't like the words "commitment," "accountability," or "obedience." We want "easy," but it rarely brings the best results. Quality comes with hard work and time.

The lack of commitment to relationships, to families, to duty, is a tragedy in our society. Schools, daycare, and so many other programs have taken the place of parents. Both parents have to work to get that new house or car or television or electronic gismo. Are they really more important than family? And we are being told everywhere that we can be our own gods. We can decide what's right or wrong for ourselves because there is no real truth. A billboard in a European city recently proclaimed: "Truth is flexible." Wow! No accountability means no rules and no judgment. Yippee! ... *but what if they're wrong?*

One of the worst words for us has to be "obedience." *We* will decide what we want to do for ourselves. No one is going to tell us what we should or shouldn't do and lay guilt on us for breaking *their* rules! Maybe not, but there *will* be consequences for breaking God's rules. Someone told me just yesterday that he didn't believe that there was such a place as hell – in spite of its frequent mention in the Bible. My question for him is: *"What if you're wrong?"* Are you willing to take that chance? It's *eternity* at stake here!

All the positive character traits that we used to admire have come to be looked upon as old-fashioned and out-of-touch with reality. Who's promoting these ideas? Why do we follow their lead? Is it making our world a better place? Christian parents have a huge hurdle to overcome with decades of society's brainwashing. Praying parents call their children to commit themselves to Biblical truth, to be accountable to it, and to listen (obey). There's that word again tucked into "listen." And this generation does not like it. It's like the warnings that God gave to the Israelites when they were about to reenter the Promised Land after leaving Egypt and after wandering in the desert for forty years due to disobedience. When they listened to God, they were successful; when they didn't, they failed. This was especially true in the area of intermarriage with the Canaanites. God warned them over and over again, but God's people wound up ignoring Him and serving the false gods of their heathen spouses, falling away from the one true God.

Bible Reading: *Deuteronomy 7:1-6, Judges 3:5-7, Isaiah 55:9-11*
> Why do you think God is so harsh here? (no treaty, no mercy, destroy them totally...)
> *Is* God being cruel or is something more going on here? (See *Genesis 15:16.*)
> Were all of the Canaanites killed? (See *Joshua 6:25, 9:6, 14-16.*)
> What did God say the consequences of intermarriage would be?
> Did the Israelites listen to God? (See *Judges 3:5-7.*)
> Should we expect to fully understand God? (See *Isaiah 55:9-11.*)

Challenge: If you know of anyone missionary dating, warn them and pray for them.

> *"Do not be yoked together with unbelievers. For what do righteousness and wickedness have in common? Or what fellowship can light have with darkness?"*
> *2 Corinthians 6:14*

WEEK 19

"Squarehead in a round hole"

Moving from my little elementary school with fifteen or so students per grade to a high school of over 600 was a bit traumatic. I had just managed to become a relatively confident "someone" in the smaller school and here I was starting all over. By the way, when I say "someone," I don't mean a superstar or even a lowly dwarf star, but just a someone who had become content with the less-than-perfect person she saw in the mirror, who felt at relative ease in her environment, and who had a certain amount of self-assurance in her own uniqueness. I knew I was not a "nobody" (a person of little or no interest or value). I had decided long before this that there was no such person. I would be the best "square peg in a round hole" that I could possibly be. Over the years I've found this contentment to be much more valuable than popularity. Popularity depends upon other people; contentment is between you and God. Who is more trustworthy? Being placed in a new environment, I immediately defaulted into defensive mode and adopted a wallflower stance. Do you see me? Over there ... blending in against that cement block wall in the school hall ... probably not ... I was pretty good at being invisible. Until safety was assured, this was my tactic: Find out how deep the water is and if there are any rocks around before diving in.

Do you know of anyone that some people might consider a nobody?

What makes them seem so unimportant?

Have you ever felt like one? Explain.

Can you relate to the wallflower above?

Of course my sister was a senior and part of the "in" crowd so that kept her busy and uninvolved with regard to my peace of mind and inner contentment – except the times when she tried to help me come out from that wall. If I were a different person, her attempts to help me might have caused me either to consider changing my ways or to lose confidence. However, I had no interest in being part of the "in" crowd, so she usually gave up pretty quickly with little affect on me. Most of the time we just didn't bump into each other, especially in high school, so chances were that few people even knew that we were related. I knew that she was always there for me if I needed her, but we were very different. In addition to her I had at least eight to ten cousins and ten to twelve good friends from my church or town who attended my school. That meant that there were over twenty kids I could probably count on to some degree for friendship. It's doesn't hurt to have a safety net. In addition to these advantages, there was the fact that I had learned to function pretty well as a loner. Couldn't hurt either. How bad could high school be? Pretty naïve, huh?

What does being "someone" mean to you?

Is it important to you to be popular? (Be honest, now.) Why/why not?

Have you ever thought about the importance of being content with who you really are?

Are you content with who you are? Why or why not?

What does God's Word have to say about this?

> *I praise you because I am fearfully and wonderfully made; your works are wonderful. I know that full well. Psalm 139:14*
> *But godliness with contentment is great gain. I Timothy 6:6*
> *… I have learned to be content whatever the circumstances. Philippians 4:11*

There will be times in life when family and friends may fail us. I would guess that individuals have already let you down in one way or another. I have had friends, especially in high school, make me look foolish or fail to back me up when I most needed them. I have had family members get sick or die on me and desert me in that way, unintentionally. I have been disappointed in those closest to me when they failed to be perfect. Why was I surprised when friends let me down? Ever since I was a little girl I had been taught from God's Word that *"all have sinned and fall short..." (Romans 3:23)* They were simply doing and being what God said they would do and be. And ironically, I am a part of that "all." I know that I have failed my friends at times, sometimes without being aware of it, but at other times, with full or that loophole-seeking suppressed knowledge of the crime I was about to perpetrate. "All have sinned and fall short..." and I am no exception.

Can you describe a time when a friend or family member let you down?
Can you describe a time when *you* let *them* down?
Have you ever let God down? Can you share it?

People are weak. But weakness is no excuse. If we are foolish enough to let God down, how can we expect to do more for each other? Though it is awesome when we have family and friends we can count on, God warns us through Job's example to be prepared to be abandoned: "All my intimate friends detest me; those I love have turned against me." *(Job 19:19)*, and in prophecy: "Do not trust a neighbor; put no confidence in a friend." *(Micah 7:5a)*. Now Job and the end times are extreme cases and not typical, but yet possible even in our own lives. The *Psalms* are full of David's disappointment in his friends. Yet he also had his best friend Jonathan who was true to the very end. It's so important first of all to really know who God is, and secondly to know who you are *in* Christ. God is the Almighty Creator of the universe. Nothing is too difficult for Him! And we are His children through the finished work of Jesus Christ on the cross. There's nothing we *have* to do to earn that position. There's nothing we *can* do to earn that position. As His children we are so loved that even with our idiosyncrasies and foibles, and even though we keep making the same mistakes over and over (yes, even then), we are incredibly precious to Him and therefore important. Friends may abandon us, but never God.

In elementary school, in high school, in college, at work, no matter where we are, we are each "someone," someone of infinite value, someone with mighty power, someone with an incredible future, someone holding the keys to eternity for a lost and hurting world. Get it? Sometimes God does use others in our lives to teach us or to give us joy and earthly love, but ultimately, we don't need to get anything related to our self-worth from other people. So when you're entering a room full of people whose good opinion you crave and are yet unsure of, try to remember this: Walk in with the full assurance that no matter what others may say or think about you, you have a very special status: you are the child of a King! ... which makes you a princess by the way (or a prince if you're a guy). Wild, huh? We've already got all that's really important through Jesus Christ who would have died for any *one* of us. Is that amazing or what? And we have been given an incredible responsibility as His children. He has entrusted us with the commission of bringing His love to a broken world. He must have a lot of confidence in us. But don't let that scare you. Understanding that it's actually the Holy Spirit who will work through us should give us that same confidence. We don't have to do this alone.

Others *may* let us down from time to time. Others *will* let us down from time to time. Forgive them and get on with your life. It's much more fun being happy than carrying around some old hurt or grudge. And it's your choice. Happy or unhappy? ... Happy or unhappy? Is there really a choice here? Of course you may want to be a little cautious in dealing with certain people in the future because it is in fire's nature to burn, and some people are a lot like fire. Then again, try not to *be* that person who burns. It's not always easy, but do your best. It's bound to get easier with practice. And of course there are those true friends out there who are "closer than a brother" in their faithfulness and support. If you have even one of those, count yourself blessed. Cherish them and treat them well. They would be hard to replace. And forgive them too if they slip along the way. They are not the ones to keep at arm's length. You should be able to tell the difference.

Bible Reading:
Look at these heroes and how *they* let God and others down.

Eve and Adam
listened to Satan.
Genesis 3:1-7 (4:25)*

Noah got drunk.
Genesis 9:18-23 (6:8)*

Lot moved into Sodom
and Gomorrah.
*Genesis 13:12-13, 14:12
(2 Peter 2:7)**

Joseph's brothers sold him
into slavery.
Genesis 37:19, 27 (37:21, 42:22)*

Moses killed a man.
Exodus 2:11-12 (15:2)*

David stole another
man's wife!
2 Samuel 11:2, 5, 15, 27 (12:13)*

Paul persecuted Christians.
Acts 9:1-2 (9:20)*

Peter denied Christ
three times.
John 18:15-18, 25-27 (21:15-17)*

The early Christians couldn't
get along.
*I Corinthians 3:3, 11:18
(2 Corinthians 3:18)**

What did each of these people do that was wrong?
Why do you think they did these things? Discuss.
Do you think these people repented of their sins?
(See verses above in parentheses with asterisks.)
Why is that so important? (See *I John 1:9-10*.)

Challenge: Remember that if the people above could be heroes, then you can be one! Confessing and repenting of sin is the first step; so step up.

*"Love the Lord your God with all your heart and ...soul,
and...mind. ...Love your neighbor as yourself."*
Matthew 22:37-38

WEEK 20

"Crushes"

My first crush was a friend of my father. He was probably old enough to *be* my father. He was a single Norwegian guy, or maybe Danish – which for some mysterious reason seemed to be considerably better than Swedish. Some kind of sibling rivalry in there, I think. In my experience, Norwegians have always enjoyed lovingly harassing their brothers, the Swedes, about heritage. The only possible reason I have been able to unearth is that it is perhaps related to either the neutrality of Sweden in World War II or to their past aggression in Norway. Either way, it has long since stopped being a serious issue and has become a source of amusement for both. Norwegians ask "What is the one thing Swedes have that Norwegians don't have?" Answer: "Good neighbors." See what I mean? (I've also heard that the other way around…) Anyway, my father would bring this Norse "demi-god" home from work sometimes to have supper with us. He was *soo* handsome and *soo* nice. My sisters and I all immediately fell in love with him. We had no choice.

Before he started to work at a defense plant, my father was a floorlayer. By trade, Dad's friend was a mason, a bricklayer. I remember my dad telling us stories of jokes he would play on this younger man. If he knew this friend was coming in next to a job site, Dad would leave *Lifesavers* candies hanging from strings near the framed opening for a fireplace after he'd finished measuring a house for flooring. They had a great friendship. Then, one day, it happened. The demi-god brought someone along with him when he came to visit us. I had to admit that she was very pretty and very nice. I really couldn't discover anything negative about her. Sadly I realized that I would probably have to give up my prior claim, step aside, and let her have him. I was, after all, only about seven or eight years old.

My next crush was a guy from my church in my sister's class. He was smart and athletic and artistic … and not bad looking either. Of course, as in so many of these cases, he had no idea I was alive except as his friend's little sister. One of the first times I remember him noticing me was a time I wish he hadn't. I was still in grammar school, but my sister had started high school. I was probably in seventh or eighth grade. I had found a little lizard and was trying to scare my sister (not too difficult) by walking toward her carrying this lizard while chanting, in what I imagined a very scary voice, "I'm a momma lizard." Ouch! I did this several times before I realized that a couple of older guys were hiding in my breezeway listening to the entire thing and enjoying it all way too much. Double ouch. I have *never* lived this event down. *Never!* It still comes up in conversation.

My chances of impressing this guy were now next to nil, so it was a couple of years before I even considered trying. As a freshman, I would try to impress him with my sketches of monsters. They were actually not bad if you liked one-eyed weirdly shaped people/animals complete with 3-D shading. They were indeed unique, if nothing else. How many young girls, as a pastime, sketch monsters to impress older guys? If he wasn't impressed, he should have been. He at least did a good job pretending to be. He was patient with me and helped me to design an annual calendar for the planet Mars for Earth Science complete with solstices, equinoxes, and illustrations. No monsters. Then he started to date an older girl, who I had to admit was also pretty and nice. Strike two.

Those were the only two real crushes before I went away to school in Minnesota. There were a couple of boys I thought were cute and one that I actually dated once or twice, but nothing as long-lasting as those first two. I was selective about my crushes.

Who was your first crush? Why did you like him?

Did you do dumb things to impress him? Explain.

Have you ever humiliated yourself in front of someone you liked? Explain.

Crushes can really hurt because almost by definition they are apt to occur when we are pretty young and they frequently have little hope of panning out into anything serious. Often they are one-sided with the target totally unaware of the bliss felt by the admirer if simply in the presence of the admired. For this reason we must remove blame from the unknowingly admired if he (or she for the guys) should inadvertently dash to pieces the hopes of the admirer while in the course of everyday life. (Whew!) We also must remove blame from the admired person who discovers a crush, but just doesn't feel the same. It's not something that's inevitably mutual. This can't be helped. If you are caught up in a one-way crush with no sign of it becoming mutual, I can only give you one piece of advice: Get over it and move on! Sorry, but that's the way it is. God's got something even better for you.

Have you ever been unrequited in love?

How did you get over it (assuming you were smart enough to do so)?

Were you able to get good advice from anyone?

What was that advice?

I guess I was fortunate because I never went so "head-over-heels" about someone that I got hurt (close, with my future husband once). I think all of the death that touched my young life may have helped me to understand how unimportant so many seemingly important things really are in life. At any rate, I rarely dated unless the guy was exceptional, and I had no intention of getting remotely serious until I was about … twenty-eight . Yes, twenty-eight – that was my target age for starting to think about a serious relationship. I had a plan. For that reason (and others) I think I may have been a little intimidating as a potential date.

How *did* they date in the Old Testament? Check out:

Isaac: *Laban (the father) and Betheul (the mother) answered, "This is from the Lord, we can say nothing to you one way or the other. Here is Rebekah, take her and go, and let her become the wife of your master's son, as the Lord has directed"... Isaac brought Rebekah into the tent of his mother, and he married Rebekah. So she became his wife, and he loved her; ... Genesis 24: 50-51, 67*

Jacob: *Jacob was in love with Rachel and said, "I'll work for you seven years in return for your younger daughter, Rachel." ... When morning came, there was Leah! ... " Why have you deceived me?" "Finish out this daughter's bridal week; then we will give you the younger one also, in return for another seven years of work." Genesis 29:18-27*

Ruth: *... go down to the threshing floor ... uncover his feet and lie down. He will tell you what to do. ... "Spread the corner of your garment over me, since you are a kinsman-redeemer (type of Christ)." ... So Boaz took Ruth and she became his wife. Ruth 3 and 4*

Esther: *"Let a search be made for beautiful young virgins for the king." ... Esther also was taken to the king's palace and entrusted to Hegai, who had charge of the harem. ... Now the king was attracted to Esther more than to any of the other women, and she won his favor and approval more than any of the other virgins. So he set a royal crown on her head and made her queen... Esther 2:2, 8, 17*

Hosea: *"Go, take to yourself an adulterous wife and children of unfaithfulness... So he married Gomer... Hosea 1:2-3*

So much for dating in the Old Testament. Arranged marriages seemed to be the M.O.. Isaac and Rebekah had never even seen each other when she willingly went with his servant to a far-off country to marry him. And is dating ever even mentioned in the New Testament? If girls in Bible times had crushes (which I expect they did), they were probably rarely considered in the match-making process (e.g., *Fiddler On The Roof*). How would you like to have your husband chosen for you without ever having even seen him? How would you enjoy lying at his feet to offer yourself as his wife, or being chosen from a harem? What if God told you to marry a prostitute? Yikes! Any struggles you might have with dating kind of pale in comparison, don't they? On the other hand, there is something to be said for these arranged marriages – many of them turned out quite well.

As I mentioned in an earlier week, dating should be considered a serious prelude to marriage. Like Gideon in the Old Testament (*Judges* 6), you could put out a metaphorical fleece to ask for God's guidance. Of course you already know His main criterion – faith in God. You shouldn't even *begin* dating someone who doesn't share your faith. I wonder how that might change the whole dating scene for Christians? Most of the pressure and conflicts of dating would be gone. We would take more time to get to know someone before dating them. Now there's an idea!

Bible Reading: *Jeremiah 29:11-13, John 15:7, Psalm 40:1*
    Do you believe that God has plans for your life?
    How do you discover these plans?
    Are you a patient person? Any examples?
    Do you ever try to do things *for* God? Explain.
    Do you think God considers crushes in His plans?

Challenge: You might want to check out a good Christian book
            on the topic of dating – like *I Kissed Dating Goodbye*
            or *Boy Meets Girl* by Joshua Harris, or *Love, Sex and
            Dating* by Andy Stanley.

*"Delight yourself in the Lord and he will give you the desires
of your heart. Commit your way to the Lord; trust in him
and he will do this."*
                                                    Psalm 37:4-5

"Everything that has breath"

took violin lessons for a few years while I was in elementary
school. I played duets with a friend in church occasionally, but I
never really excelled as a violinist. I had a string (ha!) of bad luck
with teachers. The first, who taught out of her home in my town
and had mostly piano students, was so thrilled that she had a violin
student that she took me to Boston Pops' concerts to motivate me.
That was cool. Sadly, she was pretty old and stopped teaching. My
next teacher was a man a couple of towns away who taught in a
studio where there were several rooms and teachers and many
students learning to play all sorts of instruments. He decided to
move to Florida, and since he owned the studio, it closed. My last
teacher was a woman who had a signed picture of Jascha Heifitz,
the great violinist. She taught in a semi-dark room, had lost much
of her hair for some reason unknown to me (cancer?), and made
me examine the picture of Heifitz periodically to learn posture
and to inspire me. She also stopped teaching while I was still her
student. I had this feeling that I might just have been too much
for these violin teachers, that I was the one who had triggered the
demise of their teaching careers. My sisters still tease me about
my bad luck – and about a dog that howled relentlessly outside my
window one night as I practiced. (That crazy dog would not stop,
no matter how I tried to scare him off.)

I was hoping to continue playing the violin except neither of my
high schools had orchestras. My first school had only a band – no
violins. That meant I either studied on my own or took up another
instrument. The band director was relatively new and was trying
to make a fledgling band into a great band. High hopes. When I

approached him with my dilemma, he suggested I try the clarinet, since he needed someone in that position. I set aside my violin for a while. Because I could read music, I learned quickly and was accepted into the band within a few short weeks. I progressed to the alto-clarinet and then the bass-clarinet whose low mellow sounds were more to my liking. I loved to see how all of the parts eventually came together in a song, once we learned it. Prior to that it could be downright discouraging, if not frightening.

I got to know the small group of people who made up my corner of the band: the clarinets, bass clarinets, oboes, trombones, and percussion. You see, when we had a particularly heavy percussion piece, I would switch over to help out percussion, playing the cymbals, the timpani, or even the lyre during parades. I didn't mind the variety. I actually liked it. I still love a parade today if it has a good marching band to get the adrenalin going. I dated one of the saxophone players a couple of times. He was nice, but I was only going out with him because he was my sister's boyfriend's cousin (whew!) and they thought we should double date. I think my sister was trying once again to "help me out." I enjoyed being in the band.

Were you ever in a band or orchestra?

Was it fun? If so, what made it fun?

What instrument(s) did you play?

Were you really good? or just average like most of us?

Isn't it amazing when it all comes together right before a concert?

The Bible has a lot to say about music. For instance:

...Praise him with the sounding of the trumpet, praise him with the harp and lyre, praise him with tambourine and dancing, praise him with the strings and flute, praise him with the clash of the cymbals, praise him with resounding cymbals. Let everything that has breath praise the Lord. Psalm 150

David and the whole house of Israel were celebrating with all their might before the Lord, with songs and with harps, lyres, tambourines, sistrums, and cymbals. 2 Samuel 6:5

Once, the day before a big concert, the two lead bass clarinetists both came down with chicken pox and I (the rookie) was left alone to play our solo in a song ironically entitled "Relax." I was appalled that I should be playing a public solo this early in my career, but the band director assured me that I would be fine. To this day I can hum that solo in its entirety, in spite of the fact that that evening I took liberties that were shocking as I tried to get my shaking fingers to move quickly through the notes of this rhythmic Latin song. The good thing is that I managed to keep the funky beat going as I "rewrote" the solo that night. The band leader and the other instruments backing me up must have wondered through the entire solo what on earth I was doing. After the concert, my instructor just smiled and said something like: "Well, we managed to get to the same place at the same time with very few people knowing that we were not playing the same piece of music." Thank God I never had to do that again.

Our director was pretty tough with his rules and regulations for staying in the band. We couldn't miss even one parade during parade season. Many of them happened on weekends and during holidays, so it wasn't always easy. When one of my aunts died, he made me bring a note from home to go to her funeral. I think he thought I was just trying to pull a fast one. He worked us hard and it paid off. We went to a band competition at the University of Connecticut in Storrs at the end of my second year in band and I think we might have even come in second. I remember that we did a medley that included the nursery tune "Where, Oh Where, Has My Little Dog Gone?" right in the middle. During that portion of the song the entire band had to wander aimlessly around the field still playing the song while pretending to look for a lost dog. We then had to come together in perfect position at exactly the same moment to once again march in place and time. For the first time *ever* (even in practice) we did it flawlessly. Talk about dumb luck.

Have you ever been really, really nervous about something you had to do in public? Explain.

How did you get through it?

What does God recommend?

> *I can do everything through him who gives me strength.*
> Philippians 4:13
> Peace I leave with you; my peace I give you. I do not give to you
> as the world gives. Do not let your hearts be troubled and <u>do not</u>
> <u>be afraid</u>. John 14:27
> So we say <u>with confidence</u>, "The Lord is my helper, I will not be
> afraid. <u>What can man do to me</u>?" Hebrews 13:6

Was luck, hard work, team work or all three involved?

What does God's Word have to say about this?

> <u>Whatever you do, work at it with all your heart, as working for the</u>
> <u>Lord, not for men.</u> Colossians 3:23
> <u>Two are better than one</u>, because they have a good return
> for their work. ... A cord of three strands is not quickly broken.
> Ecclesiastes 4:9-12

Being in a band or an orchestra is a real responsibility. When everyone is doing his/her gifted thing, and doing it well, the result is awesome. However, if we fail to do our part, or try to do someone else's part, or constantly bicker about our part, the result can be awful. Not only can we make ourselves look bad, but we can make the whole band look bad as well. And the leader is disappointed in us and embarrassed by our performance. Can you see the parallel to working for the Lord? We are each a member of the "body of Christ" with different roles to fulfill. We need to make room for everyone in that body to have the opportunity to be used by God in great and small ways.

So often we focus only on ourselves and the latest opportunity to use our gifts that we forget that there may be others around us with the same gift just waiting to be used. We even step forward to be used in areas in which we are not that gifted. We try to help someone we look upon as less able than we are by doing their jobs for them. Think about it. That's stealing. It's stealing the blessing, the joy, the opportunity to grow, and the feeling of being a viable part of a healthy community. Do your thing to the best of your ability without grumbling. (Grumbling kind of reverses the blessing. How can you grumble and have joy at the same time?)

And stay away from the opportunities set aside for others. Rather, encourage them to join in and to shine. When we work together in harmony, the results can be awesome. And we will then bring honor and glory to our Leader.

When I went away for my last two years of high school, there was no band or orchestra. I was disappointed but not enough to stay home. I played my violin a little with a good friend who I travelled with in a trio. We would wedge small hair combs onto the strings of our violins up against the bridge to mute them and make our mistakes less apparent. I haven't really played it much since those days.

Bible Reading: *Romans 12:3-8, I Corinthians 12:4-11*

Is anybody in a band/group endeavor ever really indispensible? Discuss.

Have you ever tried to do someone else's job for them?

What was your reasoning?

How do you think they felt?

Are you happy for others when they excel?

Why is it important to remember that we are all working together?

Challenge: Encourage someone else to use their gifts in some way.

"So do not fear, for I am with you;do not be dismayed, for I am your God. I will strengthen you and help you; I will uphold you with my righteous right hand."

Isaiah 41:10

WEEK 22

"The narrow gate"

was naïve enough not to know that being part of a "Youth for Christ Club" might be less than a cool thing in the eyes of some of my new peers in public high school. For the longest time it never even occurred to me. *Of course* I'd be in the club that honored God and that all my friends were in. I joined a few other clubs as well, each without much of a "wow" factor as it turned out. I have no idea why I joined those other clubs – probably because someone asked me. I might as easily have joined the Yogurt Club or the Tree-Pruning Club, if there had been such. You see, I loved to try new things and I had a wide range of things I liked to do, a range that became a problem later in life as I struggled with what *exactly* to do. I have been called a "Renaissance" woman several times in my life. I think that means that I have a wide variety of interests – so, why didn't they just say that? I have to admit though, that I enjoyed the mystique in that word.

Anyway, this Youth for Christ Club met weekly in the science teacher's room. Science teacher, go figure. (No offense to science teachers, but most of the ones I later worked with were not especially interested in Christian clubs.) I can't remember exactly what we did each week in this club, but it was primarily kids from my church along with a handful of others. I know we read from the Bible and prayed, but I can't remember if it was more like a Bible study or a church service or something completely different. What may be a surprise to you is that several of the most popular kids in the school went to this club. In any event, we took a stand for our faith by having the club and by being active members. Years later in life a man who had gone to high school with me and whose children I now had in some of my classes came up to me and told me that though he had thought us a little odd back in high school, he remembered our little club when he later gave his heart to the Lord as an adult. He said that it had been a brick in the foundation God was laying in his life. Cool. That man eventually became a state superior court judge!

Describe a time you took a public stand for the Lord.
Were you alone or with a group?
Were you ridiculed? How?
What was the outcome?
Were you glad you took the stand? Explain.
What does the Bible say about taking a stand?
> So then, brothers, *stand firm and hold to the teachings we passed on to you*... 2 Thessalonians 2:15
> Resist him (Satan), *standing firm in the faith,* because you know that your brothers throughout the world are undergoing the same kind of sufferings. I Peter 5:9
> All men will hate you because of me, but *he who stands firm to the end will be saved.* Mark 13:13

There are lots of things to take stands for or against, and teen-agers are tested in this area more often than most. Do I try drugs or alcohol? (Do you want someone else making important decisions for you while you are "under the influence"?) What will my friends think if I don't join them? (Are they really your friends if they pressure you to do something you don't want to do?) Can it really hurt just once ? (How many times does it take to get pregnant?) If I don't go all the way with him, will I lose him? (Does he really care about you or just what he can get from you?) Everyone does it, right? (Do they?) It's OK if I really love him, right? (Isn't love patient?) Everyone cheats, so what's the big deal? (Do they?) Sound familiar? To me it sounds a lot like, *"Did God really say?"* in *Genesis 3:1* when Satan tempted Adam and Eve. He is still asking that same question today in many different ways.

Questioning whether or not you should do something should immediately raise a red flag in your mind. Why am I questioning it? Something or Someone must be telling me to stop and think about it. God's Word is pretty clear on these issues. And I know there are many more questions out there. You probably already know the answers to these, and I will be addressing each of them specifically in later weeks, but meanwhile, here are some verses to get you thinking:

Do I try drugs or alcohol?

The acts of the sinful nature are obvious: sexual immorality, impurity and debauchery, idolatry and witchcraft, hatred, discord, jealousy, fits of rage, selfish ambition, dissentions, factions and envy, <u>drunkenness, orgies, and the like</u>. I warn you, as I did before, that those who live like this will not inherit the kingdom of God. Galatians 5:19-21

What will my friends think if I don't?

<u>If I were still trying to please men, I would not be a servant of Christ</u>. Galatians 1:10b

Can it really hurt just once?

But among you <u>there must not even be a hint </u>of sexual immorality, or of any kind of impurity, or of greed, because these are improper for God's holy people. Ephesians 5:3
<u>Do not set foot on the path of the wicked</u>… Proverbs 4:14

If I don't go all the way with him, will I lose him?

<u>Love is patient</u>, love is kind. It does not envy, it does not boast, it is not proud. It is not rude, it is <u>not self-seeking</u>, it is not easily angered, it keeps no record of wrongs. Love does not delight in evil, but rejoices with the truth. <u>It always protects</u>, always trusts, always hopes, always perseveres. 1 Corinthians 13:4-7
<u>Do not be yoked together with unbelievers</u>. For what do righteousness and wickedness have in common? Or what fellowship can light have with darkness? 2 Corinthians 6:14

Everyone does it, right?

Enter through the narrow gate. For wide is the gate and broad the road that leads to destruction, and many enter through it. But <u>small is the gate and narrow the road that leads to life, and only a few find it</u>. Matthew 7:13-14

It's OK if I really love him, right?

It is God's will that you should be holy; that you should avoid sexual immorality; that <u>each of you should learn to control his own body in a way that is holy and honorable</u>, not in passionate lust like the heathen, who do not know God. I Thessalonians 4:3-5

Everyone cheats, so what's the harm?

No one who practices deceit will dwell in my house; no one who speaks falsely will stand in my presence. Psalm 101:7

If you give in to the seduction in these questions, you will suffer regret later. Ethics are not situational as many would have us believe. If everyone was able to decide right and wrong for herself and it varied with each situation, there would *be* no "right" or "wrong" and the world would be in chaos. I know that it's nearly useless to talk about later regrets to many young people because later seems so far away. What's important is the "right now" and it's hard to imagine even a year or two from now. I know. I was there. And contrary to some of the evidence I have shared with you so far about my young life, I was tempted just as much as you are now. I was a regular kid in spite of chess club and being a "mama lizard." *I really do get it!* And I want to help you to avoid some of the scars carried by others who have gone before you. *Please listen.*

My pastor tied a string from a window on one side of the church to another on the other side up in front of the sanctuary one Sunday. He told us to imagine the string going on forever out the windows. Then he drew a dot on the string somewhere in the middle and asked if anyone could see the dot. No one could see it. He said that the string was eternity and that the dot was our earthly lives. He asked if our focus was on the string or the dot and if that's where it ought to be. What about you? It's the eternal versus the temporal. The dot is surely important – we are in this world for a short time and should do our best for the Lord here and now – but the only thing we can take with us when we die is another person. Is that foremost in our minds? Do we live as if telling others the Good News is the most important thing we could do? The world promises us freedom but ends up enslaving us. Some call following God a form of slavery, but in the end it is what truly frees us. It frees us from all of our sins and from sin's consequences.

Does it bother you to think that there might really be an inherent unwritten moral law of right and wrong to which we all are somehow accountable? C.S. Lewis says that moral law is deeply rooted within each of us. It is apparent in many ways on a daily basis. And that law is more like a Person than a set of laws. We can almost hear it speaking to us, urging us to do the right thing.

Do you believe in absolutes, in right and wrong?
Why or why not?
Do you believe they can change with the circumstances?
Give an example.
Who decides what is truly right or wrong?
Are you living for the present or for the eternal?

Bible Reading: *John 8:31-47*
What is it that sets men free? Explain.
Why do you think Jesus' words upset them so much?
They are Abraham's descendants, but are they his sons? Explain.
Who is Jesus telling them is their real father?
If your parents are Christians, does that make you one? Discuss.

Challenge: No matter what you may have heard, the Bible says that it's not okay to take part in the sins listed above. If you have fallen into any of them, change your habits now!

"It is for freedom that Christ has set us free. Stand firm, then, and do not let yourselves be burdened again by a yoke of slavery."
Galatians 5:1

"The turn of a phrase"

It's interesting how the same phrase can have so many meanings depending upon who's saying it and how it's being said. "You seem like a smart kid." is one of those phrases. Seems innocent enough, but in high school, it could be heavy with implication. If the older boy I had a crush on had said that to me, I would have been thrilled at the compliment because he was definitely a smart kid. If one of the less motivated students at my school had said it to me, I might have hesitated, wondering what he was about to ask me for. If one of my teachers had used it, I would have waited for the "so why on earth did you dangle a participle on a hexagon's outer electron shell?" That's the "who" saying it, but try a little experiment with the "how." Let's assume it is being said with emphasis on one of the six words:

"*You* seem like a smart kid." (emphasis on the first word) could mean the speaker is singling you out in a complimentary way.

"You *seem* like a smart kid." (emphasis on the second word) could mean that the speaker is in doubt of your "smarts."

"You seem like a *smart* kid." (emphasis on the second to last word) might indicate that the speaker thinks you're a smart-aleck, arrogant.

"You seem like a smart *kid*." (emphasis on the last word) is probably a put-down. The speaker mocks your youth.

You can see how someone might hesitate to be called a smart kid. One's educational promise could be in doubt at any moment due to the turn of a phrase. And now with emails and texting, the

119

opportunities to misread a person's intentions are greater than ever. On several occasions I have been misunderstood in my emails. That's why I always say that if you have something important to say to someone, say it in person, so there will be no doubt of your meaning. A reader might put the emphasis on a word for which you may not have intended it. The intonations in your voice and the facial expressions help to tell the whole story. Additionally, there will be no written record of your mistaken intention that can be shared with others as evidence of an alleged crime.

When I was a little girl, I was visiting at my aunt's house where she had just poured a couple of cups of very hot water for both her and my mother for tea. I reached up on the table to discover what was in one of the cups and pulled it down unto my chest. Immediately I screamed and immediately my mother pulled off my t-shirt. Big mistake. Never pull off a piece of clothing from someone who's just been scalded. The skin tends to come off with the shirt. Do what my sister did as a counselor at a youth camp: A young girl had dropped a bowl of hot spaghetti sauce on herself, so my sister (a nurse) threw a pitcher of cold water on her. Now the people in the dining room only saw the water get thrown. They of course thought my sister had really lost it and that the cold water was the reason the girl was crying. Though not immediately apparent, this was the smart thing to do and really helped to prevent serious burns from developing. Meanwhile, as a child I had to go through a few weeks of treatment with ointment and gauze. Memorable.

So how does this tie in with how you say things? Easy. I was burned by hot water as a child, but I've been burned by words many times since. I'm not sure which hurt more. There are people out there who seem to enjoy making others feel bad through hurtful or witty words. It may be an environmental by-product – this is what they've grown up with so it seems natural and acceptable. Or it may have become a well-established personal habit that they've just never really considered from another person's perspective. Some grow out of it, but others develop it into a fine-tuned art through which they continue to belittle others. Sarcasm becomes their brand of humor. Some even manage to do it with passive-aggressive silence – the kind that screams volumes. I'm not sure if it's a sadistic thing in which they enjoy seeing others hurt or if it's an attempt to inflate their own egos due to a poor self-image. All I do know is that some people are very good at it and I have learned to keep clear of them. Their words hurt more than boiling water. And there isn't always a pitcher of cold water around to make it feel better.

Have you been hurt by the words of others? Explain.
How do/did you respond? Zing some words right back at them? Go home and cry? Hold a grudge? Report them to the "authorities"? Badmouth them? Other? Explain.
What should you do? (*Colossians 3:13-14*)
What does the Bible have to say about the words we speak?
(There is) ... a time to be silent and a time to speak... Ecclesiastes 3:7b
A man of knowledge uses words with restraint.... Proverbs 17:27a
Simply let your "Yes" be "Yes," and your "No," "No" - anything beyond this is from the evil one. Matthew 5:37
Let your conversation be always full of grace, seasoned with salt, so that you may know how to answer everyone. Colossians 4: 6
In everything set them an example by doing what is good; in your teaching show integrity, seriousness, and soundness of speech that cannot be condemned, so that all who oppose you may be ashamed because they have nothing bad to say about us. Titus 2:7-8

There was a time when I went through the entire Bible and underlined everything that warned of unrestrained speech. (I tend to talk too much.) Do you have that problem? Some call it "motormouth." I'd like to think that it's gotten better, but I haven't given up working on it. I know that I am now less apt to blurt out whatever comes into my mind without first thinking it through. "Think before you speak." It's a good motto. I also like the saying: "God gave you two ears and one mouth; so listen twice as much as you speak." At this point in my life, I would recommend listening even more than that.

There was a young Christian girl I went to school with who was someone I always thought of as "fragile." She was very sweet but she had a pretty low self-image. She began to enjoy the attentions of a young man who seemed somewhat unworthy of her. (Sorry, if I judge here.) She graduated from high school and I later heard that she committed suicide. Rumor had it that there was a pregnancy in the mix. Knowing how judgmental others can be (especially on this topic years ago), I could imagine that her life was very difficult and that the rumors were even more nasty than those I heard. What an awful thing suicide is, such a heartache. She must have felt that her hope of a happy life was over – or that she had somehow cataclysmically failed to be the person she should have been. She was too confused to understand that none of us are the people we should be and that God can take any situation and restore it to joy. This is exactly why Christ came to earth – to heal the sick and the wounded, not the healthy. I imagine that the words of others had contributed to her despair. Shame on us for hurting anyone with our words. Our words can cause great tragedy. I am so sorry for the times I have been guilty of hurting with words. Words are like the feathers shaken out of a pillow on a windy day from high on a hilltop. There's no getting them back again. That's another reason for thinking first.

I guess I don't get it. I may talk too much but I can't imagine beating up on someone who is already down with abusive words. She knew her mistake and it was between her and God. Sharing this through the gossip chain could be even more harmful than personally coming down on her. You can never be sure how things will be communicated down the line. It's like that childhood game called "telephone." One person whispers something to the person next to her, who whispers it to the next, and so on down the line. The last person openly shares the secret which is usually quite different from the one originally shared. Try it sometime. It's an eye-opener. Gossip is warned against in the Bible. (*Ephesians 4:29, Psalm 141:3*)

Some might say that this young woman should have aborted her child for her own mental health. But I could never use this to encourage an abortion. That's just getting "out of the frying pan into the fire." The baby did nothing to deserve death and the mother would eventually feel even worse if she aborted her child. Besides, the Bible says that God alone is the giver/taker of life. (*Deuteronomy 32:39, I Samuel 2:6*) However, I do use this as a reason to bring shame upon those who should have come alongside this young girl to help her to move on from the pain and guilt into God's love and forgiveness, doing everything they could to help her to do what was right for both the baby and herself. Maybe someone did try to help her. I hope so. But so often judgment is all that's offered. She needed compassion and love to help her through this. If she was not in a position to raise a child, there were many who would have loved to do this for her. What is wrong with the Christian community that doesn't help those in need? – especially those among their own "family"?

We need to be so careful of what we say. We may be pushing someone into fatefully bad decisions through our misuse of words. Have you heard the old nursery chant: "Sticks and stones can hurt my bones, but words can never hurt me." Not true. I'm not sure how that came into use as a childhood chant. You can tell that the child chanting that doesn't even believe it. It's more of an attempt to get back at the one doing the hurting. Words *can* hurt – more than boiling water!

Bible Reading:

The Bible has so much to say about our speech:

It tells us to seek wisdom in *James 1:5, Proverbs 25:11, and Ecclesiastes 10:12.*

It tells us to have spiritual conversation in *Deuteronomy 6:6-7, Malachi 3:16, Ephesians 5:19-20*

It tells us to use restraint in our speech in *Job 6:24, Psalm 34:13, Proverbs 13:3, James 1:26, and I Peter 3:10.*

It warns us against lying in *Proverbs 6:16-19, Leviticus 19:11, Colossians 3:9, Acts 5:4b and Psalm 34:13.*

Have you ever hurt someone with your words?
Have you asked them for forgiveness?

Do NOT try to vindicate yourself in an apology. In other words, don't try to get yourself off the hook by explaining why you did what you did. All too often that only makes the situation worse. Just say you're sorry. Confession really is "good for the soul." *Proverbs 28:13* says "He who conceals his sins does not prosper, but whoever *confesses and renounces them* finds mercy." Did you catch the "and renounces them" in there? I think the Catholics can teach us something in this area, though as a Protestant I would suggest that a good trustworthy friend would do just as well as a priest (no offense to my Catholic friends here), and confession directly to God is always the first step. *James* 5:16a says "Therefore confess your sins to each other and pray for each other..." There is a personal accountability in confessing to a friend that you would not otherwise have that might help in the "renouncing" step. Most importantly, we have *Hebrews* 4:16 which says "Let us then approach the throne of grace with confidence, so that we may receive mercy and find grace to help us in our time of need." The curtain separating the holy of holies from the holy place in the temple was torn down with the death and resurrection of Jesus Christ. We can go boldly to God's throne without fear.

Challenge: If you need to apologize for hurtful things you've said to someone, do it now!

"Therefore confess your sins to each other and pray for each other so that you may be healed. The prayer of a righteous man is powerful and effective."
James 5:16

"Campfire stories"

I can remember going to Bible camp many times during my preteen and teen years. I loved it! I have been a Christian for pretty much all of my life, but it was during a meeting at camp in a tent with wooden benches and sawdust on the floor that I was first convicted of sin. Though I can't remember a time when I didn't love the Lord, there were seasons in my life when the Holy Spirit convicted me and brought me into a fuller, more mature understanding of who God is and what He expects of me. Sitting in the tent listening to Pastor L. talk about sinners and their need for salvation, I can remember thinking, "Yeah, those sinners should be ashamed of themselves making Jesus die on the cross for them and causing so much trouble." I was pretty frustrated with those sinners … until I gradually started to understand that I was also one of *those* sinners. Whoa. I started to squirm in my seat.

Without a second thought I found myself walking down to the front of the tent to ask for forgiveness. I quickly experienced that divine joy that the disciples felt on the Emmaus road in *Luke 24:32*. Years later I recounted that moment in a short poem: "My heart was 'strangely warmed' as we communed along the way. And I felt I travelled with Him on the dusty road that day. He opened to me the Scriptures. I began to comprehend. And this time as He turned to go, I recognized a friend." There began my appreciation for *John 15:15* where Jesus calls us His friends. Through the Lord's grace I have felt again and again in this life that mysterious warmth in those little glimpses of God and of heaven. "Thank you, Lord." Years later I was also able to thank Pastor L. for his faithfulness in making me aware of my culpability in Jesus' death. Recognizing my guilt was a necessary step in growing into a mature faith.

I had always known that I was capable of sinning, but I didn't think I was one of *those* sinners, the ones who nailed Him to the tree. I loved the Lord and prayed to Him all the time. He was my *raison d'etre* (reason to be). How could I be one of *them*? But I hadn't fully understood the whole "all have sinned" part in *Romans 3:23*. It's funny because I knew I needed Jesus. I always felt Him there with me and would have known if He wasn't there. Almost before I can remember I had sincerely accepted Him as my Savior, yet without completely understanding exactly *why* I needed Him and what I had been saved *from*. The faith of a child I guess. "All have sinned." Period. Each one of us has virtually committed *every* sin, in thought, word, or deed. We are all *those* sinners. I went forward and confessed my sin that night and have been confessing my sins to God ever since. (I can't seem to stop sinning. Pretty disappointing.)

When did you give your heart to the Lord?

Where were you when you made a confession of sin?

If you haven't yet, what are you waiting for?

What sins do you think you are guilty of? Discuss.

Is it possible that you are guilty of them all? Discuss.

Does the Bible really say that we *all* have committed *every* sin?

> *Everyone has turned away, ... there is no one who does good, not even one. Psalm 53:3*
> *All of us have become like one who is unclean, and all our righteous acts are like filthy rags; Isaiah 64:6*
> *You have heard that it was said, "Do not commit adultery." But I tell you that anyone who looks at a woman lustfully has already committed adultery with her in his heart. Matthew 5:27-28*
> *Whoever keeps the whole law, yet stumbles at just one point is guilty of breaking all of it. James 2:10*

So even our thoughts can convict us. But don't let these verses discourage you too much because God, in His great love for us, has taken care of this. He has made a way out. In *Psalm 51* David asks for mercy from the Lord, confesses his sins, and recognizes that only God can restore him to a right relationship and a pure heart. In *Psalm 32* David talks about the blessing of being a for-given man and how important it was and is to confess sin. Read those psalms in your quiet time and try to grasp the emotion with which David is speaking. Most importantly, understand that there *is* forgiveness, forgiveness for any and every sin we have already committed and are yet to commit.

As a teacher, I once made a continuous graph on my overhead graphing calculator made up from several separate equations that represented my walk with the Lord. It had uphill climbs (diagonal lines, or exponential curves for the really tough times), times of confusion (sine and cosine waves), plateaus (horizontal lines), and other notable periods in my life all mapped out in an effort to share lessons learned with those listening. I'm sure my students thought I was a very strange math geek, but more importantly, I think they may have remembered it. What would your graph look like?

Camp was a time to learn and grow spiritually, but it was also a time of fun. We went swimming, boating, and water skiing; we played a myriad of sports/games and got to learn all kinds of new things. I broke my wrist in three places at camp! That's something I'll never forget. My first time ever waterskiing, I managed to get up on the skis and go around the lake a couple of times. Then we started in toward the shore, but no one had told me ahead of time what to do coming in to the dock and no one was directing me now. They weren't even looking at me. As I came in toward the dock I realized that I was going too fast and that I was going to ski right into a boat if I didn't do something. So I let go of the rope but never thought to fall over – it all happened so fast. I held my arm out to try to prevent the skis from damaging a boat in front of me and my wrist cracked!

The irony was that I had to wait for over an hour to go to the doctor because the nurse's shift wasn't over and she wasn't sure my wrist was broken – in spite of the fact that *the bone sticking out from the wrist* could only be held in place by wrapping a *National Geographic* securely around my wrist and taping it tightly in place. Sheesh. (I have forgiven her.) A doctor and his nurse pulled simultaneously on my elbow and my hand to get the broken bones to pop back into place (ouch!) and then plastered me up with a cast that went around my elbow and included my hand but not my fingers. I went through two more casts that summer as I abused them. But at least I got to quit my summer job sewing tobacco leaves onto lathes. (weird job, huh?)

I went to a lake with the first cast and put a plastic bag securely over it so that it would not get wet as I walked out to a little island that we liked to picnic on. The water only got to chest depth so I figured I would hold my arm above my head and I would be fine. I tripped. The water filled up the secure(?) bag, and the tape holding it in place made it difficult to remove said bag, thereby thoroughly soaking the cast. They replaced that cast with another which I did a pretty good job on by sticking a metal hanger down it to relieve the horrible itching. It was somewhat lacerated on the top, but it did the trick until they put a little shorty cast on at the end.

The girls at camp slept under the camp dining room in basement rooms with bunk beds, low ceilings, and lots of spiders. The boys were in a different building with a heavenly host of bats (the flying rodent type) to help stir up trouble. I remember hiding out in the bushes one night as a counselor tried in vain to discover who was running around outside after lights out. There were actually several of us. The discipline was not all that tight. When I got a little older, a small group of us sneaked across the road onto a golf course where we laid down on one of the greens looking up at the full moon when someone (might even have been me) got the bright idea to switch the flags in a couple of the holes – which seemed harmless enough at the time. Now that I golf myself I can understand the seemingly undue fuss over it the next day. Years later when I was a counselor and then a camp director I always knew just where to look for missing kids. When they asked me how I knew where to find them, I would say, "That's where I would have been."

I think *every* kid ought to go to Bible camp. Churches and individuals should help *every* young person to get there. Many

Christian camps have scholarship funds just for that. Did you know that most people (well over 90%) who come to the Lord, make a commitment before the age of 21? and many at Bible camp? After that hearts begin to slowly harden making it tougher to "melt" them and "mold" them like the song says. That's why I've always been so involved in youth camps over the years. Not only are teenagers (the campers) and young adults (the counselors and staff) the coolest people in the world, but the teen years are also the best time to introduce someone to Jesus. For a few years after high school, I did a lot of guest singing at Bible camps. I felt compelled to be a good role model then and rarely sneaked out at night, and I have to admit: it was nice not to have to worry about getting into trouble for being a rascal.

What kind of camps have you attended?
Have you ever broken the rules? Explain.
What were the consequences?
Have you ever felt compelled to be a good role model? Why?
What do you think the Bible says about that?
Don't let anyone look down on you because you are young, but set an example for the believers in speech, in life, in love, in faith and in purity. I Timothy 4:12
In everything set them an example by doing what is good. In your teaching show integrity, seriousness and soundness of speech that cannot be condemned, so that those who oppose you may be ashamed because they have nothing bad to say about you. Titus 2:7-8

We are witnesses to the world of God's love, but we are also role models for those Christians who are younger – both in age and in their faith. Sadly, I have not always been the best example. I was often a bit of a scamp. It's a good thing I came to the Lord early in life because that kept me from doing even more stupid things. Just as the verse at the end of this week is often used to encourage the unbeliever to come to the Lord, it can be used to encourage the believer to confess sins committed and good deeds omitted, be forgiven, and do better on a daily basis. That's why the Lord's Prayer includes *"forgive us our debts (*sins*) ..."*

Bible Reading: *Psalm 51:1-14*

What is David asking for in this psalm?

Why does he say that sin is against God and God only?

So then, why do we need to ask forgiveness of others?

When does David say he began to be sinful?

What does David believe God can do for him? (verses 10 and 12)

What does he fear?

I searched for verses on forgiveness in the Bible only to find that most of those dealing with forgiveness between individuals put the onus on the offended person. We are called more often to *be* forgiving than to *ask* for forgiveness. Maybe because asking for forgiveness is the natural by-product of a forgiving heart? The verses telling us to *seek* forgiveness are directed toward God – because all sin is ultimately against God. This however, does not let us off the hook in apologizing, because the Bible also calls us to be reconciled (onus on us) to one another. (*Matthew 5:24*)

Challenge: Whatever sin you are holding inside, confess it and turn away from it.

"If we confess our sins, He is faithful and just and will forgive us our sins and purify us from all unrighteousness."
I John 1:9

WEEK 25

"Out east"

Would God have approved of our teenage ideas for having fun? Sometimes yes and sometimes no, I would guess. I know He would have liked our sing-a-longs at the parties at my house when we sang Christian choruses. Though I'm not sure how He would have felt about secular rock groups in general, I think He would have liked that we cleaned up the lyrics when we sang their songs. I think He would have enjoyed lying on the golf green across from our Bible camp looking up at the moon with us, but He probably would not have liked us breaking the camp rules in sneaking out, and possibly not our prank in switching the flags around on the golf course holes. No, some things He may not have liked at all – like our tendency to periodically gravitate out east in our town to race cars. That was a little dangerous. And we've already seen what he thinks of taking chances (in week one).

With the Corvettes, GTO's, Roadrunners, Mustangs, Camaros, and assorted other fast cars belonging to our youth/young adult group, we obviously had an interest in speed (the "going fast" kind). I remember blocking off the road with cars on both ends of the rarely used straight stretch of road in the "hollow" at the northern end of the reservoir or "out east" in the state forest heading into Massachusetts. Then two cars would line up side by side on one end, and the race would begin. If any other cars came toward this stretch of road, the cars blocking the road would flash their lights and the race would subside. It was all very scientific. And we were very fortunate that no one ever got hurt (not even close as far as I know). What is it they say? "God looks out for fools and little children." ? something like that. I guess we were both in a way...

131

What are some of the things you do to have fun?
List them in one of these three columns:

GWA	MGWA	PGWNA
"God Would Approve"	"*Maybe* God Would Approve"	"Probably God Would *Not* Approve"

Which column has the most entries? Is this a problem for you? Is there a way that you could move things from a column on the right into one on the left without a lot of difficulty? Sometimes it's simply a matter of cleaning up the words.

Challenge: Consider picking a couple of things above to move to the left.

What would God think of our attempts at fun?
Folly delights a man who lacks judgment, but a man of understanding keeps a straight course. Proverbs 15:21
Therefore do not be foolish, but understand what the Lord's will is. Ephesians 5:17

Often with fast cars comes the ability to work on these cars, and the guys in our youth group (especially my cousins) were no exception. Sometimes I would hold the light as they went deep into the engine to fix a problem or to make the car a little more competitive somehow. I picked up a few things that came in handy later in life and got a lot of free work done on my car when I most needed it in college. I didn't need a car before college because I was at a boarding school in the Midwest that didn't allow me to have a car. Once I started college, because my hometown was so remote from anything resembling civilization, a vehicle was a must.

I had a thirty minute commute on my recently purchased motor-cycle to my college's nearest campus. I also worked close to the campus for twenty to twenty-five hours a week during my first two years. Whenever the weather was too nasty to ride my motorcycle I hitched a ride with my oldest sister who worked near my school. But right before my junior year I bought a used '65 Mustang for $400 and put about five hundred and fifty miles a week on it com-muting to my college's main campus which was about 50 miles from home. After driving it for two years, I turned around and sold it through the paper for $400. Not a bad investment. I also learned a lot from that car – like how to start my car by holding the butterfly valve open with a screwdriver. It had its quirks.

The guys in town liked to drive their fast cars and sometimes they drove them too fast. It's amazing how patient God was with us in those days. I remember going down the highway with a singing group from our church to give a concert at a church over an hour away. The group I was then in had about twenty members so we had several cars headed down a relatively empty highway on a sunny Sunday afternoon. One thing led to another and within a short time, three or four of the cars had been pulled over and were getting tickets from a policeman who must have wondered at the number of speeders who had all appeared at the same time on an empty road. (Probably hit his monthly quota right there and then.) He seemed unimpressed when I mentioned that we were headed to a church down the road to give a concert. Still got the ticket. In retrospect I probably shouldn't have mentioned the church thing because the tickets didn't reflect well on Christians.

Sometimes we play with fire – and cars are a prime example. The last thing I would ever want to be, would be the reason another human being dies. Cars are deadly weapons when used without wisdom. They're like loaded guns. And teenagers have the worst records. The number of young people who are involved in car acci-dents each year is staggering. Sorry, but it's no wonder insurance rates are higher for teenagers. Some states are even considering raising the age to get a license in an effort to save lives.

Do you have your license? How old were you when you got it? For how long have you been driving?

Do you have your own car? Did *you* pay for it?

Have you ever exceeded the speed limit by more than five mph? ten mph?

Have you ever had an accident? Was it your fault? Explain.

Have you ever gotten a ticket? For what reason? Explain.

Did you try to talk your way out of it? How? Were you successful?

What does God have to say about this?

> Remind the people to be subject to rulers and authorities, to be obedient, to be ready to do whatever is good, to slander no one, to be peaceable and considerate, and always to be gentle towards everyone. *Titus 3:1-2*
>
> Everyone must submit himself to the governing authorities, for there is no authority except that which God has established. The authorities that exist have been established by God. Consequently, he who rebels against the authority is rebelling against what God has instituted, and those who do so will bring judgment on themselves. *Romans 13:1-2*
>
> "...Give to Caesar what is Caesar's, and to God what is God's." *Matthew 22:21*

The very worst thing that could happen to a driver of a car would be injuring or worse, killing someone. I heard about a teenager who accidentally struck and killed a man on a small country road. The sun was in his eyes and he didn't see the man. More experience may have taught him to slow down in that situation – or to wait. I pray for that young driver whenever I think of him. It can't be easy living with that. And the penalties have become quite severe if found drinking while driving. Fortunately, he wasn't.

In the Old Testament, even accidental death was grounds for the family of the victim taking the guilty party's life. "Cities of Refuge" were set up just for that reason. (See *Joshua 20:1-6*.) These were actually used successfully for hundreds of years. But you had to live within the city limits until you stood trial AND (if found innocent of intention) until the present high priest died ...

which could be many long years. If found guilty, it was "an eye for an eye."

If there is one vice that I have been especially guilty of, it is speeding. I grew up around fast cars and people who knew how to drive them. I lived in a remote town that had no police force and open, empty roads. It was a lethal combination and I came to enjoy the challenge of driving fast. I have learned over the years that this is not what God expects of me. I have learned to value the lives of others as well as my own more. I have slowed down – not because I've gotten scared or too old – but because it's the right thing to do. Paul talks in *Romans* about the struggle within us between our two natures, the human nature and the Godly nature He is giving to us as we grow in Him. I have always been encouraged by Paul's honesty, to know that I'm not the only one struggling.

Bible Reading: *Romans 7:14-25*
> Do you ever struggle with doing the right thing as Paul did?
> Do you find yourself doing the opposite of what you want to do as a Christian?
> What does Paul say is the reason for this?
> What two things are at war in Paul?
> To whom does he look for rescue?

Challenge: Examine what is going on inside you. If you have this battle as Paul did, do as he did in crying out to God for help.

"You are the ones who justify yourselves in the eyes of men, but God knows your hearts…"
Luke 16:15a

WEEK 26

"Psycho, and other bed-time stories"

could hardly believe that my mother was allowing me go to work for my uncle at a Christian college in Westchester County just north of New York City for two whole summers when I was only 16 and 17 years old. I guess she figured I was in a pretty safe environment and that my uncle would be keeping a careful watch over me. Little did she know ... It was just a short ride into the city with all of its attractions, and I found myself drawn there pretty often. And though my uncle was an awesome guy, he was way too busy to be watching me every minute of the day. Then again, I was basically a good kid, so maybe he really didn't have to?

My uncle was the food service manager at a Christian college in Westchester county. During the week, each kitchen staff member helped to prepare the food and work the meal line for the summer students (mostly commuters) and the college staff with meal plans. Everyone worked on Saturdays, because each Saturday evening there would be a dinner and concert for over 600 people. We were the crew who helped to prepare all of the food for the buffet. We would peel and clean over 100 pounds of shrimp and roll about 150 pounds of Swedish meatballs for baking. My uncle called them Norwegian (his wife) meatballs in Danish (himself) sauce. On second thought, it may have been 150 pounds of shrimp and 100 pounds of meatballs ... whatever. We were taught how to embellish the many salads with artistic designs of edible garnishes, and we waited tables at the dinner. I served a few tables which usually included the head table where the president of the college and the guest artist sat. I took my position as waitress/entertainer quite seriously. As a result I got pretty good tips – which I had to share with everyone else. Bummer.

The buffet table was a work of art with each plate of delicious food decorated so beautifully that one hated to see the first guest go through the line to use fork or spoon to despoil the symmetry and artistic design of the salads and other food dishes. But it would surely happen – very quickly and quite thoroughly. The scene was complete with a fountain of punch spilling down its colorfully lighted tiers on a side table and a beautiful ice carving in the center of it all. Saturday was the busiest day of the week. Sunday was my day off. Otherwise, the schedule varied little each week.

I could probably write an entire book about my adventures over these two summers. Like the time I broke a cardinal rule of the college and went to a movie, *The Sound of Music,* and got turned in to my uncle by my own cousin! Or the evening I locked an aggravating guy (who had thrown dirty floor mop water on me) in a tunnel that ran from the road down below up to the kitchen in the basement of the main building. He was the guy my sister was engaged to (a couple of times) a few years later. The night watchman later let him out. There was the morning I threw an uncooked meatball out of a nearby kitchen window and admired its tenacity as it stuck to the front license plate of the college president's car for the next week. "How in the world…?" Or the night I joined a group of friends (all girls) up on the top floor of the main building to watch Alfred Hitchcock's movie, *Psycho.*

It was summer, so the main building was mostly empty with only a few female students and summer staff (including me) staying on the second floor. The top floor was especially scary with its twists and turns through the winding low corridors of the empty attic of this ancient whale of a building. We found a TV in an unused lounge and settled in for the scare of our lives, enhanced by the unnoticed approach of a handful of guys from the men's dorm, across the roof, along the ledge, to our lounge, where they began tapping on the window. Talk about psycho! We didn't see them coming so "yes," we rewarded them with the scream they were hoping for.

The most noteworthy story from those two summers of my life has to be the bizarre visit one moonlit night (full moon) to a grave-yard of fictional fame in a nearby sleepy town on the Hudson River. Six of us, three couples, loaded into a VW beetle and headed out for a scare. I'm not sure why teens and young adults enjoy scaring themselves, but... We parked the car on a nearby street and walked into the main gate of the very impressive cemetery, which was somehow both enticing and foreboding at the same time. Maybe it was the night, maybe the graves all around us, but no one spoke above a whisper. We barely spoke at all. Before we got to the bridge of renown (though not the original one of Washington Irving's day) located inside the park, two of our companions casually disappeared. Once at the bridge, we could see lights up on the other side. We sneaked up closer to see a circle of flames with a small group of people moving about within it. All kinds of thoughts raced through my head – *none of them good.*

Evidently the same thoughts must have occurred to my three companions because we were all suddenly running noiselessly back out of the cemetery. I *actually* experienced the cliché of "feet barely touching the ground." En route our two missing friends appeared from among the gravestones (to scare us, I think); but immediately assessing the seriousness of our anxious and speedy flight, they breathlessly joined in without a word. Nearing the exit, we saw flashlights and heard voices, so we hid behind the grave-stones all around us. It turned out to be several policemen who were running toward the bridge we had just left. We separated into twos and somehow managed to get through a side entrance and return to the car. Fortunately my friend and I got there first because he had the car keys, and the policeman who listened to our "out for a moonlit stroll" story and told us to leave right away, might not have looked favorably upon our full story. Again, fortunately, we saw the rest of our party right around the corner and they were able to jump into the car without further incident. We didn't do any-thing illegal, but we definitely did something dumb.

What do you think was going on in the cemetery? Share.
What would you have done if you had been there? Discuss.

It was probably someone dabbling in the occult (witchcraft or some other cultic event) under the full moon, which seems to be a prime time for that type of activity. (At this point in time they have legitimate moonlit tours of the cemetery, though it is a bit macabre for my taste now.) Why do people get involved in the occult? Curiosity? Is it that attraction to danger or the thrill of fear that we have talked about? Maybe it's because the supernatural gives evidence of something God-like which can be deceptively enticing. People are probably drawn into the occult while trying to fill within themselves that "infinite abyss...that can be filled only... by God Himself." (quote from Blaise Pascal, mathematician of "Pascal's triangle" fame) They desperately want that hole filled, but are not willing to consider God. He might expect them to change. If they were really honest, they would admit that there is a longing for God built in to each one of us from birth. They don't recognize God as the desire, but they hunger for things to be good and right; they hunger for true happiness, for joy. Only God can offer these. Satan imitates God to a certain point which makes him all the more intriguing. But after the initial introduction, things start to skew far from the God for Whom we yearn. People try so many things to fill their heart's cry for their Creator and Savior. I remember once reading a book, *The Beautiful Side of Evil,* that exposed the ability of evil to disguise itself as good. A young woman (true story) got caught up in the occult thinking it to be of God, only to come face to face with evil.

We didn't really want to stay around the cemetery to find out what those lights were, and the rush of police into the cemetery made it an even less attractive option. There was nothing in the paper over the next couple of days, so we never discovered the truth about the lights. One thing I did learn was that I had NO interest in the occult and never wanted to get that close again.

What does God say about the occult?

> He sacrificed his own son in the fire, *practiced sorcery and divination, and consulted mediums and spiritists*. He did *much evil* in the eyes of the Lord, provoking him to anger. 2 Kings 21:6
> Furthermore Josiah *got rid of the mediums and spiritists*, the household gods, the idols *and all the other detestable things*. 2 Kings 23:24
> But the cowardly, the unbelieving, the vile, the murderers, the sexually immoral, *those who practice magic arts*, the idolaters and all liars – their place will be in the *fiery lake* of burning sulfur. This is the second death. Revelation 21:8

What are some seemingly innocent ways people might become involved in it?

Have you ever used a Ouija board? Discuss.

Do you know anyone involved in the occult?

Do you need to warn them?

What does God say about things like our cemetery visit?

> Brothers, *stop thinking like children*. In regard to evil be infants, but in your thinking, be adults. I Corinthians 14:20
> Therefore *do not be foolish*, but understand what the Lord's will is. Ephesians 5:17

So, was I done being dumb yet? Hardly. I was too fearless. I was young and never even considered the dangers and possible consequences. I was invincible and ready for almost anything! It was fortunate for me that my mother never had a hint of my escapades, or I would certainly have spent the remainder of my summers back at home. Yet ... we visited no more cemeteries.

Bible Reading: *Proverbs 4:14-15, James 4:7-8a, I Peter 5:8-11, I John 4:1-6*

What does *Proverbs 4:4-15* warn us of?

What does *James 4:7-8a* tell us is a good way to resist evil?

How active is Satan in all of the evil we see in our world? (*I Peter 5:8-11*)

What should we do to be prepared?

I John 4:1-6 tells us to do what?

This we can do with three tests:

message (v.2b- Does it contradict Scripture?)

audience (v.5- Who is listening?)
character (v.6a- Who is the message giver?)

If you come across something that seems a little off spiritually, use these tests. Compare what is said to Scripture, look at the people buying into it (Are they people of wisdom?), and check out the speaker (Is he/she trustworthy? How do you know?). And pray.

Challenge: If you know someone who is dabbling in the occult, warn them of what the Bible says, and be sure to stay away from it yourself.

"Be very careful then, how you live – not as unwise but as wise, making the most of every opportunity, because the days are evil. Therefore do not be foolish, but understand what the Lord's will is."
Ephesians 5:15-17

WEEK 27

"Extra credit"

should probably stop telling stories of my summers working in New York, but there are a couple more that might be of "educational benefit." For instance, there were those late nights we would all go into the city after cleaning up after the banquets on Saturday nights. I would go with my friend from the cemetery and we would leave at about ten o'clock at night. We usually went down into the village (Greenwich Village). One night we came upon a scuffle (probably more common in the Viet Nam war era) in Washington Square all started by a monkey climbing a tree. Someone went up after it into a tree that wasn't supposed to be climbed I guess. A heated debate ensued. I must have felt invisible as I stood there watching a small group of students and policemen interact physically, either in order to make a statement or to successfully enforce the law. It got a little rough and I just stood there and watched. What *was* I thinking? God's angels were busy protecting me that night, but I was pushing it.

We frequented a bistro nearby called "Café Wha?" My friend would bring his guitar because they often let people come up on stage and perform during "open mic" times. One of the girls in our party offered to get hypnotized one night! Not sure if I believe she was actually "under," but I think she wound up acting like a chicken or some type of barnyard bird, maybe it was a duck. I couldn't believe she would even consider offering to be hypnotized. Being a little younger than most (and a little smarter than at least one I'd say), I again just watched.

What do you think of hypnotism? Discuss.

What does the Bible say about letting anyone into your mind?
Dear friends, do not believe every spirit, but <u>test the spirits</u> to see whether they are from God, because many false prophets have gone out into the world. 1 John 4:1
<u>Be very careful</u>, then, how you live – not as unwise but as wise, making the most of every opportunity, because the days are evil. Therefore, <u>do not be foolish</u>, but understand what the Lord's will is. Ephesians 5:15-17
... we <u>take captive every thought to make it obedient to Christ</u>. 2 Corinthians 10:5b

My dictionary says that hypnosis is "a mental state of heightened suggestibility characterized by trance-like sleep." One's attention is fixed slowly in one direction – that of the hypnotist. It is historically linked to séances and was used by Hindus, Buddhists, witchdoctors and shamans. Under its power it is difficult or impossible to distinguish between fact or fantasy, truth or error. Bottom line? We need to be very careful any time that we are invited to open or clear our minds in the relaxation techniques out there today (e.g., hypnosis, yoga, meditation, drug-induced states, etc.). Some are simply Eastern religion in disguise and should be avoided for that reason. Others may include mind-altering drugs that could become addictive. Though some may relax us and even produce spiritual revelations, psychic powers or euphoria, they may also produce anxiety, depression, or worse. The spirits they contact are not of God. As Christians we never want to clear our minds totally because we want the Holy Spirit to be *ever-present* in our hearts and minds. Clearing our minds can open the door to all kinds of uninvited guests. Talk to your parents and your pastor and pray about anything like this before you take a step toward it. Don't be deceived!

My friends from my summer job at the Christian college were few in number but of a great variety in spite of that. There was the girl who took me to "Wing Ding" events – Christian events for young adults filled with music and fun, all taking place in a big barn filled with hay and havoc. She was a great Christian and lots of fun. There was the guy I went out with once or twice who had our whole lives planned after the second date, leading to ... no third date. And my best friend was a girl my age who was so much fun that she ended up getting kicked out of the college a couple of years later – not for doing anything all that terrible – simply for the sheer number of trivial infractions she amassed.

There was also this guy who may have been the best dancer I had ever seen. He was *very* handsome and lots of fun. He and I went into a store one day to buy furniture for our apartment. We were not a couple and did not have an apartment, but we wanted to see if we could raise a few eyebrows. We did. Not sure that that was a smart thing to do at that point in American history. I think we thought we were taking a stand for civil rights. You see, he was black and I was white. I could never understand the big deal over those adjectives because he wasn't exactly black and I wasn't exactly white (more like brown and tan). But these words seemed to work on some level to contribute to our basic descriptions. To me those adjectives were just like "short" or "tall." He *was* tall, by the way. And he was a good friend.

Have you ever been a victim of racism or prejudice? (no matter what your race or ethnicity)
Has anyone you know? Explain.
Has racism/prejudice become less or more of an issue in the USA over the years? Discuss.

My friend from the cemetery was of German descent and has already been mentioned a couple of times. He had most of my attention for a while. First of all he was "wow" cute and very interesting. He was going into his senior year of college and could have dated anyone, so people were probably surprised when he asked me out. Then again I was a pretty safe date because I had no intention of getting serious for the next ten years or so. He was the guy I went with to the cemetery and to the café. He was a little crazy to bring a seventeen year old country girl into the city that late at night, even if there were five or six of us in our group. I don't think I was ever even slightly bored on an adventure with him.

Ever date an older guy? (This is more of an issue in high school.)
How did/do your parents feel about it?
Do you have any friends like the ones I just "introduced" to
you? Explain.
Maybe you are like one of my friends?

It's important to have good friends you can count on. My friends
in New York may have been a little careless at times, but they were
good people who were, in the "macro" sense, making wise decisions in their lives. Though we've since lost touch, I bet they are
all living for the Lord right now. Like me, they enjoyed adventure
and fun, but they had limits, lines they wouldn't cross. There were
things that were simply taboo. I never knew any of them to get
drunk or take drugs of any kind. I don't think any of them were
sleeping around (and we probably would have known); and they
seemed to have healthy family relationships. I may have been
more cautious than they were, but I was also the youngest and
firmly convicted when it came to crossing my lines. My two summers working in New York were a lot of fun and I learned so much
about what *not* to do next time – things I might not have learned if
I'd stayed at home – like the dangers of hypnotism and the importance of taking a *meaningful* stand against racism/prejudice and
getting involved in other important causes. Yet when I think of all
that could have gone wrong… Yikes! It's so cool that God chose
to help me through that time in my life in spite of my foolish escapades. Our God is awesome!

Who do you know who is a "wealth of knowledge"?
What is the difference between knowledge and wisdom? Discuss.
Who are the wisest people you know?
What makes them wise and not just knowledgeable? Explain.
Are any of them your age? Your friends?

I've known a lot of smart people in my lifetime, but only a
handful of people who I would consider to be wise. Wisdom is

145

more than just a knowledge of facts and figures and techniques for doing something well. It is a deep understanding of what it takes to make good choices in life on a regular basis. It's being able to look at the big picture and see the consequences of those choices, weighing them against other choices to bring about the best outcome for all involved. "Wisdom is proved right by her actions." (*Matthew 11:19b*) It's not tied to a person's level of education. Someone with very little education or learned skills could be very wise. And it's the wise person whose company we should seek and whose advice we should listen to. My friends and I were often unwise. But there is always hope – the Bible says that advancing years teach wisdom. (*Job 32:7*)

What is the Bible's advice on friends?
He who walks with the wise grows wise, but a companion of fools suffers harm. Proverbs 13:20
A man of many companions may come to ruin, but there is a friend who sticks closer than a brother. Proverbs 18:24
A friend loves at all times, and a brother is born for adversity. Proverbs 17:17

Bible Reading: *I Samuel 18:1-4, 23:16-18, 2 Samuel 1:25b-26, 9:6-7*

What does it mean to "love him as himself"?

Was Jonathan jealous that David was to be king instead of him, the king's son?

Can love between two friends be as strong as the love of husband and wife without crossing into homosexuality?

How long did David and Jonathan's friendship last?

Challenge: Find and be a good friend. It takes work.

"*Do not be misled: 'Bad company corrupts good character.'*"
I Corinthians 15:33

WEEK 28

"...walk beside me, and be my friend" (Camus)

My first summer in New York had spoiled me for the quiet life in Connecticut, at least for the immediate future. I was half way through my high school education and I had always hoped to go to the school that my mother had graduated from in Minnesota. Trouble was, boarding school was expensive. However, one of my brothers and both of my sisters had been offered the option of attending the school, so my mother was determined to work it out for me as well. I managed to get a small scholarship and a job in the school's kitchen which would take care of half of the cost, and my mother would take care of the rest. I understood that there would be no trips home for Thanksgiving, Easter – any holidays other than Christmas. And there would be no unnecessary phone calls, which meant "emergencies only." (Long distance calling was expensive back then.)

My oldest sister had lasted for only about a month due to homesickness. A couple of her free-spirited friends from Connecticut had been sent home right at the "get-go" which probably contributed to her decision. The younger of my two brothers decided to go for his senior year, so he had only one year out there, but he did graduate from the school. My closest sister in age went out for her junior year only. I was going out for my junior year with every intention of graduating from the school. The school had an excellent academic reputation with top students from all over the nation and beyond. The school also had an outstanding vocal music program which interested me. Their sports program for girls at that time was even worse than in my other school, so I could forget any real challenge there. And they had no band or orchestra – which was a more serious disappointment. (Both are *very* much improved at this point in time, by the way.) Weighing my options, taking into consideration the pros and cons, I still had no doubt that I wanted to go to this school in Fergus Falls, Minnesota. I had been planning this for years and would do whatever I could to help this to happen.

> Was there ever anything you wanted so badly that you would do almost anything in your power to get it or to make it happen? Explain.
> Describe a time you had to weigh things very carefully to make a big decision.
> What does the Bible have to say about big decisions?
>> *Ask and it will be given to you; <u>seek and you will find</u>; knock and the door will be opened unto you. for everyone who asks receives; <u>he who seeks finds</u>; and to him who knocks the door will be opened. Matthew 7:7-8*
>> *… But Jehoshaphat also said to the king of Israel, "<u>First, seek the counsel of the Lord.</u>" I Kings 22:5b*
>> *<u>You guide me with your counsel</u>… Psalm 73:24*
> Do you enjoy new adventures or fear them? Why?

My pastor said he had the perfect high school roommate for me from his old church in Chicago. I said, "Sure." I didn't know her any better than anyone else, so it didn't matter to me one way or the other who I roomed with. At least she had one solid recommendation. I was leaving behind only a few close friends. Many of the guys (i.e., cousins and friends) I hung out with were either away at college or had been drafted into the army and were on their way to either Viet Nam or to Europe. They would be gone for at least two years. My best friend was closing in on marriage of all things. She had been "otherwise engaged" for months now. I had drifted away from the other church girls my age over the past two years, partly due to the fact that we weren't in any of the same classes at school, and partly due to the fact that we didn't seem to have many common interests outside of school. I had no serious concerns in leaving home. It was time to move on. I was more than ready for my next adventure and looked forward to a change like this. I felt sure that God had something special in store for me as I entered this new chapter in my life.

I had grown fiercely independent during my life, perhaps to a fault, but this is probably what helped me to survive and even to overcome many of the challenges in my life. Having no father and no grandparents, and having experienced serious concern over the possibility of losing my mother during a number of episodes she had had in the hospital over my teenage years, it became absolutely imperative for me to learn to trust in the Lord with all my "heart, soul, and mind." He would never leave me. I almost expected the other people in my life to let me down in some way – not a good thing. I think this made it more difficult for me to get really close to people or to make friends quickly. I hated wasting time so I never put a lot of effort into seeking out kindred spirits because I didn't think I'd find any.

In spite of all of this and thanks to God's intervention, I discovered some amazing people who became exceptionally good friends during my two years away at boarding school. I opened the door slowly and was pleasantly surprised with the result. I began to make some of the best friends I would ever find in my lifetime. I consider several of them to be my closest friends even to this day. These friendships grew even sweeter after we graduated and found ourselves living hundreds of miles apart. It makes you kind of wonder, doesn't it? C.S. Lewis said "Friendship is born at the moment when one person says to another, 'What! You thought that too? I thought I was the only one.'" You will never get to that place unless you open up to the possibility.

Do you have many true friends? a best friend?

What are their best qualities?

Which of the fruits of the Spirit do you value most in a friend? *love, joy, peace? patience, kindness, goodness? faithfulness, gentleness, self-control? (Galatians 5:22-23)* Why?

Can you think of an example of each fruit in action? Discuss. What kind of a friend are you? Explain.

I'm not sure that I made a very good friend. First of all, it's that independence thing from when my father died and I tried not to need people too much. True friends like to be needed, need to be needed. It makes all of us feel as if we're contributing something to a relationship. I also had a problem committing to things that didn't interest me. I got bored way too easily at most organized events that many of my friends seemed to enjoy. (Maybe it was undiagnosed ADHD?) Often I would find myself wishing I could just curl up with a good book under or in a tree, or go out for a ride on my motorcycle through the autumn leaves, or well, anything except sitting in an auditorium listening to the topics that were being shared. I admit that there have been diverting exceptions. And all of the topics were excellent topics – I had just either heard them too often or had zero interest in them. I'm not proud of this. I was tough to please. You have probably guessed by now that, as a friend, I could be a challenge. But seriously, don't you ever feel that way?

For the most part I haven't always fit in very well. I guess I always felt a little different. I know there were many excellent events out there, but I always felt that I needed to focus the little time I had in areas of my greatest need or interest – which were not necessarily widely shared. Friendship, however, was something I cherished and knew I *needed* to put more time into. How could I be a better friend? I found it easiest when a friend was in need. I liked to help if I could. See that? I too liked to be needed. It was hardest when I was asked to join in something that I had no interest in. It was difficult to feign enjoyment in an activity that "bored the socks off me." (Did I just say that out loud?) Maybe if I focused more on my friendship and less on the activity? That might help. I don't want to be that me-centered person we are encouraged to be on a daily basis on television, in ads and on the radio (e.g., "…and you're worth it!"). I knew that that was not God's plan for me. I may still be somewhat hopeless, but I will keep trying.

In spite of me, I have a handful of faithful friends who have been my friends almost from the moment we met. (They are worthy of sainthood.) Somehow we connected quickly on a deep level. We either had strong common interests or strong similar personalities. One in particular really surprised me because I never would have guessed that we had much of anything in common in my first impression. She just seemed way too classy. Just goes to show... In each of these friendships we have strong common spiritual beliefs. We don't necessarily see each other often right now because our lives have become so busy with family and commitments. And most of us live several states away from each other. But when we do get together, it's as if we had just seen each other the day before. We pick up right where we left off. I think heaven will be like that when we see our friends and family there. It will be as if we had seen them yesterday.

Overall, I would have to say that my very dearest friend in life was probably my mother. Yes, you can be mother and daughter and also friends at the same time. She was my confidant and the "go-to" person when I had relationship questions. (Her brother, my uncle, was my "go-to" person for theological questions.) Mom always gave me wisdom and told me when I was being stupid or stubborn. Hmmm. And I still enjoyed hanging out with her.

Friendship at times comes in unusual places where you might never expect one. People from different backgrounds can become the best of friends. I have been surprised more than once finding gems where I least expected them. I have also had friends who do not share my Christian beliefs; but I find it difficult to get as close to someone who doesn't "get me" on the spiritual level. That's the level that really matters for all of eternity. To think that they will not be in heaven is almost unbearable. I have made attempts to share the awesome gift of salvation with them, but it is now between them and the Holy Spirit. You can only push so much. Hopefully seeds were planted that will prosper.

Bible Reading: *Ruth 1:15-18, 2:11-12, Matthew 1:5b*

What had just happened in Ruth and Naomi's lives?

Ruth obviously loved her mother-in-law. They were very good friends.

How does she show this in chapter one?

How does Ruth take care of her mother-in-law in chapter two?

Did God reward her for this? How?

Challenge: Call or text a good friend and find out how you can be there for her/him.

> *"Two are better than one, because they have a good return for their work. If one falls down, his friend can help him up. But pity the man who falls and has no one to help him up!"*
>
> *Ecclesiastes 4:9-10*

WEEK 29

"The drop-off"

My mother and my oldest sister decided to make a vacation of it when they drove me out to boarding school. My two sisters, my mom and I took a road trip. We spent nearly two weeks traveling out to the Midwest via Niagara Falls into Canada and down through Michigan, over to Iowa and South Dakota, down through Nebraska to Colorado, and up around through Utah, Idaho and Wyoming to Montana and North Dakota, finally reaching Fergus Falls, Minnesota, where they dropped me off as we circled back toward the East.

Niagara Falls was incredible – so much power! I remember a strange sensation as I almost felt the falls pulling me down into them. A group of Italian sailors visiting there asked to have their pictures taken with my sister and me. That was interesting. In South Dakota we got to see Mt. Rushmore – very cool. All I could think of was that old movie, *North By Northwest*, where Cary Grant climbs all over the top of the presidents' faces and noses. We rode horses through the "Garden of the Gods" in Colorado. Since I was pretty fearless and had ridden before, I was chosen to ride the spirited horse. Up where the trail narrowed on the side of a good sized hill, he decided to rear up a bit on his hind legs and pursue a separate path. (The whole "separate path" thing somehow struck a familiar chord in me, so I wasn't overly critical of him.) There was no backing up once he started along his chosen path, so the guide told me not to worry because he'd wait for us where the two trails came back together. They did converge a short time later and we made it safely down to where my mother had chosen to wait rather than risk danger. She never knew until we returned that

153

the keg she was sitting on was filled with live rattlesnakes! How ironic was that?

We swam in the Great Salt Lake in Utah. The beach we went to had lots of stones but it was easy to float in the salty water. In Wyoming we stayed in a motel in which our room had an extra door going into an adjoining room. The other room was rented out to two men, at least one of whom had a gun. I saw it when his jacket partially opened as he entered his room. As an added precaution to a locked door, we put two dressers and a chair between the questionable door and the opposite wall to prevent anyone from entering our room through that door. It was only in the morning that we noticed that the door opened in toward the other room; the dressers and chair had done little good, except that they allowed us to sleep ... and would have made breaking in quietly unlikely.

Entering Montana, we came through Yellowstone Park. We had been hoping to see a grizzly bear all along the way, but saw none. Toward the end of the day we started seeing more bears than we cared to see and were becoming more and more concerned. We should have been through the park and to our exit when we realized that our map (no GPS's back then) was missing a road. We had turned "right" on the "wrong" road, a new one that wasn't even on our map. We had to backtrack and try again, exiting the park much later in the day than planned. When we got to the gate, it was already getting dark. We were thrilled to see our first human being in over two hours. We asked the ranger where we could get a room for the night. He said to follow the Beartooth Highway along the top of the mountain and we'd see the lights of Red Lodge, a quaint mountain town, as we came down through the pass about an hour or so ahead. There were a couple of hotels there and this late in the season there should be rooms available.

The lights of the village far below us looked so inviting ... when suddenly they disappeared! The town seemed to have vanished into thin air! As we continued down the mountain and finally entered the town, it was being lit by candles and lanterns. There had been a power outage and it was going to take some time to restore it. In spite of this, we managed to find a cozy rustic hotel and were brought by candlelight up to our room in the new section of the inn where construction was still going on. Thick plastic was hanging in front of one hallway to keep the dust to a minimum. Some of the students who had worked in the park for the summer were having a "Christmas in August" farewell celebration in the lounge and invited my sister and me to join them. We had a great time going on a hayride, sitting by the huge fireplace, and enjoying the festivities of the night.

On the eastern side of Montana, we got to see our mother's birthplace. She was born in Wolf Point where there were many Blackfoot Indians. My grandparents had run a grocery store there and again later in North Dakota. We found her first home with little trouble even though the main street in Wolf Point had moved a few blocks away from where it had once been. Her house was now on a quiet back street, making its false front, typical in these older western towns, seem seriously out of place. (A smaller house with a slanted roof was made to appear much bigger by simply adding a square false front to it that made it look more like a city building of at least two or three full floors.)

Since my grandparents had been so busy – Ma running the store and Pa travelling with a preacher friend – my mother and her brothers and sisters, had a nanny named Shutah, a Blackfoot Indian. She would chew the children's meat for them to soften it up, until my grandmother suggested she use a knife to cut the meat into smaller pieces. A family of Blackfoot Indians was now living in my mother's old home as we drove up to it. I knocked on the door and asked if we could take a picture. No problem. A bunch of adorable little faces smiled out through the overly large storefront window. My mother then quickly looked up an old friend and we got on our way.

In Grand Forks, North Dakota, we looked for the home my mother had moved to during her teen years. Her house was on the same street as the school that I was about to attend – before the school had moved to Minnesota. This was where my mother

155

had attended the boarding school, though she was able to live at her home just across the street. Stories of this school and home flooded my mind as we drove down the street – like the time my mother's older sister came into the store and literally ripped a skirt that belonged to her off of my mother's body. My mother, a teen-ager then, had to hurdle the store's counter to get into her house through the door behind the counter in order to avoid being seen by a group of her classmates coming in through the front door of the store. It was kind of fun to imagine my mother doing that. Even back then, sisters struggled to get along.

Finally, we drove on to my destination and I was dropped off a couple of days early at the boarding school because my sister had to get back for some reason – probably a date. I was about to begin two of the most exciting and memorable years of my life. I knew that this was going to be a major turning point in my life. I was very excited.

Have you ever gone on a long adventurous trip like this? Share. Have you ever thought you were not safe when you actually were? Explain.

Have you ever been dropped off to begin a new adventure all on your own? Explain.

When I arrived at school there were three footlockers with my name on them stacked right there in the front hall. We had sent all of my bedding, towels, winter clothes, etc. on ahead so we wouldn't be crowded in the car, and three small footlockers were not a lot considering everything packed inside them; but the football team, who had arrived early for practice, would never let me forget the "gigantic" pile of trunks stacked high in the hall all bearing my name in big letters. I had started with a bang. For better or for worse, half of the guys in the school already knew my name. Oh well... I was able to get unpacked and thoroughly moved in before my roommate came and the rest of the students began to arrive over the next two days. I also got a head start on my new job – working in the kitchen. Yeah!

Have you ever been the new kid in school or elsewhere? Did it take long to feel at home? Explain.
What does the Bible say about feeling at home?

> Dear friends, I urge you, *as aliens and strangers in the world*, to abstain from sinful desires which war against your soul. *I Peter 2:11*
> By faith Abraham, when called to go to a place he would later receive as his inheritance, obeyed and went, even though he did not know where he was going. By faith he made his home in the promised land *like a stranger in a foreign country; he lived in tents,* ... For *he was looking forward to the city with foundations, whose architect and builder is God*. *Hebrews 11:8-10*

There is so much beauty in this world around us, so many glimpses of God's creativity; but more and more I feel as if I am an alien and a stranger in this world. I know, I know, I *am* pretty strange. But, seriously, don't you feel misplaced at times? (as I did in my multivariable calculus class in college?) I think it's because we anticipate, we long for, that better world, that "inheritance" that God has prepared for us after we fulfill His plan for us here. Solomon says that God "has set eternity in the hearts of men." (*Ecclesiastes 3:11*) Still, some Christians actually fear the thought of heaven. Why, I wonder? Abraham is a good example for us. He never owned a home, never really put down roots, and he looked to the Lord for everything. He obeyed God as many of us wish we did and he kept his eyes focused on his heavenly home to come. Not that he wasn't here in an earthly sense; he just knew better than to put his trust in the things of this earth – like jobs, houses and land, family, position, money, etc.. His trust was in the Lord. Don't buy into the lie that you need anything besides the Lord. Obedience to Him brings blessings, but *He is all we need!*

Bible Reading: *Genesis 11:31-12:5, Hebrews 11:8-10*

What was the difference between Terah's and Abraham's responses to God's call?

Have you ever been uprooted and moved far away from home? Was that very difficult? Explain.

Why do you think Abraham never had a permanent dwelling in this new land?

Abraham had a good life, so why was he looking forward to heaven?

Challenge: Are you looking forward to heaven?
Make that more of a positive focus.

"...they were longing for a better country – a heavenly one. Therefore God is not ashamed to be called their God, for He has prepared a city for them."
Hebrews 11:16

"Workin' in a coal mine"

O kay, I wasn't actually working in a coal mine, but we did have a coal shoot which had been adapted into a potato shoot, since coal was no longer the heating source of choice at the boarding school I attended. The kitchen was in the basement of the main building and the dining room was along one end with high windows on three walls. My responsibilities in the kitchen varied as I rotated through the different jobs available. One week I would be on the serving line, another assigned to pot washing. I would also switch onto the dishwashing team or the dining room clean-up crew. We took turns taking care of weekly duties like peeling potatoes which needed to be done to prepare for supper in the evening.

The serving line was pretty easy and kind of fun. The cooks were here most of the time – portion control I think. Pot washing was a bear of a job because the pots needed a lot of elbow grease and yielded a lot of grease too, which made this ... a greasy job. There was a professional dishwashing machine which needed to be filled and run and emptied all through the meal as students finished eating. This job was better than "pots and pans," but still pretty hot and messy from all of the steam. Lastly, the dining room clean-up was not too bad of a job if you could handle the kidding. There was one girl who worked in the kitchen who would beg me to trade jobs with her whenever she saw any of the athletes (notorious teasers) lingering long after everyone else had left. They could get pretty carried away if they thought they were getting the reaction they hoped for. I rarely gave them that satisfaction, and I was pretty good at throwing the joke right back at them so they didn't bother me all that much. Maybe my comfort level had to do with the many hours spent hanging out with all of my male cousins back home?

Peeling potatoes was a nuisance because it happened at the best time of day to be doing something fun, right after school. The first step was collecting the potatoes (the worst part of the job) from the dark and damp "potato room." This room was bad – it had no windows and was poorly lit, unheated, and eerily dank. It probably could have been used in a scene from a horror movie. Periodically, a farmer would come with his truck and drop many pounds of potatoes down the old coal shoot into this room below the street level. Obviously there would soon be some squishy rotten ones in there. I can still remember the feeling when I reached into the dimly lit pile of potatoes and accidentally picked up a yucky, soft one. At certain times of the year that room was ripe with the smell of rotting spuds. And sometimes the room had to be cleaned out. Horrors! This was one reason to avoid getting "squelches." (See week 32.) After collecting several buckets of potatoes, we would drop them one bucket at a time into a peeling machine that took off all of the skin but not the deeper eyes. They would be removed manually later. Or not. This machine had sharp pieces of metal on its insides and the potatoes would bounce against these in a flow of water as the machine revolved. Timing was a critical element or the potatoes would become golf-ball-sized quickly. "Oh, for fun!" (Midwesterners put an "Oh, for" in front of all kinds of adjectives to describe things: "Oh, for cute. Oh, for sweet. Oh, for whatever…" It was good material for mocking them … all "for fun" of course.)

Though we did get teased a lot working in the kitchen, I don't remember taking any abuse over needing to work to pay for school. Many students were from farms and though fairly well off, they appreciated hard work. Others didn't have to worry about the cost of anything much, but were never snobs. The kitchen workers had to leave classes a little early, eat lunch really fast, and get into our places before the rush. I hated going to class after breakfast and lunch without having had the luxury the other kids had of cleaning up and getting a fresh start for the next three to four hours of school. We often came slightly late to class with a little bit of the meal still stuck to one of our elbows or to our clothing in a spot that had evaded notice. I learned to joke about it – that I had smuggled a snack into class for later when I got hungry. The evening meal was better because we had no classes before or after supper. On the other hand, I always had to be back for supper even if all of my friends were staying downtown (about a mile's walk) to eat or to shop.

How old were you when you had your first real job?
Was it as glamorous as this one? What was it?
Were you ever embarrassed by it? Explain.
How long did it last?

You can get used to just about anything and I quickly got used to working in the kitchen. It became a regular part of my daily schedule. And this was definitely better than my babysitting job a couple of summers before. We worked every meal every day unless we were in bed sick or away. We could hire someone on our own to take our place if we chose to do so, but that rarely happened. There was a seminary or Bible college student who worked in the kitchen each semester to help pay for his schooling who was our "boarding boss." There were a couple who were exceptionally patient and really good with teenagers. They had us working hard, but managed to have fun with us as they also worked hard. We gave an awful lot of grief to one who had a lot to learn about working with high school students, though the kitchen workers were not nearly as hard on him as the other kids coming through the lines. Some of the boys were merciless. I remember ketchup and mustard on the ceiling at one meal. He was nice enough, but young. They knew how to push his buttons and get him red-in-the-face mad. As long as they could get that reaction, they kept playing the game.

At the end of my senior year I organized a strike. Yes, you heard me right, a strike. (Lord, forgive me if this was bad.) We made posters on sticks and carried them around in front of the school asking for some time off during the year. This would not help me since I was soon to graduate, but it would help the next year's crew. I don't know if I would have dared to do this earlier; I would have been unwilling to risk the improbable but possibly warranted outcome of losing my job which was essential to me staying at the school. Looking back now, we should have tried asking for a meeting as a first step, but we went straight to the picket line. Impulsive. On the other hand, we were a very polite strike force. We were simply trying to make heard a concern that would most likely go unnoticed otherwise. We brought a lot of humor into our signs and into what we were saying, while trying to get the message across that three meals a day, seven days a week, week after week, without a break, was a lot to ask of teenagers. We were quickly invited in to talk. (I imagine a picture of us picketing in the news would have brought unwelcome publicity, though that never occurred to us at the time.) During our hearing, I think we even had a couple of the members of the school's "supreme council" smiling behind their serious demeanors. They listened and treated our request with respect. The next year would change. Hooray! Organized labor here we come!

Who were/are your most memorable bosses? Describe.
What makes a boss good? Discuss.
Are you a good employee?
What does God's Word have to say about relationships in the work force?
Whatever you do, work at it with all your heart, as working for the Lord, not for men. Colossians 3:23
Submit yourselves for the Lord's sake to every authority instituted among men; whether to the king, as the supreme authority, or to governors, who are sent by him to punish those who do wrong and to commend those who do right. For it is God's will that by doing good you should silence the ignorant talk of foolish men. Live as free men, but do not use your freedom as a cover-up for evil; live as servants of God. Show proper respect to everyone: Love the brotherhood of believers, fear God, honor the king. Slaves, submit yourselves to your masters with all respect, not only to those who

are good and considerate, but also to those who are harsh. For it is commendable if a man bears up under the pain of unjust suffering because he is conscious of God. I Peter 2:13-19
"If a man will not work, he shall not eat." 2 Thessalonians 3:10

God's Word is pretty clear about submitting to authority, even if it's unjust. Of course, we are not slaves, and we usually have a choice regarding where we choose to work. The problem with that is that there are those who jump around from job to job regularly because they feel that they are being treated unfairly everywhere they go, or that there is always a better job out there. Some of these people may have a problem with authority and submitting to the directions of those above them. For others, working hard is something they have never experienced and it seems harsh to them. A friend of mine owns his own company and says that it's amazing how many young college graduates think that they should be able to start right at the top, because after all, they have a college degree! Reality check. There are a lot of young graduates and very few management jobs out there – most being given to those who have put in the time to earn them.

Do you have a tough time submitting to authority? Deal with it. Just do your job to the best of your ability. Do you have a tough time waiting patiently for a reward you need to earn? Patience really is a virtue. It used to be that people would stay at the same job all of their lives. Not so any longer. There's always greener grass just beyond the hill. But oftentimes the same problems show up at the next job. Be careful not to burn bridges as you leave a job. The best thing is to leave a good name for yourself wherever you go, and "silence the ignorant talk of foolish men." Remember that you represent Christ. Also, you may need a friend down the road who can give you a good reference. Check out *Proverbs 12:11, 20:13,* and *Ecclesiastes 9:10* for advice on hard work.

Bible Reading: *2 Thessalonians 3:6-15*
What does Paul say about the idle person?
What "rule" did he give to the Thessalonians?

What is it that we should never tire of?

Someone once said "Find a job you love, and you will never have to work again." What does this mean? Is it true?

Can you have a change of heart toward a job? How?

Challenge: Take an honest look at the reasons you might not like your job (or chore). Think of a way you can improve your attitude.

"A man can do nothing better than to eat and drink and find satisfaction in his work. This, too, I see, is from the hand of God"

Ecclesiastes 2:24

WEEK 31

"Dormed"

Junior Year

During my first year at the boarding school I had a room on the fourth floor, at the top of the building. I was actually kind of fortunate to have agreed to room with my pastor's friend's daughter. Not only did she turn out to be an extraordinary roommate and friend, but because she had been there her sophomore year, she had had the opportunity to choose her room the year before. Our room was the second one from the top right corner when looking at the building from the front lawn of the school. It was a nice size and had some cool, funky angles going on with the roof. I liked it. We were just around the corner from the bathroom and had little interference from the girls' deans who hesitated to climb from their second floor office all the way up to fourth floor to remind us of the dorm rules, unless it was absolutely necessary. My roommate and I did what I would like to think an exceptional job in decorating our room, and we kept it very neat and clean. I admit I'm a little OCD or "Monk"-ish (You know – the guy on TV.). I would make sure all of our towels were lined up evenly on the back of our door before I could go to sleep at night. Fortunately, that was one of the only outward indications of my obsessive behavior. I think.

We had an interesting wall (only on fourth floor) separating the girls' and the boys' dorms that could be moved back and forth in the hall to accommodate more girls or boys as each year might require. This door was the prime spot for sending notes between the two dorms at night. As a result, girls would line up on our side night after night to pass or receive notes. There was a mirror on this wall that at one point developed a patch of lost reflection. After being teased by the boys about our pajamas and bath towels, we finally realized that the patch was actually a window that the boys had scratched on the back of the mirror through a hole in their side of the wall to see into the girls' dorm. I put a band aid over the hole only to later discover the hole outgrowing the band aid. The deans eventually had to be made aware of the problem. We were not willing to sacrifice our privacy to keep the secret. The problem was remedied. The scratch "healed." Of course at one point the entire wall fell down! The expressions on all of the faces was a missed photo opportunity. Can you picture it?

I was frequently engaged in shenanigans like dumping pails of water down the stairs at marauders from the third floor. There was a trap door in the very high ceiling near the top of those stairs that was intriguing, and easily opened ... if standing on a dresser. It was rumored to lead to the attic where, if one didn't mind squeezing through a couple of access holes in fire walls over the droppings of generations of mice, one might reach a stairway that led to a flat portion in the center of the roof totally hidden by the many gables along the edges. Perfect for sunbathing ... so they said. We only let a few girls in on this theory and we managed to keep it a secret until the next year when a heavy padlock showed up on the trap door. Meanwhile, in the attic, they suggested that one could also gain access to the school's main tower that could be seen miles away from several vantage points. Rumor has it that in that tower, in a spot where the sun shines in through a small crack, one might even find my name, right next to my older brother's. I wonder how that got there?

From time to time during my junior year I would visit other rooms when we were supposed to be in our own rooms studying, rarely, if ever, getting caught. However, I do remember hiding under a friend's bed down on third floor one night while the head dean sat on the bed joking around with the two senior girls in the room. I had jumped under the exceptionally low bed to avoid detection, and was later convinced that the dean knew I was under the bed the entire time, staying there a long time to make me as uncomfortable as possible. It worked. This dean was not only smart, but also a lot of fun. She was really the perfect dean for me. I think she got me. The girl I had stopped by to visit kept quietly laughing inside as she sat there listening to the dean, with only the continual, yet nearly imperceptible bouncing of her body to give away her nervous fear of being caught.

Do you have any obsessive/compulsive habits? Explain.
What does the Bible say about the most extreme of these
    behaviors?
      ...The man who fears God will <u>avoid all extremes</u>. Ecclesiastes 7:18b
Did they have fun in the Bible?

In *John 2:1-2* we see that Jesus attended a wedding celebration.
    (I bet He was fun to be with.)
In *2 Samuel 6:14-15* we see David "dancing for all his might"
    in joy over the ark.
In *Romans 14:16-18* it says "Do not allow what you consider
    good to be spoken of as evil." (Some people are quick to
    judge. Pray, and weigh their input.)
In *Romans 13:13* it says to "behave decently." (This rules out
    the unhealthy fun.)

Senior Year

The start of my second year was a surprise to many since at the end of my junior year I had been asked by the head dean to be a senior (peer) counselor. Go figure. This put me in a prime room on third floor right at the top of the stairs between the two fire doors. It was a big square room with two large windows overlooking the front of the school. Great location – except that the deans' office was directly below. In this room I turned over a new leaf, to a certain degree, and started to consider the fact that I was now a role model. The head dean had pulled a fast one on me. Like I said before – smart lady.

The worst I did this year was to sabotage the dorm intercom through which the deans were reportedly able to listen in on our conversations. At first I tried to put a straight pin through the two wires to short it out. I got caught when my new roommate tested it while I distracted the dean. "Hey, Swensen!" she yelled into the mic. She chose to use my last name (really?) when she tested the microphone (still working) which was a dead giveaway that we were surely up to something. Since the dean had no clue why my roommate was talking into the mic, the consequences were minor. Since plan "A" did not work, I resorted to a temporary fix. Every once in a while I would put a little transistor radio, tuned to no station at all and playing only static, behind the speaker/monitor on the third floor. This resulted in a loud buzzing noise whenever the intercom was accessed for that area. The next morning I would take it down. I'm sorry to say that the dean and the janitor could never figure out what was wrong with the system, and after several attempts to address the problem *during the day,* they finally gave up.

Confession: I would skip church occasionally – not because I didn't like church or because I had something better to do, but just for the challenge. On a dare I went to church one winter night with just a slip and underwear on under my coat. (Whoa, what a rebel!) Again, I had those lines I wouldn't cross. I wouldn't sneak outside the building at night because that would get me into BIG trouble. I knew the guy/girl rules for dating were a ticket home if broken, but I never considered breaking those anyway. Life was interesting. There was always somebody ready for fun when I was, and I think I brought a little excitement into some otherwise woefully quiet lives. A job well done.

Do you have lines that you won't cross? Are they in good places? Explain.

Are you rebellious, mischievous, or totally content to follow the rules?

Are you happy with that? Why or why not?

Jesus had boundaries. He set aside time to be with His Father (*Luke 5:16*). He didn't give in to family pressure (*Matthew 12:46-50*). He was able to put His disciples in their place (*Matthew 16:23*). He didn't bow to pressure from the king (*Luke 23:8-9*). We need to set aside time to be in God's Word so that we understand His will for us, and to weigh the pressures of family, friends and society before we let them push us into something we believe we should not do.

I know that we are supposed to follow the rules and I admire people who seem to do it perfectly, but I can't help but think that God enjoys the goofballs in life too, because He made us. He made us with an overactive sense of humor and the need to make people laugh. Good clean humor doesn't seem to be a bad thing. It can even cheer people up at times. I don't think it's condemned anywhere in the Bible... I'd like to think that, like one of my uncles, who was a church elder and our resident "Moses" while I was growing up, God would smile just a little when I said something funny or got caught in a faux pas. And that, like my uncle, his foot would tap ever so slightly during my latest song even if it were a bit more contemporary than the church was ready for. And yet ... we really do need to know where to draw our lines. Going too far past them could be harmful, or fatal. Fortunately my limits included mischief, but nothing beyond that. How about yours? *Romans,* chapter 14, shows us that not all of our lines will be in exactly the same places on the non-salvation issues, but that's okay. If you have a vice, no matter how great or small, you need to stay away from its particular temptations with some strong boundary lines. Others may not have the slightest problem in those areas. Their lines are different from yours.

Remember that "joy" is much more lasting than "fun" or even "happiness." In *Nehemiah 8:10b* it talks of the joy of the Lord being our strength. *Psalm 16:11* tells of the joy in knowing God's will. *Isaiah 35:10* points to the everlasting joy of Heaven. And *I Peter 1:8-9* proclaims the joy of salvation. True joy is tied to obedience, following God's commands (*Luke 11:28*). Fun, laughter, and even happiness are little pieces of true joy, but only joy can continually endure in spite of whatever else is going on in our lives at the moment. True joy is a gift from God.

Bible Reading: *Exodus 28:31-38, Numbers 20:8-12,*
                       Exodus 20:1-17

> The Old Testament is full of rules and regulations, especially about the temple.
>
> What was the penalty in *Exodus 28* if the high priest did not follow the rules for bells?
>
> Do you think he followed the rules?
>
> Did Moses follow God's command in *Numbers 20*?
>
> What was the result?
>
> Are rules good or bad? Do they steal our fun? happiness? joy? Explain.
>
> Is it good to have penalties for breaking rules? Why/why not?

Challenge: Join me in trying harder to follow God's rules – which leads to joy!

> *"Do not merely listen to the word, and so deceive yourselves. Do what it says!"*
>> *James 1:22*

WEEK 32

"It is reputed..."

Reputations are easily trashed, but not as easily redeemed. Do one dumb thing and you are labeled for life. Try to make up for that and you would probably have to do at least ten smart things. Maybe many more. And reputations start early in life. I bet you could give me a quick overview of all of the children that are a part of your life. Know any kids who are precocious, talented, spoiled, hyper-active, or really sweet? Any whiners, clowns, or athletes? Reputations begin in childhood and can often last for life!

What kind of reputation do you have?
Who do you think of when I say funny? smart? foolish? stubborn? loving?
What adjectives do you think of when I say Eve? Noah? Samson? Rahab? Judas?

In Minnesota I was a prankster and had a hand in most of the fun taking place around me. We had water running down two flights of stairs when we got going in the girls' dorm water fights. Of course that just meant we had to clean it up afterwards. But the stairs needed a good washing from time to time anyway, right? (Then again I hate to think of the possible damage done to the underlying structure of the stairways...) When you messed up in the dorms you might either get an immediate punishment like being "dormed" (restricted to the dorm), or you might get "squelches" (units of punishment that you had to work off). Each squelch was one hour of work, usually in the dorm – or worst case scenario: the potato room. Some pranks resulted in multiple squelches. I had

171

spent several hours cleaning public areas in that dorm by the end of my first year there.

As a junior I auditioned for and acquired a spot in the a cappella traveling choir. (There was also a larger fall choir that didn't travel and that you didn't have to try out for.) This was a coup since everyone wanted to take two or three weeks off in the spring (missing some school even) to travel to the Pacific Northwest (i.e., Minnesota to Washington to Oregon and back with a bit of Canada thrown in as a bonus). While on tour, I wound up staying in a home somewhere in Montana with my roommate and two guys, guys who just happened to be dating us. Someone was not paying attention when the host homes were assigned because they would never have put people dating at the same house if they had noticed it. The people we stayed with were older and very nice. They gave us money to go bowling downtown, a walk of several blocks.

While bowling, we decided that we were thirsty and needed soft drinks. The problem was that the only place to get a couple of Cokes was in the bar in the back of the bowling alley. No big deal. I would get the drinks. While standing at the bar waiting for our soft drinks, who should enter the bowling alley but our principal, one of our chaperones. He didn't know me very well, refused to listen, assumed the worst, and sent us all back to our host home with angry words. We headed out into a surprise snow storm (in April!) and had difficulty finding the house from which we had started. The houses looked a lot alike and we hadn't really paid attention. When we finally found the house, the principal had already called to be sure we had gotten back, and by now was livid. The next day I was given the privilege of sitting next to him on the bus for the rest of the trip. Really? None of the others had to sit with him. He also informed me that I may as well forget being in the choir the next year, and that if it didn't cost so much I would have been on my way home right then. And I didn't even like alcohol. Talk about being labeled. It didn't get much worse than that. And the worst part was that I was innocent! (That's what they all say, right?)

"It is reputed..."

What is your reputation at school? in church? with your friends? Which one is most accurate? Or are they all the same? What does God say about reputations?

A good name is more desirable than great riches; to be esteemed is better than silver or gold. Proverbs 22:1
A good name is better than fine perfume, ... Ecclesiastes 7:1a

You can probably imagine what the principal thought of me, but in the dorms I think I was known for fun and mischief, and with my teachers for being a good student but somewhat of an inconsistency. The head dean evidently had faith in me because she chose me to be a peer counselor who would be assigned several girls to mentor in a counseling group each week. At the beginning of my senior year when the principal saw my face amidst those of the counseling team, he pulled the dean aside and had a few words with her. Evidently she was quite persuasive, because I was not asked to leave.

As a matter of fact, I moved on to become an integral part of one of the school's small singing groups used for P.R.. Choir was then a shoo-in. My trio jelled so well that we actually wound up traveling and singing together for over four years on and off, ... but that's another story. What was interesting was to see the gradual change in the principal's attitude toward me as I began to become a public relations' asset for the school. Before the end of the year I was *possibly* even one of his favorites ... yeah, maybe not. Not that that was a big deal to me, but it did come with some nice perks. The funny part was that I had not intrinsically changed at all. This had always been who I was. He had never really gotten to know me before. My dean had.

I hadn't thought much about reputations before this. Reputations can be hard to live *with* or hard to live *up to*. They could affect my life for good or for bad. I began to realize how valuable a good reputation could be. I also began to understand that my reputation affected more than just me. It affected my family, my Christian school, my church, and my God. Wow! The dumb things I did could make someone choose not to go to my school – or worse – not to reach out to God. This was a real responsibility! I certainly did not want this responsibility, but here it was in spite of that. I was being forced to grow up, and I wasn't sure that I liked that.

A young girl I knew had gotten pregnant with her boyfriend. She was the pastor's daughter, so the whole church was drawn into the drama. She knew that what she had done was wrong but probably thought, as many do, "It's my life and I will live it as I choose!" She began to see the effect of her action on herself and on others and repented in front of the whole church at a communion service. That took courage. Her boyfriend insisted on standing up with her. She said the very thing I just said – that she never realized how what she had done would affect her parents, her family and even her church. The forgiveness given to her was immediate and healing. As a matter of fact it was that forgiveness that later brought her boyfriend to the Lord. He told me that he was so blown away by the church's forgiveness and love that that was the moment he began to understand God's love and to reach out for it. He became a true man of God.

My first roommate was voted "the sweetest girl in the school." My second was one of the biggest rascals (but that was unofficial). One guy, whose company I enjoyed, was known as a "schmoozer," and another as a "big teddy bear." They both made me laugh. Every school has its assortment of brainiacs, gossips, and flirts. Some girls are known as "easy" and some boys as "trouble." There are "brown-nosers" and "bookworms," along with all the other commonly found types on any campus. Each has a reputation either to be proud of (in most cases), or to live down. Mine wasn't sterling, but it wasn't something I had to live down either. I guess it was deserved. When I asked a friend why someone had written a "#1" on my legs in a picture in my yearbook I was told that the boys' dorm had voted my legs #1 in the school. I wasn't sure how to react to that honor. I discovered later that other attributes had also been voted on. Hmm. And here I was with zero expectation of ever coming in first for anything! Astonishingly, that was my only win. Of course I could only guess what they thought of me as a person. I was pretty sure I wasn't a top date choice. I was probably a bit intimidating as I was 5'10", rarely hesitated to say what was on my mind, and was clearly uninterested in dating most (not all) of the guys at the school anyway.

Does it *really* matter what others think of you? Why/why not?
Does it even *really* matter what *you* think of you? Why/why not?
What does God think of you?

> For God so loved the world that <u>He gave His one and only son</u>, that whoever believes in Him shall not perish but have eternal life. John 3:16
> I no longer call you servants, because a servant does not know his master's business. Instead, <u>I have called you friends</u>, for everything that I learned from my Father I have made known to you. John 15:15
> For you did not receive a spirit that makes you a slave again to fear, but you received the Spirit of sonship. And by him we cry, "Abba, father." The Spirit himself testifies with our spirit that <u>we are God's children</u>. Now, if we are children, then we are heirs – <u>heirs of God and co-heirs with Christ</u> … Romans 8:15-17

Do you deserve your reputation?
Do you deserve God's esteem for you? Explain.
What would His "class superlative" (nickname?) be for you?

We can see that the Bible considers a good reputation valuable. But reputations can be false if based upon gossip and/or misinformation. I try to have a rule to set reputation aside and find out for myself who a person is. Oftentimes, I discover amazing people with false reputations based upon one person's mistaken conceptions. Then the gossip train takes the rumor away to grow even worse down the line. But there is something more important than reputation as we can see here:

Bible Reading: *Revelation 3:1-6*
What is the difference between reputation and character?
Which one is more accurate in describing you? Why?
What was the reputation of the church in Sardis?
What was actually true of this church?

What three things are the remedies for this problem in verse three?

What does verse six mean?

Challenge: Examine yourself. Is your character better or worse than your reputation?

"Even a child is known by his actions, by whether his conduct is pure and right."

Proverbs 20:11

WEEK 33

"The master key"

During my junior year I dated a super guy for a few months. Everybody liked him. He was smart and cute, thoughtful and talented, and an awesome Christian. He was also in possession of a master key to the building. When I discovered this, I was shocked, and that didn't happen often. He didn't seem the type. Well, he gave me a copy of the key and I did find it handy on a couple of occasions. For one thing I found it handy during the mission conference. We had over twenty mandatory mission services/ classes in one week! I managed to skip ten or eleven of them -– a record, I think. I used the key to open the trunk room on fourth floor. I (and a friend or two) would go into the trunk room with a pack of Rook cards and some junk food, and hang out until everyone had left, at which time we would go into our rooms to sleep. It was all pretty harmless. I remember one time when we watched the dean through the old skeleton keyhole double-checking our rooms, looking under our beds and in our closets. She knew we hadn't come down the stairs, but she couldn't figure out how we had disappeared. I guess she never thought to ask. I would have confessed the whole sordid thing.

I used the key a few more times to skip church, but it really wasn't much good for anything else because I had those lines I wouldn't cross. Near the end of my senior year my first roommate asked me to help her skip church one Sunday night. She said she had decided to skip with me because she wanted to do it just once before she graduated and she didn't want to get caught. I was flattered, ... though I was about to corrupt "the sweetest girl in the school." That never really occurred to me at the time. All

177

went as planned and she got to be a rebel for a night. It had been challenging rooming with this personification of sweetness, but somehow this helped. She was human after all. How sad is that? I felt better because she wasn't perfect. There's a definite character flaw in there for me.

Toward the end of my senior year a rumor had gotten around that there were now several master keys floating around the school. The principal was "in the know" and he offered a deal. He said that if anyone having a master key put it in an envelope and slid it under his door at any time, there would be no questions asked and no punishment. Hmmm. Of course I could have thrown mine out or stashed it away somewhere I suppose ... but did he know who had them? Probably not. Oh well. I walked into his office and handed him my master key. He was openly surprised. I said, "I only used it to skip church, nothing else." He asked where I had gotten it, but I said I couldn't divulge that. Someone had used a key to break into the kitchen a couple of times, and I assured him that it wasn't me or my source. I admitted that I had heard of a couple of other keys out there, but I had no idea who had them. I told him that I preferred giving him the key face-to-face rather than sliding it under his door to let him wonder who had had it and what they had used it for. I guess he respected that. I never heard another word about it.

How many times a week do you go to church?
Do you ever get tired of going to church?
What is it about church that makes some of us want to skip it at times?

Twenty plus missionary services/classes in one week was exceptional. But that was only during the mission conference. The usual number of services in one week was more like seven or eight: chapel every weekday morning, which was usually light and sometimes even fun, and two services each Sunday at the local church, plus the fairly frequent special service that came along. *I was a kid!*

Sometimes I guess I just got bored ... so I skipped church. Now if you want some insight into Satan's attempts to derail us from Sunday services read C.S. Lewis' Book, *The Screwtape Letters*. If you can't relate to some of the thoughts going through some of his character's minds, you're just too perfect to be reading this book. (I borrowed that idea from Lewis.)

Going to church is obviously not as important as having a personal relationship with the Lord, but it *is* something we are reminded to do in God's Word: "Let us not give up meeting together, as some are in the habit of doing, but let us encourage one another – and all the more as you see the day approaching." *(Hebrews 10:25)* I would sometimes complain to my mother that church was boring and she would tell me that enjoying church requires us to take a part; that every sermon has something in it for each of us if we just look for it. We need to make an effort to dig into the pastor's words or the Scripture passage used and find God's special message for each of us. I can't tell you how much that helped me. It's like resolving a little mystery now for me to find the hidden message just for me. Taking notes on the sermon also helps. Mine contain graffiti. I once used my notes to make an anniversary poster for my pastor. He seemed to enjoy the collage with "designer" sermon notes overlapping in the background and pictures of special events on top.

How important is it to follow the pastor's sermon? Explain.
Do you have any special trick to keep your attention in church? Please share.

More often than not at this point in life, I don't need to hunt for the message, but at times I still do. You can complain about the pastor's messages, the music, and the people in the church, etcetera; but chances are, if you're in a Bible teaching church, *you* are the biggest part of any problem you might have. Try constructively helping and stop complaining. No church is perfect and there may even be times when leaving is necessary, but too many families bounce around from church to church because they can't seem to pick a good one and stay with it through thick and thin, joining in the work to spread the message of God's love through Jesus Christ. Somehow their toes get stepped on and they move on. Children learn that the pastor, the choir, the church, is flawed. (Big surprise?) And they drift away later in life because they were never taught the importance of committing to the church in spite of its flaws. And the parents wonder what they did wrong. I heard it said once that the family who keeps hunting for the perfect church may eventually find it, only to discover that the minute they begin attending, it is no longer perfect.

Do you go to church for what you can get out of it or for what you can contribute to the body of Christ and God's great mission? Think about it. And when you do contribute, does it have to be your way, or can you follow the lead of those God has placed in authority over His church? Or maybe you go to church because it's the right thing to do and your family has done it for generations. You get a good feeling for having done such a good thing. There's nothing personal about church to you because you never discovered how to really engage in it. You're missing out.

It's ironic that I used a master key to skip church. A master key is kind of what church is all about. When we attend a Bible teaching church, we hear from God's Word, the key to opening all the doors of understanding that God has placed before us. The Bible is the key to knowing how God wants us to live; it's the key to a life of peace, joy and love; it's the key to solving the problems that plague our lives here on earth. It is *the* "master key."

In what ways does going to church help us?
… Come, let us go up to the mountain of the Lord, to the house of the God of Jacob. He will teach us his ways, so that we may walk in his paths Isaiah 2:3
Blessed are those who dwell in your house; they are ever praising you. Psalm 84:4

What does the Bible have to say about itself?
For the word of God is living and active. Sharper than any double-edged sword, it penetrates even to dividing soul and spirit, joints

and marrow; it judges the thoughts and attitudes of the heart.
Hebrews 4:12
Your word is a lamp to my feet and a light for my path. Psalm 119:105
All your words are true; all your righteous laws are eternal.
Psalm 119:160

According to the Bible, we should be learning God's ways in church, and we should be worshipping Him there. I guess that corresponds primarily to the sermon, and the music. Musical worship comes in so many forms – it could be a praise team, a choir, an orchestra, special music, or the song played during the offering. But worship is not necessarily restricted to music. We can worship the Lord through serving in the church, through giving of our time and talents and tithes. There are good churches out there with all kinds of musical styles, each right for different hearts of praise. But beware of the church whose pastor attempts to be politically correct, who avoids actually teaching certain topics from the Bible because someone might be offended. Find a good church that teaches God's truth without apology. And get involved, using your gifts for the Lord!

Bible Reading: *Acts 20:7-12*

How long do you think this service lasted?

Have you ever been to a service that lasted over three or four hours?

Were you able to stay alert through the entire thing?

What kinds of things go through your mind in church? Discuss.

What happened after Eutychus was brought back to life?

Challenge: Try my mom's suggestion and dig for God's special message just for you next time you go to church.

"Let us not give up meeting together, as some are in the habit of doing, But let us encourage one another – and all the more as you see the Day approaching."
Hebrews 10:25

WEEK 34

"and in this room..."

"The Sweetest Girl in the School"

How did I ever wind up rooming with a princess from Chicago? She was petite and cute, had beautiful girlish clothes, and spoke in a sweet princess voice. When her father and mother pulled up to the school in their black Rolls Royce with a fur coat over her mother's shoulders and a second one in the back seat, I knew I was "not in Kansas anymore." *(Wizard of Oz)* They took us out to dinner and I felt like royalty, or at least I imagined I did. This was like nothing I had ever experienced back home. I concluded that my roommate was indeed a princess. And *everyone* liked her. She followed the rules. She did her homework on time. She got good grades. Every few weeks she received a beautiful new outfit from home. She had everything necessary to succeed. And she really *was* the sweetest girl in the school.

I remember that our room was nearly always immaculate, that I dumped more cold water on her during water fights and over the top of the shower than she ever deserved, and that she became a dear sister to me in every way. When she asked to skip church with me, I was determined that it would all go well. I would have felt awful if I had let her down. The skip was a success and she had her dive into mischief. After high school my first roommate and I visited often, and she even lived in Connecticut for a few months when I was first married. I consider her one of my best friends to this day. I probably would have roomed with her my senior year as well, but when another good friend asked me to room with her, I thought, "That could be fun." and I made the switch. I was fortunate with roommates.

"The Rascal"

I was mischievous, but my second roommate took it to the next level. She did things I hesitated to try (for the record, none all that terrible), and she often got caught. I think she wound up with more dorm squelches than she could have worked off in a lifetime. She was dating a "townie" who was the source of half of her squelches. She was constantly getting caught car-riding with him, a no-no, or going to the movies with him, another no-no.

Interestingly, she and I were the two tallest girls in the school which meant that we could sometimes share clothes. Back then I was what my sister-in-law called emaciated. I was 5'10" and about 120 pounds – thin. I wore a size 5, a size I never saw again after that year. Short dresses were in, but the school had mandatory hem lengths. My roommate and I would spend the weekend taking all of our hems down, per order of the dean, and then putting them right back where they had started. Shame on us! I had this theory that even with my hems six inches above my knees, I still had as much leg left as most girls started with. It really does make sense if you think about it. The deans would ask us if we had taken our hems down and we could honestly answer, "Yes." No one ever thought to ask if we had *left* them down. Not exactly honest was it? Ouch. I might have been a good lawyer … and that is not a compliment. I have reformed since then.

This roommate was a little tougher to get along with than my first one and I take *at least* half of the responsibility. Maybe we were too much alike? She wanted the window open at night, even in cold weather, but she didn't want to sleep in the bed near the window. Really? I was not used to weather this cold. At times it would get so cold in northwestern Minnesota that the little hairs inside the nose would literally freeze! But that would be a little too cold for an open window even for her. We fussed over this and other things, but nothing to cause a rift in our friendship. Yet, I have never laughed more with any other friend. She has a gift for making people laugh.

The number of hours I started to put in practicing with my trio became a problem. I was "in seventh heaven" (pretty happy) just practicing with these girls and spending more and more time in the practice room but less and less time going through with the plans that my roommate and I had concocted. It wasn't that I stood her up exactly; I just never found time to agree on the specific details for our plans. I'm afraid I let her down. She would tease me about that – still does. Meanwhile, as I was often practicing, she started spending more and more time with her boyfriend or other friends. Our friendship was changing. I guess our priorities were shifting. We were no longer on the exact same wavelength as we had been the year before. She was certainly one of my favorite people still and we had great times together, but we had begun to drift apart a little.

Do you have any friends who are sweethearts? any rascals?
Are you finding some friendships changing? How?
Do you need to do something to strengthen a friendship?
Do you have any ideas?
Do you have any friends who are a good influence on you? a bad one?
What kind of friends *should* you surround yourself with?
> ...*walk in the ways of good men* and *keep to the paths of the righteous. Proverbs 2:20*
> ... *you must not associate with anyone who calls himself a brother but is sexually immoral or greedy, an idolater or a slanderer, a drunkard or a swindler. With such a man do not even eat. I Corinthians 5:11*

Good friends are so important in our lives. They have a huge influence on us when we are young, and they contribute to our character all through our lives. When I was younger, my friends were mainly my cousins; as I got older I discovered friends outside of family. I have always been *very* fortunate in my friends. Though all very different, they have touched my life in many positive ways and I thank God for each one of them. As a mother, later in life, I considered surrounding my children with good friends one of the most important things I could do for them from the time that they were very young. I truly believe that this has been one of the most influential things in helping them to become the women of the Lord that they are today.

Bible Readings :Were these famous friendships in the Bible good for each other? Explain.

David and Jonathan (*I Samuel 18:1-4, 19:1-20:42, 23:16-18*)

…Jonathan became one in the spirit with David, and he loved him as himself… And Jonathan made a covenant with David because he loved him as himself. Jonathan took off the robe he was wearing and gave it to David, along with his tunic, and even his sword, his bow and his belt …Saul told his son Jonathan and all the attendants to kill David. But Jonathan was very fond of David and warned him. …Jonathan spoke well of David to Saul, his father… David …went to Jonathan and asked, "How have I wronged your father, that he is trying to take my life?" "Never!" Jonathan replied …"whatever you want me to do. I'll do it for you … if my father is inclined to harm you, may the Lord deal with me, be it ever so severely, if I do not let you know and send you away safely." David bowed down before Jonathan …they …wept together. Jonathan said to David, "Go in peace, for we have sworn friendship with each other in the name of the Lord."… Jonathan went to David at Horesh and helped him find strength in God.

Job and friends (*Job 19:1-6, 21*)

How long will you torment me and crush me with words? Ten times now you have reproached me; shamelessly you attack me. If it is true that I have gone astray, my error remains my concern alone. If indeed you would exalt yourselves above me and use my humiliation against me, then know that God has wronged me and drawn His net around me….Have pity on me, my friends, have pity for the hand of God has struck me.

Ruth and Naomi *Ruth (1:16-18)*

Don't urge me to leave you or to turn back from you. Where you go, I will go, and where you stay, I will stay. Your people will be my people and your God my God. Where you die, I will die, and there I will be buried. May the Lord deal with me, be it ever so severely, if anything but death separates you and me.

Paul and Silas (*Acts 16:22-25*)

The crowd joined in the attack against Paul and Silas, and the magistrates ordered them to be stripped and beaten… he put them in the inner cell and fastened their feet in the stocks. About midnight Paul and Silas were praying and singing hymns to God, and the other prisoners were listening to them.

Mary and Martha (*Luke 10:38-42*)

...a woman named Martha opened her home to him (Jesus). She had a sister named Mary, who sat at the Lord's feet listening to what he said. But Martha was distracted by all the preparations that had to be made. She came to him and asked, "Lord, don't you care that my sister has left me to do the work by myself? Tell her to help me!" "Martha, Martha," the Lord answered, "you are worried about many things, but only one thing is needed, Mary has chosen what is better, and it will not be taken away from her."

Which one of these friendships is closest to yours with your best friend?

Do you ever wish your friendship would change? How?

Is there something you should do to help that happen?

Is there anyone for whom you would give your life?

Is there anyone who would do that for you? (not just friends your age)

Challenge: Think about this deeply: Who are your *real* friends?

"Greater love has no one than this, that one lay down his life for his friends. You are my friends if you do what I command."

John 15:13-14

WEEK 35

"Many a true word..."

I had always been a bit of a comedian, but I had just come from a school where I had been amongst the top students academically to a school where I was suddenly pretty average. I probably could have moved up a bit if I had wanted to start working harder, but I was smart enough to know that even with that, I would never make *the* top, or even close enough to make it worth it. There were a lot of really smart kids in my class – several national merit scholarship finalists and semi-finalists. Hmmm... So, I decided that court jester was a good alternate path to walk. That was my unofficial class superlative according to what a good friend wrote in my yearbook. At first I was insulted by the title, but then I got to thinking... The jester in Shakespeare acted the buffoon but usually had the keen insight and poignant dialogue that revealed the truth. (too much?) Anyway, I decided it was, after all, a compliment. I'd rather not know if it wasn't. I call it "blind bliss" – one of the main reasons I stay pretty happy.

Wikpedia has this to say about court jesters: "In Shakespeare's *Twelfth Night*, Feste, the jester, is described as 'wise enough to play the fool.' Indeed, to be successful in the job of King's Fool the holder had to be anything but a fool in the modern meaning of the word... In literature, the jester is symbolic of common sense and of honesty; notably in *King Lear*, the court jester is a character used for insight and advice on the part of the monarch, taking advantage of his license to mock and speak freely to dispense frank observations and highlight the folly of his monarch." He's the one who proclaims with a smile: "But the emperor has no clothes on!" So, though playing the fool, the role of court jester was only a façade. I liked that. I decided to embrace that role.

I managed to stay on the honor role with rather inconsistent grades. If my grades began to slip, I would simply work a little harder and bring them up. I remember making a tape recording for my speech class in which I had an argument with my conscience. I had to time the whole thing very carefully because the tape relentlessly played my conscience with no delay for any unforeseen change in timing. The tape interacted with the real me in class. It worked perfectly. I forget who won the argument, but I think I did.

Art class was one of my favorites. I had to hand in a "Friday sketch" each week. My sketch was pilfered once or twice by a good friend, the adorable schmoozer, who would sign his own name to it and leave me to quickly come up with another. I think he's a policeman now. No surprise. I did an oil painting of a city alley which got thicker and thicker as my classmates kept painting graffiti on my brick walls and I kept painting over it. Finally, I decided to leave the graffiti as part of the picture and I tried to make it look real. It came out pretty cool and I gave it to a friend. I heard it wound up in the football coach's family room thanks to the good memories in the graffiti. Go figure.

I did almost no work in chemistry one quarter. I would sleep in the last row right behind a big guy for concealment. I got my very first C on a high school quarterly report card – totally deserved. Math and English were still easy for me. I think I had had some excellent teachers early on who took me through the most difficult stuff and left me ready for anything later on. So, I did the minimum amount of work to stay on the honor roll, which also helped me to be able to go on tour with my trio on and off during my senior year. Even later as a teacher I was convinced that some kids put too much effort into grades. There are more important things in life – like family, friendships, and sharing God's love.

If you have graduated, did you have a class superlative? Did it suit you? best dressed? most athletic? most likely to...?

If you haven't graduated or didn't get one (only a few do), what
   might it be/have been?
What is/was your favorite class in high school? Why?
Do/did you do your best in high school? Why/why not?
Do you think it's okay not to? Explain.
What does the Bible say about that?
> *Do your best to present yourself to God as one approved, a*
> *workman who does not need to be ashamed and who correctly*
> *handles the word of truth. 2 Timothy 2:15*
> *Whatever you do, work at it with all your heart, as working for the*
> *Lord, not for men. Colossians 3:23 (I want this one on my tombstone*
> *some day.)*

How did my teachers put up with me? I started way back in
elementary school trying to lighten the atmosphere with humor,
and I often wound up sitting in the hall or the principal's office as
a result. My first two years of high school were pretty quiet, but the
next two brought me right back into jester mode and I went in for
the fun over and over. The sad part is that I'm not sure how funny
I actually was … probably not all that much. I used to wonder if
I had some deep-seated problem that made me the way I was;
but the fact of the matter was: I was an inordinately happy, fairly
well-adjusted young person. I think.

There was at least one role of court jester that I was always
sure suited me – getting people to laugh at themselves or at me –
it didn't matter which. I knew it was more fun to have a heartfelt
laugh at life's incongruities than it was to cry or complain or sulk
or … well, just about anything else I could think of.

Of course not all laughter is the same: the coarse laugh after
a joke in bad taste, the cruel laugh at someone else's bad fortune,
the nervous laugh in attempting to hide something, the desperate
laugh of a person in mental anguish. These are not the laughs I
was hoping to provoke through humor. I'm talking about the fun-
filled laugher of people enjoying life and the irony of their own
eccentricities. Life is so much more fun when we choose to take
pleasure in it. The King James version of the Bible even says that
"a merry heart doeth good, like a medicine…" (*Proverbs 17:22*)

189

So, it's *good* for us to enjoy the laughter of a merry heart. Kind of like eating fruit or drinking milk. Two things that I always liked that were also good for me – very cool.

Who is the court jester in your circle of friends?
(Remember this is not necessarily the funniest person.)
Does this person use humor or irony to get the truth across?
Is the truth more palatable when drenched in humor? Explain.
What does God's Word say about all of this?

> *A cheerful heart is good medicine, but a crushed spirit dries up the bones. Proverbs 17:22*
> *Therefore each of you must put off falsehood and speak truthfully to his neighbor, for we are all members of one body. Ephesians 4:25*

Sometimes we use humor to share a serious concern thinking that it will be accepted more readily. Sometimes that's true. But we need to be careful not to use humor when it's inappropriate. Sarcasm is often very cruel, and laughing at the coarse jokes we see in television/ movies today is not something we should enjoy. I know I am guilty of this on occasion. I like to think that my jokes were (still are?) timely and in good taste, and I like to think that my unofficial class superlative was meant in the very best of ways. I have taken pains to convince myself and perhaps even you that this was the case. In all honesty, I'm sure there were times when my humor was either poorly timed, poorly phrased, or poorly directed. Being the "court jester" is a role that is fraught with difficulty in determining when and whether to use humor ... and whether the jester is being mocked or is doing the mocking ... and if there is much of a difference. In summation of my lengthy defense, I must quote Shakespeare as he directed us to the truth in one of his greatest plays: "The lady doth protest too much, methinks!" (*Hamlet*)

Bible Reading: Do you see humor in these verses?

> *2 Chronicles 21:20:* ("to no one's regret") That didn't have to be in there. But it's humorous.

Exodus 32:7-11: ("your people" hot potato) Both God and Moses disclaim the Israelites and pass them off to each other.
Jonah 4: (the vine story – especially verse 9b) The entire book of *Jonah* is full of humor looking at his childish behavior.
2 Samuel 21:20: (six fingers…six toes) Is the author trying to keep our interest here by throwing in this fact?
Ecclesiastes 3:4: ("time to laugh") Here we are given permission to laugh at humorous or happy things.

Challenge: Work at keeping your humor from becoming sarcastic, hurtful, self-serving, or dishonoring to God.

"He has showed you, O man, what is good, and what does the Lord require of you? To act justly and to love mercy and to walk humble with your God."
Micah 6:8

WEEK 36

"Vietnam"

The Vietnam war was heating up right about the time I went off to Minnesota. It didn't affect me as much at the beginning as it might have because my cousins and friends were getting drafted just as I was also leaving home. I would have most definitely felt their absence more if I had stayed at home missing their interaction in my daily life. On the other hand, I started to write to a few of them regularly. They mostly talked about the weather (hot or rainy) and their buddies (great guys), but they didn't say much about the horrors to which they were spectators ... or worse. One cousin was injured in a freak accident, and another was given some kind of medal for capturing a group of Vietcong. These were quiet Christian guys who had never seen or done anything like this before. They would be forever changed.

One of them, the one who wrote the most, asked me if I would write to a good friend of his over there who never got any letters. My cousin was hoping I might consider writing his buddy letters like those I sent to him, full of facts and fun, sketches and photos, and of course, humor. So, I added another pen-pal to my writing schedule. I never got to meet him, but he sent me a picture of him and his dog, and I'd like to think I brought a little bit of light into his otherwise nightmarish situation. These guys were on the front lines under the threat of attack at all times, and actually engaged in war as often as not. And they didn't sign up for it. I can't even imagine.

Do you have any friends or relatives living in danger right now? Where?

Do you have any war veterans in your life?

Do they ever talk to you about their experiences? Share. What can you do to help them with any present anxiety or other after-effects?

After high school, I went to the University of Connecticut where protests were growing as the war neared its end. Students had sit-ins and chained themselves to desks in the administration building. There were bomb scares and classes cancelled as the mood turned more and more desperate around the campus and country. It was difficult to take my education seriously as I wondered why I was even going to college. Life was so uncertain. I couldn't count on having classes *tomorrow*, never mind my friends returning from Asia any time soon. I began to question everything.

Does God ever condone war? Should Christians ever go to war?
There is a time for everything, and a season for every activity under heaven: ... a time for war and a time for peace. Ecclesiastes 3:1,8
He will defend the afflicted among the people and save the children of the needy; he will crush the oppressor. Psalm 72:4
So Joshua took the entire land, just as the Lord had directed Moses, ... Joshua 11:23

Should a "Christian" country prepare for war?
He trains my hands for battle; my arms can bend a bow of bronze. You give me your shield of victory; you stoop down to make me great. 2 Samuel 22:35
Proclaim this among the nations: Prepare for war! Rouse the warriors! Let all the fighting men draw near and attack. *Beat your plowshares into swords and your pruning hooks into spears. Let the weak say, "I am strong!" Come quickly, all you nations from every side, and assemble there. Joel 3:9-11 (*The UN has the opposite sentiment engraved on its outer wall from Isaiah 2:4.)

But what about loving our enemies?
...Love your enemies, be good to those who hate you, bless those who curse you, pray for those who mistreat you. ... Do to others as you would have them do to you. Luke 6:27-31
...If you enemy is hungry, feed him; if he is thirsty, give him something to drink. In doing this, you will heap burning coals on his head. Romans 12:20

My sister and I used to joke about that last verse. When we treated someone nicely who we thought had been unkind to us, we would whisper to each other, "burning coals, burning coals..." I think it started right after our dad died and people said all kinds of silly things. I'm not sure that that was the right attitude to take, but it made us laugh when we wanted to cry ... or scream. Some people complain that the Bible contains contradictions like this verse telling us to be good to our enemy while also imagining heaping burning coals on his head. But like this verse, life is full of contradictions. Check these out and discuss them:

war/peace	*...war will continue until the end... Daniel 9:26b*
	May the God of peace... Hebrews 13:20a
life/death	*...I have come that they may have life...*
	John 10:10
	For the wages of sin is death... Romans 6:23
blessings/curses	*I will bless those who bless you, and whoever curses you, I will curse. Genesis 12:3*
good/evil	*Good and upright is the Lord... Psalm 25:8*
	...but deliver us from the evil one (Satan)... Matthew 6:13b
humility/pride	*... walk humbly with your God. Micah 6:8*
	... take pride in himself, without comparing... Galatians 6:4b
bondage freedom	*...you have ... become slaves to God... Romans 6:22*
	no longer call you servants... (but) friends... John 15:15
love/hatred	*...a time to love, and a time to hate... Ecclesiastes 3:8*
	Hate evil, love good... Amos 5:15
meek/bold	*Blessed are the meek for they will inherit... Matthew 5:5*
	...the righteous are as bold as a lion. Proverbs 28:1
faith/unbelief	*"...I do believe; help me overcome my unbelief!" Mark 9:24*

How is it possible for these seeming contradictions to coexist? Is it possible for them to work harmoniously together? Is it possible for them to actually be the same thing? Don't fall for accusations of contradictions in the Bible. The context and the big picture help us to understand God's purpose and God's truth if we just take the time to discover them. It is often helpful for me to remember that we live in a broken world, broken by us. God had a perfect plan for us, but because we chose not to follow it, sin and death and judgment have come upon our world and ourselves. *So in God's Word we read both of His perfect desire for us and of the contradictory consequences of sin.* His perfect plan will recommence in eternity.

My pastor once said in a sermon, *"A text* out of *context* is often a *pretext* to promote one's own opinion." According to Jonathan Cahn's book, *The Harbinger,* after the tragedy of "9/11" in New York City, on three separate occasions, leaders in our country quoted from *Isaiah 9:10*: "The bricks have fallen down, but we will rebuild with dressed stone; the fig leaves have been felled, but we will replace them with cedars..." These verses might seem encouraging until you look at their context. Because of their pride and arrogance, this is the beginning of a prophecy of doom for the northern kingdom of Israel who thought they didn't need God. Our country's leaders didn't do their homework and were actually setting our nation up to be cursed by God! So often things in the Bible are misrepresented by those who haven't taken the time to understand the big picture.

A principal once asked me, a teacher, to write up a statistical review of our school's results on a standardized test. I smiled and asked, "What would you like it to look like?" He looked at me quizzically. I told him that I could take those results and show nearly opposite results if I had a mind to. People do it all the time. If you're observant and know what to look for, you can spot data whose scales have been manipulated to give false impressions. You can also see texts out of context in almost every newspaper. However, our God is consistent throughout the Bible, both Old and New Testaments. His commandments, given to Moses on the mountain, don't change; they are repeated and more fully developed at the time of Christ in the New Testament. His "contradictions" are anything but contradictory in light of who He truly is. He can stand up to our examination.

Bible Reading: *Deuteronomy 20:16-18, Judges 2:10-13, Joel 3:9-16, Revelation 14:19-20*
Does God sometimes seem unfair in your life? Explain.
Is He unfair in *Deuteronomy 20:16-18*? Why?
Are these innocent people? (See *Genesis 15:16*.)
What is the warning in verse18 of *Deuteronomy 20*?
What does *Judges 2:10-13* reveal?
What battle is *Joel* speaking of in chapter *3:9-16*? Explain.
(*Revelation 14:19-20* shows the outcome of that battle.)

This is one of the questions that people seem to stumble over often: " Why does a good God allow innocent people to suffer?" ... and even direct His people to cause this to happen? It's hard for us to understand. Judgment is a necessary part of justice. A holy God cannot allow sin to reign supreme. History has shown us that it is only through judgment that goodness does abound. The people in *Deuteronomy* had been warned and given hundreds of years to shape up, but they ignored the warnings and continued to sin. Just as many do today. And those whom the Israelites did not destroy, later did pull God's people into sin just as God warned. When people ask where God is in this broken world, I often respond: "God is a gentleman. We have told Him to go away. We have removed all evidence of Him from our schools, politics, justice system, and entertainment. He has 'left the building.'" Obviously He has never left the believer, but I'm not sure about some parts of our world...

Challenge: If you think God has been unfair in some way, think about who He is and what "fair" treatment would actually mean for all of us.

"The grass withers and the flowers fall, but the Word of our God stands forever."
Isaiah 40:8

WEEK 37

"Adventures in counseling"

My mother was a great story-teller. When we were little in the old house, my sister and I and our two cousins who lived next door, would sit on the end of mom's bed while she was straightening up the room and we would beg her to tell us a story. My mother would sit down with us and make up stories as she spoke. They were most often tales of princes and princesses, knights and damsels in distress. No one could tell a story like her. Our two cousins fit right between my sister and me in age – four school grades in a 2 ¼ year age span – and they were great friends of ours. We were together nearly every day. We would throw a blanket over their clothesline, peg down the four corners with clothespins and then sleep out in our fabricated tent. Back then, I hate to admit it, we only received a couple of channels on our black and white television set with little choice in programs. People hadn't gotten to the point yet where they used TV sets or electronic games as babysitters, so we had to invent or discover fun things to do. Novel idea. We became pretty creative when left to our own resources.

When I became a teenager Mom didn't make up tales of adventure anymore. For one thing, she was too busy working or too tired *from* working. For another, she probably tried to use the little listening time we gave her to tell us the more important things that moms need to share with their growing children. I once asked her later in life why she didn't talk more to me about the facts of life. She said that I would cover my ears or run out of the room singing "la, la, la, ..." loudly whenever she tried. Though I didn't remember doing that, I could certainly imagine having done that. I distinctly remember when I first became a "woman" being afraid of sitting on a boy's lap in a very crowded car while the "plague" was upon me because I was not quite sure even then how everything worked. Can you believe it? I probably should have listened better to my mom because I was misinformed on a couple of critical facts for longer than I should have been. Uff-dah. (Norwegian for "Oy-vey.")

But I was a tomboy, and all that stuff was something I figured I wouldn't need to know until I neared death ... or my twenties, which was practically the same thing. And oh yeah, I did eventually get the facts squared away. It's important to get the facts straight from an adult you trust. I remember wakening to hear a particularly graphic explanation of perverted sex while I was counseling teens at Bible Camp. One young girl knew way too much about this topic and was very happy to share. I told the girls that since they wanted to talk about sex, we might as well get it straight. I talked about God's plan for us and about the fact that people take God's plans and twist them in many unhealthy ways until they become sin. We looked into God's Word on the topic. A couple of weeks later, at home, I got a letter from one of the mothers. I was afraid she might be upset about my talk with the girls because it necessarily went a little deeper than I would normally go, but she was thanking me for interceding and inviting me to visit them in New York.

When I was young I would watch my mom as she counseled the young people who hung out at our house on weekends. There were young adults who would stop by specifically to see her with no desire either to see me or my siblings, or to join in the fun downstairs. She would drop everything to listen. I did have a good role model to learn from, and it served me well to pay attention from time to time, though never realizing what was happening.

Did anyone ever tell or read you stories?
What were your favorites?
How did you learn the facts of life? Discuss.
Were those facts given from a Biblical perspective or from a humanistic one? (It's important to know the difference.)
Where do you go for counsel?

*Blessed is the man who does not walk in the counsel of the wicked
or stand in the way of sinners or sit in the seat of mockers. But <u>his
delight is in the law of the Lord</u>, and on his law he meditates day
and night. Psalm 1:1-2*
*If any of you lacks wisdom, he should <u>ask of God</u>, who gives
generously to all without finding fault, and it will be given to him.
James 1:5*
*The way of a fool seems right to him, but <u>a wise man listens to
advice</u>. Proverbs 12:15*

I got along pretty well with my mother. We talked more and more as I got older. Oh, we bumped heads a couple of times, but we had been through too much together (e.g., the loss of her husband/my father) to let that ever cause a breach in our relationship. After I graduated from college she was probably my best friend. I was fortunate. Some of my friends did not have good relationships with their mothers. Not sure whose fault that was, theirs or their mom's... I could never quite understand why they couldn't work things out, but then again, they didn't have my mother. I suppose if I had felt that I could never please her, if she had had issues constantly with my friends, or if she had shown me no affection or attention, I might not have had as good a relationship with her as I did. At the same time if I hadn't understood that her occasional criticism was constructive and given in love, if I had brought home friends who made her worry for my safety, or if I wasn't as sure as I was that she loved me in spite of myself, our relationship may have been different then too. We need to look at both perspectives. She knew how to listen, and how to give good advice. Parents are oftentimes our best counselors. But we need to communicate with them on a regular basis to keep those lines open. We need to be able to talk about *anything* that is bothering us, even if it's awkward.

How is your relationship with your mother (or stand-in "mom")?
Does it need a repair job?
Do *you* need to initiate that?
What can you do to make it better?
What would God have us do with regard to our moms?

*Honor your father and mother – which is the first commandment
with a promise – that it may go well with you and that you may enjoy
long life on the earth. Ephesians 6:2-3
Listen, my son, to your father's instruction and do not forsake your
mother's teaching. Proverbs 1:8*

I guess the counseling thing was in my blood because I did become a peer counselor in high school. I did my best to lead a weekly Bible study and to be there for the girls in my group, though I'm not sure I ever actually helped any of them. I went on to counsel as a youth group leader, at Bible camp, when I taught school, and when I directed the teen events at our Christian camp in Mt. Bethel, Pennsylvania. *I constantly asked God for wisdom,* because the importance of teaching God's truth and of giving wise advice should never be underestimated. I hear from many of the people whose lives I have been able to interact with in a teaching or counseling capacity, and I am so thrilled to see what God is doing with them today! It's heartwarming to be used by God even in the smallest way to help someone else. What an honor.

Check out these verses:

James 3:1 will make you think twice about counseling anyone.
*Not many of you should presume to be teachers, my brothers,
because you know that we who teach will be judged more strictly.*

Proverbs 4:7 and *23:23* show the importance of seeking wisdom.
*Wisdom is supreme; therefore, get wisdom. Though it cost all you
have, get understanding.*

Philippians 1:6 should encourage you as a counselor.
...he who began a good work in you will carry it on to completion...

Bible Reading: *I Kings 3:1-15, 4:29-34*
What three building projects was Solomon involved in?
How did God appear to Solomon and what did He say to him?
What *specifically* did Solomon ask for from God?
Why did that please God? Explain.
What was the first thing Solomon did to thank God?

God came to Solomon, David's son, in the Old Testament in a dream because He was very happy with him, and God said, "Ask for whatever you want me to give you." Solomon's reply was, "...give your servant a discerning heart to govern your people and to distinguish right from wrong..." God was so pleased with Solomon's request that He granted him wisdom. And on top of that God gave him riches and honor. There is a very famous story of Solomon's dealings with two women who both claimed to be the mother of a baby. He could tell who was the true mother because she was the one who would rather give up her child than have the baby cut into two equal pieces as Solomon had suggested. Though Solomon was certainly not perfect, he became renowned for his wisdom throughout his world. And the God of Israel was honored through this. It is from the Lord that all wisdom comes. And every time we display His wisdom in our actions, we honor Him.

Challenge: Ask God for wisdom. Especially when you are making a tough decision or giving advice to a friend.

"In everything set them an example by doing what is good. In your teaching show integrity, seriousness, and soundness of speech that cannot be condemned, so that those who oppose you may be ashamed because they have nothing bad to say about us."

Titus 2:7-8

WEEK 38

"I never saw such a woman"

Remember how I told you about my mother's talents? She could play the piano like a professional. She was an artist; and *she could sew*. My senior prom dress was amazing; no one had anything like it. I saw it in a magazine, but it was crazy expensive. I showed it to my mom when I was home for Christmas and we went together to get just the right material for the gown. It had a soft, ivory colored, tailored bodice with graceful overly full sleeves caught up in extra long cuffs with covered buttons on them. The skirt was ivory and very full without being bulky, with large soft brown polka dots on material that would just about melt in your mouth. The waist had a light brown, extra wide cummerbund that matched the polka dots and accentuated my then small waist and my height. It was truly an ethereal dress and, in spite of the polka dots (which I'm sure some of you are still wondering about), to this day I think it was the prettiest dress I have ever worn (with perhaps one exception).

Other than short skirts, I was pretty modest. My boyish figure made that easy. However, I was never one to hesitate to try something different with my apparel. My senior class prophecy was that I would open "Swival's Mod Clothing Store" in New York City after college. ("Swival" was the nickname I was given in high school after playing a football player in a Homecoming skit at the start of my junior year. A few of the girls, dressed in full football gear, were announced as "Swival Swensen, Jinx Jensen," etc. and ran out onto the field to the cheers of a few of the actual football players in cheerleading garb, complete with pompoms. Such fun.) Little did my classmates know that the two reasons I made some of my own clothes were the cost factor and the fact that this was one of the only ways I could get sleeves, skirts and pants' legs long enough. Back then "one size fits all" was the theory for girls' clothing. I often bought boy's jeans to get them narrow enough *and* long enough at the same time. Otherwise, girls' jeans got bigger as they got longer, and one way or the other I was in trouble. I really wasn't into sewing for the sheer enjoyment of it.

As a high school freshman I had taken a home economics course which included sewing, but when I had to actually wear the jumper I had made in school (part of the class requirement), I was horrorstruck. I had reworked that v-neck so many times that it was raw with pulled stitches and attempts to redo it properly. This first attempt at serious sewing yielded less than satisfactory results. However, when I started singing with my trio in Minnesota, we needed coordinated outfits to wear on tour. The expense would have been prohibitive if I hadn't set my mind to improving my skills as a seamstress. We wound up making three or four outfits each. I still have them and if they weren't several sizes too small, I might even wear one or two now. They are very cool. Okay, maybe a bit dated. Alright, alright, I probably would never wear them again. And don't look inside at my work. Yikes! It's amazing what can be hidden inside.

Did you ever have a special dress or outfit that surpassed all else? Describe.

Did you like your prom dress? What was it that you liked about it?

Would you consider yourself modest? Why or why not?

Do you find it hard to get clothes to fit right? (gorilla arms like me?)

What does the Bible say about clothing?

*"I also want women to dress modestly, with decency and propriety..."
I Timothy 2:9*

I put on righteousness as my clothing; justice was my robe and my turban. Job 29:14

She is clothed with strength and dignity; she can laugh at the days to come. Proverbs 31: 25

And why do you worry about clothes? See how the lilies of the field grow. They do not labor or spin. Yet I tell you that not even Solomon ... was dressed like one of these. Matthew 6:28-29

My experience with sewing did come in handy down the road. Later in life I wound up making several outfits for my three little girls, and yes, some of them were matching. Sorry, girls. When they were little, I made them *Little House on The Prairie* outfits complete with pinafores and bonnets. I had fun making my girls' prom dresses, and the bridesmaids' dresses for a couple of weddings. I was especially honored to make each of my daughter's wedding gowns. I continued to sew some of my own outfits and random clothes for friends and family. Eventually I began to work full time teaching, and clothes started to come in assorted lengths for women, so I rarely sewed after that.

None of my daughters sew much in spite of their many gifts, but I'm hoping that that might still change. I have the greatest hope for the youngest. It's good to have as many skills as you can acquire in life. They come in handy. And everyone should be able to sew on a button or sew a straight line. I read the description of the "wife of noble character" in the last chapter of *Proverbs* and I am encouraged that she was such an incredibly independent person, not at all like the wives I would have imagined back then. I thought they would all be quiet little mice, veiled and walking a couple of steps behind their husbands with little to do but make themselves look pretty and create beautiful but useless embroideries. Either that or they would be vassals who spent hours slaving over their chores, working in the fields, grinding grain, making meals, and keeping their children and the dirt floors of their homes clean and in order. Neither role seemed appealing to me. But look at the roles listed for the "wife of noble character" in *Proverbs 31*:

Purchasing Agent	Craftswoman	Chef
Realtor	Banker	Planter
Laborer	Trader	Knitter/Weaver
Philanthropist	Seamstress	Merchant
Professor	Overseer	Good mother and wife

She is also well-respected, and unimpressed by charm and beauty. Whew! That's a tough act to follow. This lady was a one-woman wonder! Can you think of any woman you know who even comes close to this description? ... which brings to mind a scene in Jane Austen's classic, *Pride and Prejudice,* where Charles Bingley innocently states that he cannot understand "how young ladies can have the patience to be so very accomplished as they all are ... They all paint tables, cover screens, and net purses ... I never heard a young lady spoken of ... without being informed that she was very accomplished!" Darcy, the leading man, agrees with the last half, but insists that the word "accomplished" is applied to too many ladies: "I cannot boast of knowing more than half a dozen, in the whole range of my acquaintance, that are really accomplished." Miss Bingley (Charles' sister) agrees, and Elizabeth, the heroine, says. "You must comprehend a great deal in your idea of an accomplished woman." They agree and Miss Bingley adds a few more items to the criteria: "a thorough knowledge of music, singing, drawing, dancing, all the modern languages ... and a certain something in her manner of walking, the tone of her voice, (and) her address and expression." Darcy agrees adding "... the improvement of her mind by extensive reading." Elizabeth returns with, "I am no longer surprised at you knowing *only six* accomplished women! I rather wonder now at your knowing *any* ... I never saw such a woman." Debate ensues until the topic is dropped.

It is a pretty long list of accomplishments and I suppose that the list would change quite a bit if we updated it. Today it might include computer skills, sports, and a thorough knowledge of the latest and best movies and CD's, among other things. Though I have to agree with Darcy that there are few who would make the cut with this list of qualifications, I also agree with Elizabeth that the expectations are too high. I would consider someone accomplished with a significantly smaller list and especially if they were exceptionally good at just one of them. On the other hand, I say again that it's good to acquire as many skills as you can in life. If you did half of what the woman described in *Proverbs* did or had half of the qualifications of the woman described in *Pride and Prejudice*, you would need all of the help you could get. In this day of fast food, amazon.com, and shopping malls, people aren't as apt to work long and hard to learn a skill, because whatever they need can be bought at a drive-up window or ordered for next-day delivery through the internet. But working hard to master a skill is still a great joy and a sense of accomplishment to the learner. And we are all impressed by those who do so. Who is not impressed by the Olympic athletes, the highly accomplished musicians and artists, and others who have put an inordinate amount of time and energy into becoming exceptional at something?

> Do you know any exceptionally accomplished women?
> What makes them so special? Explain.
> What women impress you in the Bible?

The Bible is full of impressive women. The Story of Deborah is told in *Judges* (*4:4-10, 5:31b*). The land had peace under her leadership for forty years. In *Micah* (*6:4*) and *Exodus* (*15:19-21*) we hear of the leadership of Miriam, the prophetess, who worked alongside her brothers, Moses and Aaron. Ruth asks Boaz to marry her in the book of *Ruth*. God tells Abraham to listen to Sarah in *Genesis 21*. In *Luke 1* we see the incredible faith of Mary, the mother of Jesus, when she says "May it be to me as you have said," in response to the angel's news of her imminent pregnancy. Right after that is the beautiful "Song of Mary." Other strong New Testament women include Tabitha, Phoebe, Priscilla, Lydia, Mary Magdalene, and Mary and Martha of Bethany. But one of my all time favorite stories is of the Old Testament heroine, Esther, and her incredible bravery in risking her very life for her people.

Bible Reading: *Esther 4:6-5:3, 7:10, 8:11, 10:3*
> What plot of Haman's was revealed to Mordecai, Esther's uncle?
> How did Mordecai ask Esther to get involved?
> Was this dangerous? Why?

How do verses 12-14 in chapter 4 relate to us today?
What wisdom did Esther use in getting others involved?
How did it turn out for Esther (5:3)? For Haman (7:10)? For the
Jews (8:11) ? For Mordecai (10:3)?

Challenge: Are you a woman of God as in Proverbs 31? C'mon,
develop that gift!

*"Charm is deceptive and beauty is fleeting; but a woman
who fears the Lord is to be praised. Give her the reward
she has earned, and let her works bring her praise at the
city gate."*

Proverbs 31:30-31

WEEK 39

"Practice, practice, practice!"

started singing with my trio during my junior year of high school at a big banquet at the end of the year ... except we were a quartet then. Our song went pretty well, but one of our two sopranos didn't return for our senior year. (1 quartet – 1 singer = 1 trio.) That's how we started out our senior year. When we tried to sing songs the way they were written, we ran into the same problem over and over again – the songs were too high for a mezzo-soprano, a second alto and a tenor. (We all had pretty low voices.) Our first two or three gigs sounded okay, but it wasn't really working for us. Our pianist's mom sweetly hinted that we move on, and we considered it. Then we did the smartest thing we possibly could have done. We threw away the music and we started to have fun with the songs.

Suddenly, the songs started to come alive. We put them into lower keys and did our own arranging. Our pianist, a girl from Minneapolis, was incredible. She had been invited to play in regional high school piano competitions and I think she even played in a ten-piano recital in Minneapolis or Chicago, one of those big Midwestern cities. We would ask her to take a song down a note or two and immediately she was playing it flawlessly in the new key. She could also listen to a song just once or twice on the radio and then play it by ear with all of its idiosyncrasies, which is an exceptional gift. I grew so spoiled with her playing that I couldn't understand years later why other pianists couldn't perform the same miracles. Since our trio days, she has recorded many instrumental CD's of her own arrangements under her own label. They are inspiring. As a matter of fact, I have one playing right now.

As our singing developed and our level of fun began to rise, we were requested to sing more and more often. We were delighted. Of course that meant that we needed more and more songs which meant more and more practice time. This is where I began to lose my second roommate. The little practice room off of the girls' lounge on the second floor of our dorm became a second home to us as we spent hours and hours working up new songs. I can't speak for the others, but I don't know if I've ever had as much fun just practicing. We had a tight harmony and never settled for less than the best sound that we could muster. Finding harmony in music and in relationships were strengths we developed through these efforts. Now that the songs were nice and low, it was working for us. All it really took was for us to be ourselves. Hmmm. Is there a lesson in there?

We sang a lot during our senior year. We sang at nearly every special event during the school year. Our classmates were probably getting a little tired of hearing us. We took a few long weekend tours around the Midwest and into Canada. We also sang a couple of songs at each concert on the lengthy choir tour to the East Coast over Easter break. (I did make it into the choir my senior year contrary to what the principal had threatened on tour the year before – but by now he and I were good friends – kind of.) Near the end of our senior year of high school we were asked to go on tour to the West Coast for that summer for five or six weeks. We were also asked to make a record to sell on this tour. Yikes! So now we had to get serious and pull about twelve to fifteen songs together that could be used on the record. We recorded it amid the busy graduation schedule in a small studio in Fargo, ND. How cool was that? The following summer we toured the East Coast. We recorded two more albums over the next couple of years, our last being made in a much bigger studio in New York. Can you believe how God blessed us? It still amazes me.

Do you have any friends who are exceptionally gifted like our pianist?

Does it make you feel envious, happy for them, or like leftover liverwurst?

A heart at peace gives life to the body, but <u>envy rots the bones</u>. Proverbs 14:30

Love is patient, love is kind. <u>It does not envy</u>, it does not boast, it is not proud. I Corinthians 13:4

Who is wise and understanding among you? Let him show it by his good life, by deeds done in the humility that comes from wisdom. But if you harbor bitter envy and selfish ambition in your hearts, do not boast about it or deny the truth. Such wisdom does not come down from heaven but is earthly, unspiritual, of the devil. <u>For where you have envy and selfish ambition, there you will find disorder and every evil practice</u>. But the wisdom that comes from heaven is first of all pure; then peace-loving, considerate, submissive, full of mercy and good fruit, impartial and sincere. Peacemakers who sow in peace raise a harvest of righteousness. James 3:13-18

Have you ever tried to fit a mold (singing from the book) that didn't fit? Explain.

Have you ever gotten so caught up in something that you gave it all your spare time? What?

One thing that I learned from my trio was that I was unique – and not just musically. All of the other members of my trio were quite blonde and I was a light brunette, otherwise known as a "dirty blonde." So in order to feel included when we entered a room and people remarked on the "beautiful blondes," I went into the bathroom one night on tour to bleach my hair blonde. The others waited in disbelief. To have it perfectly understood who it was being called "beautiful blondes," I actually dyed my hair a very dark brown and shocked the others as I revealed the new look. There was no sense pretending to be blonde or anything else that I wasn't. I wasn't a soprano and would never be able to hit those high notes. I wasn't trained in opera or any other kind of singing for that matter and might as well give up on those classical songs that expected more from me than I had to give. I wasn't drawn to singing hymns unless we took them and "jazzed" them up a little. I wasn't apt to do any song the way it was written. With this understood, what I could do was to take a song, put it into a lower key, change any notes that might spotlight my limits and thereby distract from the message of the words, and sing it in a style all my own. If you change all of the pronouns and verbs in those last few sentences to plurals, you could reread this to apply to my trio as a whole. We were unique; and once we discovered that that was okay, and even good, we were off and running. Never be afraid to change things up (if possible) in order to do something well. Of course, even then, we all have limits that may put some things out of our reach. (By the way ... I liked the darker hair so much that I kept it that way for over a decade.)

What does the Bible have to say about our uniqueness?
For you created my inmost being; you knit me together in my mother's womb. I praise you because <u>I am fearfully and wonderfully made</u>; your works are wonderful, I know that full well. My frame was not hidden from you when I was made in the secret place. When I was woven together in the depths of the earth, your eyes saw my unformed body. All the days ordained for me were written in your book before one of them came to be. Psalm 139:13-16
For <u>we are God's workmanship</u>, created in Christ Jesus to do good works, which God prepared in advance for us to do. Ephesians 2:10
How do you feel about your uniqueness?
Have you figured out yet what a very cool person you are?

Years later, when I got married, I tried to be the ideal daughter-in-law. In this new scenario, it took me longer than it should have to rediscover that it was all right for me to be me, that I could stop trying so hard to please all these new people in my life who were so important to me. I literally made a fool of myself on several occasions when I tried to be more like the person I thought they wanted me to be, and found that I was no good at it. So, rather than being good at being me, I failed at being someone else. It's crazy, but people do this all the time. If I had settled for being the best "me" I could be, I would have walked away with at least a partial success rather than a dismal failure. I think I might have been more readily approved of as "me" in spite of my flaws, than as a poor imitation of someone else. Once again I learned the hard way.

It's a good thing that we don't have to worry about this with God. He takes a look at our hearts and gets us right away. Check out *I Samuel 16:7* when God chooses David over his older brothers, and *Matthew 6:7-8* and *Galatians 1:10* where we are told to remember that we are serving God, not men. We may not be men's first choice, but God looks at our hearts, and He sees so much more than they do. He sees so much potential in each one of us. *Philippians 4:13* says that we can do all things through the grace of God. ALL things! And in *Isaiah 41:10* God promises to strengthen us and help us.

I don't know you, but I do know that you are an exclusive Designer original! We all are! We were made by the same God who put just as much love into the making of you as He did into anyone else. You may not have discovered the "quintessential" you yet, but that doesn't mean you're not in there. Stop trying to be somebody you aren't. Stop trying to "fit in" or "stand out." Start trying to find out how God has gifted you and what that means. It is only when you are in God's will and following His plan for your life that you will discover just how cool you really are.

Bible Reading: *Psalm 139:13-16, 23-24*
When did your life begin?
David calls God's works (in making us) what? Do you agree?
Does God have a plan for your life? How do you know?
Could you ask, as David does, for God to search you and test you? Too scary?
Why do you think David asks that of God?

Challenge: Start looking at yourself as God does.
Look inside, at the heart.

"I praise you because I am fearfully and wonderfully made; your works are wonderful, I know that full well."
Psalm 139:14

WEEK 40

"Boy am I dated!"

I didn't do a lot of dating before my junior year of high school – didn't do that much even after that on a scale from one to ten. My first kiss was at a roller-skating rink when I was about thirteen. This cute boy who I had just met and skated with walked me out to my mom's car, and right there in the headlights with my sisters watching he planted a kiss ... on my lips! I was stunned. I got teased all the way home. My first date was with a nice guy from my church who, as I found out several years later, was also the first date for several of my cousins and friends. He had lots of first dates but for some reason not as many second dates. I'm not sure why because he was a *really* great guy. Why does that seem to be a problem for some guys? Maybe there is a certain amount of truth to what Anne says in the book, *Anne of Green Gables*: "I wouldn't want to marry anybody who was wicked, but I think I'd like it if he *could* be wicked and wouldn't." I had a couple of dates during my freshman and sophomore years in high school, but none that really turned my head. There were a couple of set-ups by my sister, but you know how those go. So far dating was not something that had made a big impression on me. My second kiss was still out there.

I dated a couple of guys the summer before I went away to high school when I worked in New York at the Christian college. One had big plans for us after the second date, also our last date. I dated a couple of guys at my Christian boarding school when my naïve dating policy was: "Everyone deserves at least one chance." (... not necessarily) For a good part of my junior year in high school I dated a super guy. He was the guy who gave me the master key. He was well liked by everyone, cute, talented, smart... What more could I ask for? I really enjoyed going out with him. He was a true gentleman, very thoughtful and romantic, and I was very lucky. For my birthday he bought me my favorite perfume and the record (black plastic disc with a hole in the middle…early version of a CD), *Can't Take My Eyes Off Of You!* by Frankie Valli and the "Four Seasons." Very sweet. And it was nice not to have to worry about a date for the big events – we were an item.

Then, disaster came. He told me he loved me … *loved* me! I was *sixteen!* I wasn't even almost ready to hear those words! Maybe he thought I wanted to hear them; maybe he was just speaking from his heart; maybe all the other girls and guys were saying that to each other; maybe a million things. All I knew was that those words stopped all of the normal rhythms in my body from working together in harmony. Things just stalled inside me. Then, panic began to rise … "I had to get out of this." So I did the first dumb thing that came into my mind – a couple of days later I dumped him. Now this was dumb on several levels. First of all, I hurt him and that was the last thing I wanted to do. Secondly, we had become good friends and that was not something to just throw away. Thirdly, the end of the year was only three months away and his graduation imminent. We would both be stuck looking for dates for all of the big events at the end of the year, possibly having a miserable time in awkward or less than fun situations. Very dumb.

Have you ever dumped someone? ever been dumped?
Did you handle it well (either situation)? Explain.
What could you have done better?

I hate the word "dumped," but you know what? It really does describe how someone feels when it happens to them. More than one guy has told me over the years that the line they can't stand to hear is: "I think we should just be friends." I guess everyone hates that line; but the problem is – that's *exactly* what you hope for when you break up with a nice guy. You have learned that you don't want the affectionate relationship of boyfriend/girlfriend, but you still care very much for the guy and don't want to lose the friendship. I'm not sure that guys can handle that. I wonder if girls are better at transitioning out of affection into friendship after having dated? Not that girls can't get hurt too... My boyfriend was hurt. I tried to break up graciously, but I guess I blew it. Is it even possible to break up graciously? The entire boys' dorm was mad at me. Half of the girls' dorm was mad, and the other half happy – happy because now they could have a shot at him. I was miserable. I cried on and off for days. I realized I had blown it. Maybe we still needed to break up, especially if he was that much more serious than I was, but it could have been handled better. And we probably could have just drifted apart over the summer. Wishful thinking?

> Who do you think is better at moving on – males or females? Why?
>
> What is the best way to break up with a good friend?
>> ... *speaking the truth in love*, we will in all things grow up into him who is the Head, that is, Christ. Ephesians 4:15
>> `...faithful are the wounds of a friend. Proverbs 27:6
>
> Is it always best to tell the truth? Is it ever okay to lie?
>> *Do not lie to each other*, since you have taken off your old self with its practices and have put on the new self which is being renewed in the image of its Creator. Colossians 3:9-10
>> *Truthful lips endure forever*, but a lying tongue lasts only a moment. Proverbs 12:19

At the end of my junior year I went out with a nice guy a few times who was the most creative dater I had ever gone out with. He was one of my co-bowlers on choir tour when I got in trouble for buying a couple of cokes at the bar in the bowling alley. He always had interesting ideas for dates and we laughed from the start to the finish of each date. I liked him. He wasn't a "masher," as I jokingly called the guys who wanted more physically than I was willing to give. Later in life I was not surprised to hear that he was openly gay. I still consider him my dear friend even though we disagree on the choices he has made in life. I don't need to tell him what I believe; he knows. And he knows what God's Word has to say about it.

We are called by God to teach His truth *in love* (*Ephesians 4:15*), but to leave the judging to God (*James 4:12*). God loved us even before we asked Him to. The Bible says, *"... God demonstrates his love for us in this: While we were still sinners, Christ died for us."* (*Romans 5:8*) He loves me in spite of who I am, so how can I do less for my friend? I don't have to agree with him to be his friend, though I do pray that he will be open to God's direction in his life.

During the next summer I dated the college senior I talked about in earlier weeks – drop-dead gorgeous. Even though we were not officially a couple, I got great letters from him and responded in turn (with as much creativity as I could summon up) all through my senior year and for a few months beyond. That was enough to keep the gossips busy, especially after they got a good look at him on choir tour that year. My choir sang at the college he was attending just outside of New York City, and after the concert he came over to greet me with a hug and to take a short walk to catch up on everything. The timing was perfect. He brought me back to my choir bus just as we were leaving with everyone there to see our parting kiss – perfectly respectable for so public a farewell and yet as far as we ever went with kissing – which was the way I always liked to keep it.

I was busy with school and my trio; I had a boyfriend back home (as far as anyone knew); and I didn't need a boyfriend at school to keep my detractors (I suppose I had a few?) at bay. That really took the pressure off because there was no one I was all that interested in at school, and yet I managed to have dates for all of the important events during the year when it was nice to have one. But they were just one-shot friendship dates because there was that boyfriend back home... So I got to know better some great guys who asked me out for the big events during my senior year of high school, and I was free to have fun on our long weekend tours hanging out with the guys who came to my trio's concerts and took us out afterwards. I really enjoyed having no pressure to get serious by dating one guy exclusively before I was ready. It's like the main character said in the movie, *Gidget*: "This is the way I like it, the way I always liked it! ... You know, just kids horsing around having picnics, easy going stuff. None of that technique stuff for me!" That's the way I thought dating should be! – no pressure, as friends. Is there a way to share this concept with a guy/gal before going on a date, or is it a date-killer? Why is it so hard to keep it casual?

Bible Reading: *Philippians 2:1-5, Micah 6:8, Ephesians 4:15,*
     Matthew 7:1
 What do you think verses 3-4 are saying in *Philippians 2:1-5*?
 How does this apply to breaking up?
 How does this apply to dating in general?
 What is *Micah 6:8* saying?
 What does it mean to speak the truth in love, without judging?
  (*Ephesians 4:15*)
 How can a person speak the hard truth without judging?
  (*Matthew 7:1*)

Challenge: Bend over backwards to do the right thing if you break up with someone. Make sure they don't walk away feeling unlovable. More importantly, don't get too serious in a relationship when you're young. Keep it light, and breaking up will never be a tragedy.

"Do nothing out of selfish ambition or vain conceit, but in humility, consider others better than yourself."
           Philippians 2:3

WEEK 41

"The blind date"

I had one date that deserves its own week, even though it was only one date. Toward the end of my junior year, shortly after I had broken up with my boyfriend, a good friend from back East asked me if I would go on a blind date with his cousin who was visiting. It would be a double date. I agreed. At this point in my life, I was feeling bad about dumping one of the nicest guys in the school and I was questioning my tough standards on dating. Many of my friends seemed to be doing just fine with less stringent ones. Here I was a senior in high school and I had never even "made out" with a guy. (In my day "making out" was lots of kissing, often in a dark spot for a prolonged period of time. That's it.) I had no intention of kissing a guy just because he wanted me to, and certainly not more than once. But what was I missing? Did I want to find out? Was I even a little bit curious? These three questions had to be going through Eve's mind when Satan tempted her in the Garden.

Here was my opportunity. My blind date was a good guy who I would probably never see again. I could find out if I had "what it took" – whatever that meant – without the normal consequences in dorm and school life. After going out to eat, my friend from back home drove to a secluded spot where he and his girlfriend began to kiss. I was in the back seat and I decided to "let it rip!" I started to kiss this poor guy passionately like he'd probably never been kissed before in his life – *just to see what would happen.* (Yikes! What on earth was I thinking? It had to be temporary insanity.) I discovered one thing immediately: I did have "what it took." (It really doesn't take that much, girls.) Suddenly this nice Christian boy's hands were moving up inside my blouse and I had to block his path with my arm pressed tightly against my rib cage right below his target. He mumbled something about me being a nice girl and I heard my friend from back home chuckle in the front seat. I immediately regretted what I had done and jumped out of the car. The poor guy followed, apologizing all over the place.

What had I just done? I know this isn't popular to say but "I had kind of asked for it." I had certainly started that express train speeding down its track. But this still doesn't give a guy the right to go farther when we say, "Stop!" even if we do own part of the blame. If we are foolish enough to think that guys can simply "turn it off" when we have just intentionally "turned them on," we are very naïve. We've got a big responsibility here, girls. But the guys have an even greater responsibility because they are the ones most apt to be physically compelled to go to the next step. Guys need to guard against these situations even as the world is telling them to take advantage of them. It's kind of like playing with fire – once it's a huge blaze it's tougher to extinguish. This was one of the biggest mistakes of my young life on so many levels.

Have you ever gone on a blind date? How was it?
Have you ever wondered if it's worth it being good? Discuss.
Have you ever regretted *not* having tougher standards? Explain.
What does the Bible say about all of this?
> *It is God's will that you should be holy; that you should avoid sexual immorality; that <u>each of you should learn to control his own body in a way that is holy and honorable</u>, <u>not in passionate lust like the heathens</u> who do not know God…. The Lord will punish men for all such sins… For God did not call us to be impure, but to live a holy life. Therefore, he who rejects this instruction does not reject man but God, who gives you his Holy Spirit. I Thessalonians 4:3-8*
> <u>*I made a covenant with my eyes not to look lustfully at a girl.*</u> *Job 31:1*
> *…do not share in the sins of others. <u>Keep yourself pure.</u>*
> *I Timothy 5:22b*

Well girls, it is obviously easy to turn a guy on, but not nearly as easy to turn him off. You may have already learned that. It can get out of control fast, and if your date is not the kind of Christian that my blind date was, you may not have the strength to prevent him from going farther than you mean to go. We definitely have a power as women, and most of us have used it at one time or another. Come on, admit it: you've got the power. In our most dazzling outfit, we attempt to display or at least suggest this power. When trying to get a guy to notice us, we use this power. The power is in action sometimes even when we aren't aware of it. Fact of the matter is – we have such an amazing power that it should be considered a deadly weapon and handled with as much care as a loaded gun. So, please be more thoughtful in what you say and do, and *watch what you wear!* You might kill somebody with that outfit! ...or at least cause him to go where you don't want him to go in his thoughts. And it would be partly your fault because you know better.

My friend, whose cousin I dated, talked to me afterwards about our double date. He asked what was going on in the back seat. I told him I had temporarily lost my mind. That seemed to suffice, but he did that chuckle thing again. I never did see my blind date again (thank goodness); he was perhaps too embarrassed to return. I think I heard that he became a monk. (I'm joking.) I can imagine him using this story from another vantage point as an illustration on falling prey to temptation. I probably read as some kind of evil seductress. I wonder if he ever had a clue as to what was going through my mind as I led him down the path to mutual humiliation? I bet he's as glad as I am that we stopped when we did – or not. (He *is* a guy.)

The media and even science tells us at every turn that "everybody's doing it" and that we can't help ourselves – it's our animal nature. Not true. Unlike animals, we were made in God's image. Everywhere you look, on TV, in magazines and newspapers, movies and videos, everyone is jumping into bed with people they are not married to. The Bible calls that *fornication* (sex before marriage), *homosexuality* (sex with a partner of the same sex), and *adultery* (sex, while married, with someone other than your spouse). Check out these verses:

220

Flee from sexual immorality. All other sins a man commits are outside his body, but he who sins sexually sins against his own body. Do you not know that your body is a temple of the Holy Spirit, who is in you, whom you have received from God? You are not your own; you were bought with a price. Therefore honor God with your body. I Corinthians 6:18-20
Put to death, therefore, whatever belongs to your earthly nature: sexual immorality, impurity, lust, evil desires and greed... Colossians 3:5

Right and wrong have become reversed in our time. Wrong used to be what was done in secret, but it has gradually been brought out into the open and is often even celebrated. Right is now treated as sin once was. If we stand on what God's Word has to say we are considered prudish, judgmental or even certifiable. People mock us, because having intentionally put aside His Word, they want no reminder of it. We are looked upon as prejudiced if we have Biblical standards that guide our lives; but by their own reasoning, are they not just as prejudiced when they judge us? There is however, one major difference: we have a Source for our standards, and they have no real source and very few standards. Critics ask, "How can you claim to be right when that assumes others are then wrong?" But isn't that what everyone does? – even those whose mantra is "I'm OK; you're OK." They are assuming that if you don't agree with them, you are wrong. Isn't the idea of right and wrong inherent in the verb "to believe"? Not everyone can be right when beliefs are often diametrically opposed. But "right" (according to Biblical standards) is slipping into the shadows today and we are watching it happen before our eyes. (*Isaiah 5:20-21*) Our world lives as if many of the things that the Bible condemns as wrong are actually permissible and even "sacred" rights. And situational ethics are all the rage – sometimes right is right, but not always. Nonsense.

It's Satan in the Garden of Eden speaking to Adam and Eve: *"Did God really say... ?" (Genesis 3:1)* He would like us to doubt the truth. Yes, God *really* did say that these things are wrong. They were not the ten "*suggestions;*" they were (and still are) the ten "*command-ments.*" You want to play with fire? Then be prepared to get burned.

There's pregnancy, abortion, STD's (including AIDS), and staggering regret when you ignore God's instructions concerning sex. Your life following any of these outcomes will never be as perfect as it might have been. Not because God doesn't forgive, because He does! Praise God! But because in spite of forgiveness there will be scars. When we choose to ignore God's Word and go our own way, we can expect consequences, consequences that leave scars (emotional and physical) to remind us never to do it again.

But as I said, there is forgiveness, and scars do fade with time; so if you've got any scars, don't despair. Our God is a God of Love. He will apply the salve to the wounds Himself. Don't envy those who seem to be able to have it all. You cannot serve two masters. You either choose to obey God ... or not. Meanwhile, if you have ever had a guy force himself on you, talk to someone like your parents or your pastor. Don't be afraid to get some help. This guy may try the same thing with other girls. He needs to be stopped and called into accountability. You may think you asked for it, but nothing you did could make this acceptable. You may also discover that opening up about something like this actually helps you to get past it sooner. Your parents may show disappointment at first, but that is only because they want the best for you. God will help them to love you through this as He shows them and you what true love is.

Bible Reading: *Psalm 37:1-11, 73:2-14*

What does the *Psalm 37:1-11* above tell us not to do? To do?

This psalm tells us to wait on the Lord. How? Why?

Psalm 73:2-14 above talks about almost doing what?

What is verse 11 showing us?

Verse 13 is often the reason young Christians slip. Explain.

Challenge: Be a godly woman in action and dress.

> *"...How long will they be incapable of purity?... They sow the wind and reap the whirlwind..."*
>
> *Hosea 8:5-7*

WEEK 42

"Beyond my wildest dreams"

G oing on a singing tour for multiple weeks (twice) was the dream of this young girl's lifetime. We toured a good part of the United States and even got up into Canada a couple of times. We had a concert nearly every night after traveling for several hours each day. We usually had two concerts on Sundays and once we even had three. Either with our choir or alone, we got to sing in the West Point Chapel (awesome organ ... and the cadets weren't bad either.), the Mayo Clinic (for some person of note), on the steps of the Capitol in Washington DC (with some dignitaries present), in the Hollywood Bowl (with a handful of people wondering why we were singing so early in the morning to an empty house), in a famous restaurant on Hollywood Boulevard (with a honky-tonk piano), and in lots of churches, camps, schools, and other less typical spots. We had a blast!

My trio was made up of the three singers and a pianist, all girls. During our two long summer tours, we traveled with a pastor who gave a short message and a little talk to promote the schools at the end of each concert. Our high school, along with the Bible college and seminary on the same campus, was paying for our expenses. We were a small group and easily accommodated. Occasionally we stayed in Bible camps, colleges, or friends' homes, but more often, when we went into a town to sing in a church, one of the families of the congregation would take us all for the night. We got to stay in some of the most interesting and beautiful places. There is so much to see off the beaten track. In each part of the country people wanted to show us their special claims to fame, most of which were not on the map. And they did! It was a wonderful opportunity to learn so much more than pictures and books could reveal about our amazing United States of America.

In eastern Montana we drove out through the badlands on the ranch of the "King of the Marias" to a spot where the range gave away all around us. We were on a butte-like peninsula way up high overlooking the amazing badlands beyond. All I could think of was a commercial I had seen where a car was parked in the most unlikely spot on top of a beautiful high butte with no apparent way up. And here I was *in* that commercial! Another time, we were taken to the tops of the mountains in western Montana where we had to stop the car to let a shepherd and his flock of sheep cross the road. So cool. We continued up to our destination, a beautiful A-frame cabin sitting in a grove of birch trees overlooking an incredible view. We stayed on a misty and beautiful island off of Seattle's coast. We had lunch one day in a restaurant situated picturesquely right on top of a waterfall. There was a home in Laguna, California, with a view of the Pacific, right in the middle of movie stars' homes – and a side trip to Mexico. In Chicago we stood on the roof of a building downtown that was owned by the family we were staying with. The father gave us a personal tour of that city.

I remember a concert in Minneapolis where I was shocked when I heard the audience turn the page of the program and I realized just how many people must be sitting out in the dark multilevel auditorium to make that loud of a rustle. I became so nervous that I got the hiccups. Thankfully they stopped as we stepped out on the platform to sing and nervousness turned into sheer fright. Fright really is one of the cures for hiccups. We sang at a national youth event in Philadelphia and in several other large cities. I can still picture these places and concerts.

I will never forget the first time I heard my trio on the radio. We were headed west, traveling down the road in northwestern North Dakota flipping through the radio stations when we each took a deep breath as we heard the DJ's intro. (He was a friend and graduate from the high school we attended.) There we were, singing on the radio! I think it was KHRT out of Minot... Yikes! We heard ourselves a couple more times on the radio and were even on television a few times before it was all over. Once, on live TV in Rochester, Minnesota, when I had a four line solo in one of our songs, I drew a blank on the words and started with the third and fourth lines. Miraculously, they worked with the music, so I ended with the first and second lines. I could tell that the two other singers, one on each side of me, were anxious as to what I was doing; ... meanwhile our pianist just kept playing. There were better singers out there – but no one had more fun.

One of the dangers of not having printed music (we had words and sometimes chords) is that there was one time when our gifted pianist played one of our songs in a wrong and lower key. First our lowest voice dropped out, and soon after I dropped out, leaving our soprano singing tenor. We all laughed and started the song over in the right key. It's funny how the audience responds and met-aphorically "hugs" you with the warmth of their smiles when you make a mistake and laugh it off. Mistakes can also teach humility, an important quality to develop. At our graduation our pianist forgot what song we were singing and played the world's longest intro as she blended together the introductions to several songs, waiting for our nod to tell her that she had finally found the correct one. In retrospect, it was a nice tribute to the many songs we had sung throughout the year.

Have you ever gotten to do something beyond your wildest dreams? Explain.

Did you let it go to your head?

When pride comes, then comes disgrace, but <u>with humility comes wisdom</u>. Proverbs 11:2

<u>Pride goes before destruction</u>, a haughty spirit before a fall. Proverbs 16:18

Have you ever made a big mistake in public? Can you share it?

Are you afraid to make mistakes publicly? Why?

What does God say about this?

<u>Fear of man will prove to be a snare</u>, but whoever trusts in the Lord is kept safe. Proverbs 29:25

For <u>they loved praise from men more than praise from God</u>.
John 12:43
<u>Now go; I will help you</u> to speak and will teach you what to say.
Exodus 4:12

It's hard to express how much this time in my life affected the rest of my life. My confidence soared, not confidence that I was some kind of superstar, but confidence that no matter what I tried to do for Him, God was in it with me. Sadly, confidence is sometimes mistaken for arrogance, so many Christians go about their lives with a self-imposed "humility" that severely limits them. It can even become an excuse for doing nothing. The *arrogant* person places her trust in her *own* abilities and worth. The *confident* but *non-arrogant* person trusts in something or someone other than herself. And if that confidence is in the Lord and in His ability to work miracles through her, she has the power to do amazing things! Since we offer our gifts to God and not to men, we should step *boldly* into God's service (*Acts 4:31*) without fear and with full confidence in His ability to use us in a mighty way — and He will.

My confidence grew every time I failed because I learned that making mistakes is not fatal; it is simply part of the growth process. Hockey star, Wayne Gretsky, said, "You'll always miss 100% of the shots you don't take." You will most likely make mistakes as you engage *wholeheartedly* in life. And because I believed in giving it my all, my mistakes were usually *BIG*. To this day I still pray before I sing that God will give me the right reasons for singing and that I will put the message before the performance. All too often that can get reversed. Any time we step out in faith, there is the possibility of public humiliation, but never stepping out is worse – there's then no opportunity for sharing God's love with someone who needs it, or for personal growth. Stepping out doesn't always have to be highly public, but stepping out is a key ingredient to being salt and light.

Review: What is the difference between confidence and arrogance?
What does the Bible say about being bold?

The wicked man flees though no one pursues, but <u>the righteous are</u>
<u>as bold as a lion</u>. Proverbs 28:1
After they prayed, the place where they were meeting was shaken.
And they were all <u>filled with the Holy Spirit and spoke the word of</u>
<u>God boldly</u>. Acts 4:31

What does the Bible have to say about being salt and light?

<u>You are the salt of the earth</u>. But if the salt loses its saltiness, how can
it be made salty again? It is no longer good for anything, except to
be thrown out, and trampled by men. <u>You are the light of the world</u>. A
city on a hill cannot be hidden. Neither do people light a lamp and put
it under a bowl. Instead they put it on its stand, and it gives light to
everyone in the house. In the same way, <u>let your light so shine before</u>
<u>men, that they may see your good deeds and praise your Father in</u>
<u>heaven.</u> Matthew 5:13-16

How does God want *you* to be salt and light? What gifts has He given you to use for Him? I promise you that you will be much happier in life if you step out for Him in confidence. Don't let anything or anyone keep you from boldly serving the Lord and you will be thrilled when He uses you to lead another person into His kingdom. Did you know that that's the only thing you can take with you to heaven? Another person.

Bible Reading: *Deuteronomy 8:10-20*

What do the first few verses warn us of?

Verse 17 shows the sin that we may easily fall into. Explain.

What other gods are being talked of in verse 19?

What are the other gods of our age?

What dangers lie ahead for those who are very talented as salt and light?

Challenge: Whatever talent it is that you are using for God, always remember where it came from and pray continually that you will use this gift to His honor and glory and not yours.

"Delight yourself in the Lord, and He will give you the
desires of your heart."

Psalm 37:4

WEEK 43

"Going on record..."

I've told you a little about touring with my trio, but making records was a big part of the excitement. Our first two record albums were made in Fargo, North Dakota, in a small sound studio run by just one guy. Since we only had a piano to back us up, the technical part was not all that difficult. The first record was made at the end of our senior year of high school, so it was all ready for our West Coast tour after graduation that summer. We had most of the songs we needed for this album from a year of singing together. We sold out of the record on tour and had to make more. At the end of the summer, we each went back to our home states for college. Around Christmas time we were asked to go on a second tour during the next summer on the East Coast this time. This meant flying out to Minnesota to pull together a second album of songs. One thing that always bothered me (and here's my pride creeping in...) was that we made the records *before* our tours, and the songs sounded so much better *after* the tours when we had had time to improve upon them. I guess we couldn't get around that though. They needed the record on tour to sell it.

For our second album we flew out to Minnesota over spring break to an empty school where they put us up in the Bible college dorm, so we had several days of uninterrupted practice time. We had access to a piano and brought all of our ideas for new songs with us. We also had a couple of unrecorded new songs from the previous summer. Someone invited us out to eat once or twice and we ate out downtown a couple of times. At one point we got snowed in. The storm had distracted people and we had no way out, so we were pretty much on our own. We borrowed some popcorn from someone's stash in the lounge leaving money to cover its cost – so we got by with that for food for at least one day until they again remembered us. At the end of the week we made our second album. That summer we toured the Northeast with the new one – which also sold out. It helps to tour with them!

Our third record (which we shared with a male duo – one side each) was made out east in Long Island, New York, in a professional studio where a couple of highly popular secular bands had recently cut their records. Some of their hot-selling gold and platinum records were displayed on the wall in the entrance to the building. This time we had a whole crew of technicians and a small orchestra backing us up. Our pianist, a multi-talented man, had arranged all of the music, and we spent two entire Saturdays recording our songs. On the first Saturday the instruments were recorded. Our voices (heard only in the conductor's headset) had to sing along with them to give them the desired timing, but they were not recorded yet. The studio was just like they show on TV! There was a huge soundboard with the potential for many tracks behind a big glass window in the control room. The instruments were in the sound studio doing their thing while we were in a separate smaller glass enclosure singing along. It was time-consuming working out all of the logistics. If an instrument played a sour note at any time, the guy mixing the sound would just delete it later. And it somehow sounded as if that note was still in there and not at all sour! Very cool. (Kind of like what Jesus does for all of our sins when we confess them to Him. – "as far as the east is from the west, so far has he removed our transgressions from us." (*Psalm 103:12*) Consider them *deleted.*)

The following Saturday the voices were added. We were recording all day long and after hours of singing, the last song was feeling a little high for us by the time we got to it. So they slowed down the recording of the instruments just a little bringing the notes down within our temporarily limited range. We sang the song a little more slowly than usual in a slightly lower key and then they brought the whole thing back up to speed and back up to the correct key. If you think this is sneaky, you should see what they do today with recordings. The new technology can make your voice sound as if you were in a cathedral, and one person can play all of the instruments or sing all the harmonies one at a time to layer them into a finished product. You can make a good keyboard sound like just about any instrument you'd like, and drums are often pre-packaged. Almost anyone can sound good today with the new technologies. And today many more people are making records – only they're called CD's. I'm not sure they even know what records are anymore, ...though I hear they might be making a come-back?

Have you ever made a professional record, tape or CD? What was your experience like?

What do you think of the new technologies that can take sour notes and sweeten them and can remove all evidence of a mistake? Do you think you're hearing any of the real voices and instruments anymore? And it's definitely coming into the church. Equalizers, mixers, and special effects for reverb and what-not are standard for many churches. The first time I heard my voice with special effects I thought I had had a voice transplant! Wow! It was very cool. Though our church doesn't have all of the latest, I wouldn't mind wiring them in.

Do you have a problem with musical enhancements in the church? Why/why not?

Do you think it's okay to use whatever's available to praise the Lord? Why/why not?

For whoever is not against us is for us. Mark 9:40

The former preach Christ out of selfish ambition, not sincerely, supposing that they can stir up trouble for me while I am in chains. But what does it matter? The important thing is that in every way, whether from false motives or true, Christ is preached. And because of this, I rejoice. Philippians 1:17-18

For everything God created is good, and nothing is to be rejected if it is received with thanksgiving because it is consecrated by the word of God and prayer. I Timothy 4:4-5

I've always been an advocate of using the latest technologies to praise the Lord. We can't be afraid of new methods for getting the Word out there. I know of a young man who came to the Lord through Christian rap music, so we can't dismiss a musical genre just because we may not personally enjoy it. I do become concerned with the latest technologies in music though when the message of God's grace suffers because the method of delivery overshadows it. At times we may try to be too much like the world. We forget why we first started to sing and get drawn into "the show." If the smoke, the lights, and the special effects distract the audience from the lyrics (which are hopefully Christ-centered), then we've got a problem.

What does God's Word have to say about this?
> *Set your minds on things above, not earthly things.* Colossians 3:2
> Yet I hold this against you: *You have forsaken your first love.*
> Revelation 2:4
> *… don't you know that friendship with the world is hatred toward God?* Anyone who chooses to be a friend of the world becomes an enemy to God. James 4:4

Over the years I have heard people say that they were blessed by one of our records. I was always a little surprised … but thrilled. I guess when I started to travel and record with the trio, I was pretty young and just happy to be able to do the things I loved so much (singing, traveling the country) without it costing me more than the time it took to do these things. I was definitely doing this for the Lord, but I wasn't really thinking as much as I should have been about the reasons the school had for sponsoring our tours – for PR, to bring more students into the school to be immersed in God's Word. More importantly, I wasn't fully appreciating the big picture – another opportunity to share God's love with the world around us. Though we were given a small stipend for our time (because a couple of us would have otherwise needed to get regular jobs to earn money for college), all proceeds went to the schools, so we were obviously not in it for the money … or the fame. Admittedly, enjoyment was a big part of it.

In the next few years, as I visited the school from time to time, students now and then would tell me that it was my trio's visit to their churches that made them decide to go to my Christian boarding school. Wow! I guess the PR worked. I had been blessed down to my socks by being able to travel and sing for the Lord, but others had also been blessed. It just didn't get any better than that: "Give, and it will be given to you. A good measure, pressed down, shaken together and running over will be poured into your lap. For with the measure you use, it will be measured to you." *(Luke 6:38)* I guess I developed a better understanding of the true worth of our tours after the fact as I grew in my faith.

We all go through different stages in our walk with the Lord. We start as children all excited and engaged in carrying out great plans. But oftentimes that enthusiasm wanes and we wonder what all the excitement was about. We get older and are tempted by all kinds of things that take up our time and become gods to us. We may face persecution at school or at work from those who don't understand. We may begin to compromise to fit in or because it's just too hard to stay true to the Way. We are called back to God through some experience and we try to clean up our act. We may find ourselves compelled to share this amazing gift with others, but we face the complacency of many Christians around us. If any of this sounds familiar to you, be consoled that you are not alone, but not so consoled that you do nothing to remedy the apathy warned of in God's Word.

In *Revelation* there are seven different churches described, but they could just as easily be seven types of Christians or seven stages in a Christian's life, each with a different focus. These churches are also reflective of the different ages of the Christian church throughout history. In most cases each is first commended for what they are doing well and then condemned for mistakes being made. As you read the following two chapters in *Revelation* consider what each church is doing right/wrong and what type of "church" you are most like.

Bible Reading: *Revelation* – chapters 2 and 3

Ephesus – the new and excited Christian – hard work, perseverance, but losing first love

Smyrna – the persecuted Christian – trials, tribulations, but solid in faith

Pergamum – the compromising Christian – amoral, receptive to false teaching

Thyatira – the Christian who is barely holding on – love, faith, service, but too tolerant of sin

Sardis – the Christian who is rededicating and reforming – reputed to be alive, but near death

Philadelphia – the missionary Christian – ready to tell the world about Jesus

Laodicea – the complacent Christian – neither hot nor cold, unaware of the judgment coming

Challenge: Give generously to the Lord of your time, talents and tithe, and just watch Him "bless your socks off."

"But seek first His kingdom and His righteousness, and all these things will be given to you as well."
Matthew 6:33

WEEK 44

"California dreamin'"

We got to see a wide variety of lifestyles on our tours across the country. We stayed in farming communities, in big cities, in mountain towns and fishing villages. I got to see a calf being born on a small ranch in North Dakota, and to immerse myself for a day in a luxury lifestyle (at least to me) in a home south of L.A.. I remember falling in love with the beauty of the lakes and glaciers in the high Rockies, and with the misty enchantment of the San Juan Islands off the coast of Washington. Life was beginning to become so much more complex than I had ever realized it to be. So many different Christian lifestyles... Could they all be just as acceptable as the next?

The Midwest definitely had the most conservative youth groups. The East Coast was a bit more liberal, and the West Coast even more so. I attended a party in California where, among other things, many of the older Christian teens and young adults were drinking a good amount of alcohol. I had never been to a party before where alcohol was so widely "appreciated" – at least not one given by Christian friends. This was very different from my experience at home. I wasn't naïve enough to think Christian teenagers never drank back home, but it just seemed so matter-of-fact out there. Okay, so maybe I was more than a little naïve.

We stayed with a good friend in Laguna Beach, California, for a couple of days while on tour. We had a couple of concerts in the Los Angeles area. I had never stayed in such a beautiful house situated so impressively. Her home overlooked the Pacific and was right across the road from the beach where there was a very modern "train-wreck" of a house. Her family had dubbed the house that because it kind of looked like several train cars haphazardly piled up. We spent some time down on the beach and experienced a day in Disneyland. We lucked out there because our pianist had chipped her foot somehow and had to spend the day in a wheelchair (not exactly lucky for her). But because she was "handicapped," they let us go in through special entrances for the rides, so we got to get on each one almost immediately every time! Nice.

While staying in Laguna, I had the opportunity to sample (sip) several types of alcohol. I was curious as to what the big deal was about liquor and decided that this was a safe and opportune moment to find out. Ever been there? Now remember that though the Bible warns us about drunkenness, Jesus' first miracle was turning water into wine at a wedding, so this was not a plunge into sin. On the contrary, this was simple curiosity satisfied in a safe environment without excess. Jesus' miracle was not an open invitation to getting drunk – the Bible warns us frequently about drunkenness.

My mother would have been very happy because I hated everything. I thought it all tasted nasty. I remember being laughed at when I finally found something I liked only to discover that it was fruit juice without a drop of alcohol in it! I guessed I would never be the drinking type. And I never did learn to enjoy beer, wine, or even coffee for that matter – though I do like wine in cooking. I am still convinced that the first time people try any of it, they don't like it, and that they only keep on for social reasons, or to stay awake in the case of coffee. Same thing goes for smoking. Who likes it the first time? Why do we pursue something that has no immediate appeal as far as taste and smell go, and is proven to be unhealthy for us? I could never understand that.

Are the people you hang out with into drinking? Is it a problem? Have you tried it? Did/do you like it? Is that a problem? Discuss. Have you ever been drunk? How did you feel the next morning?

Was it wrong for me to try drinking alcohol? Why/why not?
What do you think of smoking? chewing?
What do you think the Bible says about all of this?

> *Wine is a mocker and beer a brawler; whoever is led astray by them is not wise. Proverbs 20:1*
>
> *For you were once darkness, but now you are light in the Lord. Live as children of light. Ephesians 5:8*
>
> *Do you not know that your body is a temple of the Holy Spirit, who is in you, whom you have received from God? You are not your own; you were bought with a price. Therefore honor God with your body. I Corinthians 6:19-20*

"Yes, yes," you say, "I know what the Bible says, but that was then and this is now. Besides, I'm too young to worry about that. I want to have fun and be part of the action. It's too much to ask to expect me to be that good while I'm still young. The temptations are too great. I'd be miserable and have no friends. When I get married and have a family, I'll have to settle down a little, so that's the time to start thinking about cleaning up my act." Trust me, I've been there. Now *is* the time. I was fortunate because I was never much influenced by what others thought; and since I didn't like alcohol or tobacco, it was probably much easier for me than for some of you. On the other hand, I have no regrets in this area and would love for you to be able to say that someday too. My friends who do have regrets would tell you the same thing I'm telling you: "Don't mess around with things that could be dangerous, are illegal for teens (drinking alcohol under 21; smoking under 18), cost a pretty penny, and taste and smell pretty nasty anyhow." So, what can the Bible teach us about this?

Incidents of drunkenness in Bible:

Noah (Read *Genesis 9:18-27*.)

> *Noah ... proceeded to plant a vineyard. When he drank some of its wine, he became drunk and lay uncovered inside his tent. Ham ... saw his father's nakedness and told his two brothers ... When Noah awoke from his wine and found out what his youngest son had done to him, he said, "Cursed be Canaan (Ham)! The lowest of slaves will he be to his brothers..."*

The result of Noah's drunkenness was disrespect by one of his sons who tried to draw his brothers into his sin and who then suffered the punishment of having his children cursed. Drunkenness can be a temptation that entices others to sin. Though this is an extreme example, we see it all the time with peer pressure for kids to start drinking. There are some people who can't handle alcohol at all. They make fools of themselves. And others then ridicule their foolishness, or worse – take advantage of it.

Lot (Read *Genesis 19:30-38.*)
Lot and his two daughters … settled in the mountains … lived in a cave … the older daughter said to the younger. "Our father is old, and there is no man around here to lie with us, as is the custom all over the earth. Let's get our father to drink wine and then lie with him and preserve our family line through our father … He was not aware of it … So both Lot's daughters became pregnant by their father … (gave birth to) Moab, … the father of the Moabites … Ben-Ammi, … the father of the Ammonites.

The result of Lot's drunkenness was that his daughters got pregnant by him and they mothered two sons who were the fathers of two large nations who became lifelong enemies of the Israelites. Again, an extreme example, but in less extraordinary ways we see people making really bad decisions all the time due to drunkenness.

I remember going to a college party at a nearby park that had been rented for the end-of-the-year freshman bash at the Hartford branch of UCONN. I watched as several acquaintances got drunk and started to do some pretty stupid things. The girls were the worst cases, barely clothed, tripping over things – sometimes into the pool – and getting way too friendly with guys they barely knew. I watched and thought, "and I should consider doing this *why*?" It all looked pretty sad to me. Why on earth would I want to give over control of what happened to me to chance or to another person who may not have my best interests at heart? No, thank you.

I have never been drunk in my life, not even close – which surprises people who know the stories of my more gutsy exploits in life. I think it goes back to my strong independent streak from childhood. At the same time, I doubt if anyone has had more fun in her young life. I am living proof that it's possible to have maximum enjoyment of one's life without promiscuity, alcohol or drugs.

There are other examples of drunkenness in the Bible, each with its negative consequences. And in spite of this being Jesus' first miracle, there are many warnings about drinking too much alcohol and taking part in other non-constructive actions. "Everything is permissible – but not everything is beneficial..." (*I Corinthians 10:23*)

Bible Reading: *Romans 14:19-23, I Corinthians 10:23-24,*
        10:31-11:1

In the first passage, what is "mutual edification"?

What should we be thinking of in making decisions about alcohol?

What does the first part of verse 22 mean?

What does verse 23 mean?

In *I Corinthians*, explain the tension between "permissible" and "constructive."

"All should be done for the glory of God." Explain how this works here.

Challenge: Never drink if you are under-age. Otherwise, never over-drink. (It's probably even smarter never to take one drink.) Be aware of those around you if taking a drink. Will you cause them to stumble or lose respect for God's people?

"Be careful, or your hearts will be weighed down with dissipation, drunkenness and the anxieties of life, and that day will close on you unexpectedly, like a trap."
Luke 21:34

WEEK 45

"Big decisions"

A ll good things come to an end, and high school is no exception. At graduation I was assigned to walk up the aisle to get our diplomas with a guy from Montana with whom I had won a three-legged race a couple of weeks earlier at a school field day. We had literally left the others in our dust! Now, exiting the auditorium, we were tempted to tie our legs together and go for it again. But we were growing up – and my mother was watching. We resisted the temptation. Overall my high school experience was outstanding – especially these last two years. Some of you may have a hard time relating to that. I know for some, high school was (or still is) an experience to endure. If you make it through relatively unscathed, you will be glad. For me, my junior and senior years were two of the best years of my life. I would wish you all the same.

Was (or is) high school a good or bad experience for you? Why? How could it have been (or could it be) better? Discuss. What could *you* have done (or can you do) to make it better?

Like most high school seniors I had to decide if, and then where to go to college. I had good grades and my SAT's were excellent, so I did have a few choices. I had no idea that I was a prime candidate for a scholarship, so I didn't apply for them. What did I know? I was a first generation college student and had no advice from parents or older siblings. There was no guidance counselor at my school at that time, and the East and West coast students were at a disadvantage in getting answers to questions about possible college choices. I was tired of living away from home or out of a suitcase, so I chose to go back home and go to the University of Connecticut, starting at the smaller branch nearer to home. I was accepted. Good thing, because I didn't apply to any other school. Back before UCONN became famous through basketball, it was relatively unheard of out in the Midwest, so several of my friends wanted to know why I was going to school way up in the "Yukon" in northern Canada. I explained to them that there was indeed another Yukon, spelled "U-C-O-N-N," and standing for the University of Connecticut. Today at reunions, they are all mildly impressed that I graduated from the big basketball school. Whatever.

Another big decision came along at the end of our second summer's trio tour. A country western singer had heard our trio either on the radio or on record; and he had contacted the producer of our first two records to see if we would be interested in auditioning to back him up on his next record. Wow. That would mean putting college on hold and taking a big chance. Interestingly, it was not an issue. We all knew that we had had enough of traveling and singing night after night, and we wanted the other American dream of a college education, a loving husband, two or three kids, and a nice home in the 'burbs. For me, the second step in this dream (loving husband) would not kick in until I had traveled the world and was at least twenty-eight years old ... according to my plans. Touring the country was fun while it lasted, but it was time to move on.

> Have you ever had a hard time making a big decision? What helped? Explain.
>
> Did you ask God for help?
>> But Jehoshaphat also said to the king of Israel, "*First seek the counsel of the Lord.*" I Kings 22:5
>> ... those who seek the Lord *lack no good thing*. Psalm 34:10b
>> *Make plans by seeking advice* ...obtain guidance. Proverbs 20:18

It's funny how the American dream changes over the years. I would guess my mother's dream was different from mine, especially the part about a college education and the home in the suburbs. College was not as valuable an asset for a woman in her day, and I'm not sure if the suburbs were even invented yet. She most likely wanted a few more kids than me too. (She got them.) Today's teenagers probably want exactly two kids (one boy and one girl), and their home in the suburbs is definitely bigger and more well-equipped than the one in my dream. My dream never had a whisper of divorce lurking in the background, but many teenagers in contemporary society are probably considering that possibility in the back of their minds, optimistically assuring themselves that that won't become a part of their futures. The threat of war has touched many generations, but terrorism has become a new enemy to fear. With America losing ground to other countries in manufacturing and technology, many today can only hope for job security in the future. All of these things play into the decision making process. And I believe the process gets more and more complex with every generation.

What is *your* dream?
What is the Lord's plan for you? Discuss.
Does the Bible say anything about it?

> *"For I know the plans I have for you." declares the Lord, "plans to prosper you and not to harm you, <u>plans to give you hope and a future</u>." Jeremiah 29:11*
>
> *He (the man of God) is like a tree planted by streams of water, which yields fruit in season and whose leaf does not wither. <u>Whatever he does prospers</u>. Psalm 1:3*
>
> *In my father's house are many rooms; if it were not so, I would have told you. <u>I am going there to prepare a place for you</u>. John 14:2*

Is there anything to fear?

> *Even though I walk through the valley of the shadow of death, <u>I will fear no evil, for you are with me</u>. Psalm 23:4*
>
> *The Lord is my light and my salvation – <u>whom shall I fear?</u> The Lord is the stronghold of my life – of whom shall I be afraid? Psalm 27:1*
>
> *So do not fear, for I am with you; do not be dismayed, for I am your God. <u>I will strengthen you and help you</u>; I will uphold you with my righteous right hand. Isaiah 41:10*

I have often said that there are really only two major decisions in life. The first – and most important – is to love the Lord "with all your heart ... soul ... mind." (*Matthew 22:37*) The second has two parts and has to do with marriage. Will you get married? And if so, to whom? The preeminence of the first decision is apparent throughout the Bible making it a shoo-in for first place. As far as I know, the relative importance of the second decision is not a universal idea. But because so many people today make poor decisions in marrying, and then pay for it for the rest of their lives, its importance seems to be "right up there" to me. Because divorce is so common today, fewer and fewer people have the conviction that marriage is going to be hard work and that it involves a commitment for life, *before God.* Not only do you make a pledge to your spouse, but if it's a Christian marriage, you also make a *vow before God* ("In the name of the Father, the Son, and the Holy Spirit.") – serious stuff. With a vow before God " ... (you) must not break (your) word ... " (*Numbers 30:2*).

Your husband (or wife if you're a guy) can build you up, can encourage you to succeed, can help you when you're down, and can be the key that helps to secure your children in the Lord. Or... he can tear you down, can discourage you, can bring you down, and can lead your children into the same mistakes he makes. Marriage is a very big decision and should never be taken lightly. Of course, if you *truly* love and follow the Lord with all of your heart, soul and mind, you will find a good mate, because the decision will be prayed over and made with Godly wisdom and help. Don't even consider this major commitment unless you have His approval. Make sure you get His input in all of your major decisions in life. Hint: *His* peace accompanies His approval.

In general we probably focus way too much on the temporal, the things of the here and now. Of course we need to do that to a degree, but we also need to remember that it is only the things of eternal value that will really matter in the end. And how little thought we give to them. So, when making *any* big decision, first pray.

A good checklist includes: 1. praying; 2. researching everything you can about the situation or the person of interest; 3. checking your motives – making sure you are not letting emotion cloud the facts and that your reasoning is sound; 4. getting good advice without pressure – talking your choices over with someone you trust who doesn't have his/her own agenda in the decision; 5. thinking through to the likely conclusion – without hoping for a change that may or may not happen down the road; and 6. considering all other options – asking yourself if there is a viable option, a better choice, or the opportunity to gain wisdom by waiting. And most importantly: 7. praying some more!

Bible Reading: *Colossians 3:2,15-17, Isaiah 30:21,*
Proverbs 15:31-33
What does *Colossians 3:2* tell us to do?
What does *Colossians 3:17* mean with regard to your decisions?
How should *Isaiah 30:21* affect your decision making?
What is *Proverbs15:31-33* talking about?

Do you have someone in your life who will tell you the truth in love and who has some wisdom in the area in which you are making a decision? Don't disregard your parents' advice, especially given their life experience and knowledge of who you are. Listen to them and share your thoughts humbly and without passion getting in the way.

Challenge: Try using some of the ideas above when making an important decision. Most especially pray, asking God for wisdom.

"Trust in the Lord with all your heart, and lean not on your own understanding. In all your ways acknowledge Him, and He will make your paths straight."
Proverbs 3:5-6

WEEK 46

"You talk too much!"

What can I say? It's true. All of my life I have talked too much. And the more nervous I've been, the more I've talked – which made me even more nervous. And so the vicious cycle began. As a child I chattered away about anything and everything, non-stop. When I started high school, I turned the volume down for a couple of years. It was like reading a book. You put it down for a few minutes and return to find yourself unsure of your place. But the story waits for you until you're ready to proceed. I felt as if my story was on hold for a while at the start of ninth grade. But it regained momentum soon enough. Even now, I have to remind myself that it's okay to have some dead space in conversations, that sometimes it's nice just to hang out with another person without saying anything at all. I hope I have improved in this area, but being a teacher probably hasn't helped – captive audience and all. I once went through my Bible and underlined all the verses that warn against talking too much. Not sure if it made much difference … but here are a few I found:

> *He who guards his lips guards his soul, but he who speaks rashly will come to ruin. Proverbs 13:3*
> *A man of knowledge uses words with restraint, and a man of understanding is even-tempered. Even a fool is thought wise if he keeps silent, and discerning if he holds his tongue. Proverbs 17:27-28*
> *Simply let your "Yes" be "Yes" and your "No," "No" ; anything beyond comes from the evil one. Matthew 5:37*
> *Women should remain silent in the churches. They are not allowed to speak, but must be in submission, as the law says. If they want to inquire about something, they should ask their own husbands at home, for it is disgraceful for a woman to speak in church. I Corinthians 14:34-35*

I love that second verse where it says that "even a fool is thought wise if he keeps silent." And they say the Bible has no humor. I'm hoping that that last verse was a message for *that* generation, kind of like women having to wear a covering on their heads (*I Corinthians 11:6*). It does refer to the law of that day – which may be an honorable loophole. If not, there are a lot of good people in solid Christian churches breaking the rules ... including me. Hmmm.

You would think that those verses on holding your tongue would scare me enough to straighten me out, but not so, not me. I'm a "stubborn square-head" (a phrase reserved *for* Scandinavians to be used *by* Scandinavians), and rarely does the second word, the noun, come without the first, its adjective. Change does not come easily to the stubborn. I have always felt inclined to say what I think. (Not always a good thing.) As I've grown older I've learned to control that urge a little better, but there have been times when I have wished something unsaid right after having said it. Have you ever done that? Talking got me into trouble in elementary school. It was the prime cause for most of my trips to the principal's office. In high school dropping humorous zings was again my number one reason for getting into trouble. But at least I wasn't headed for the principal's office now; those trips were reserved for much more serious offenders. On the other hand I wasn't winning any Brownie points with my teachers either.

A gift for talking came in handy in my short but notable elementary school acting career. It also came in handy in high school with oral reports and peer counseling. I joined the debate team which honed my argumentative skills, something I probably didn't need a lot of work with. I'm not sure that this gift helped much with my singing. As a high school teacher I had classes full of students who had no choice but to listen to me, and I developed my gift through my daily attempts to wow my classes both with excitement over the course content and with my latest attempt at humor. I'm not sure how well either worked out...

My conversational style would change with my audience. I would pick up a Midwestern accent instantly as I talked to a friend from North Dakota on the phone. I couldn't believe the sounds that were coming out of my own mouth! My vocabulary would soar when I talked to a writer friend of mine. My husband would chuckle in the background. Teenagers brought out the comedienne in me, and large groups of women brought out the mute in me. I'm not sure why I so easily adapted to my audience, but I think that that same ability came into play when I tried to blend in with the latest person with whom I was singing. I wondered once if all of these adaptations were a sign of weakness, a pathetic attempt to please everyone around me. *Is* that a weakness? Or is it a gift? Then again, maybe I was just good at being a chameleon. No, that wasn't it.

Do you talk a lot? Is it a problem? Why?

Do you feel that what you have to say is important? Explain.

Is it more important than what others have to say?

... Do not think of yourself more highly than you ought, but rather think of yourself with sober judgment, in accordance with the measure of faith that God has given you. Romans 12:3

Each of you should look not only to your own interests, but also to the interests of others. Philippians 2:4

Do you find yourself waiting impatiently for someone to stop talking so that you can finish what you had to say?

Love is patient, love is kind. It does not envy, it does not boast, it is not proud. It is not rude, it is not self-seeking, it is not easily angered, it keeps no record of wrongs... I Corinthians 13:4-5

Be completely humble and gentle; be patient, bearing with one another in love. Ephesians 4:2

But the fruit of the Spirit is love, joy, peace, patience, kindness, goodness, faithfulness, gentleness and self-control. Against such things there is no law. Galatians 5:22-23

Are you planning your next statement instead of listening to what someone else is saying?

He who answers before listening – that is his folly and his shame. Proverbs 18:13

... Everyone should be quick to listen, slow to speak and slow to become angry. James 1:19

"Your beauty should not come from outward adornment … Instead it should be that of your inner self, the unfading beauty of <u>a gentle and quiet spirit</u>, which is of great worth in God's sight." I Peter 3:3-4

If your answer to the second half of the first question above (Is it a problem?) is "no," but your answer to any of the following ones is "yes," then you need to rethink your answer to the first one. When I realized I would be talking a lot both in my career and in volunteer ministry positions, I began to pray for wisdom. I figured that if I was going to do a lot of talking, it would be good if I had something worthwhile to say. (You'd have to ask someone else if God answered that prayer.)

It has been said that D.L. Moody, though a powerful evangelist, did not have a command of the idiosyncrasies of the English language. *Christianity Today* called him "an awkward country boy with a grade-school education" who "became the greatest evangelist of his time." He would at times murder grammar and sentence structure. But this didn't seem to impact his ability (through the Holy Spirit) to touch a generation of people with God's message. We sometimes put too much of an emphasis on the correctness of grammar over the correctness in what it is that we are actually saying. Being too perfect in our presentation may even cause us to lose some listeners. Not that we should try to make mistakes – we should always try to do our best *given the circumstances.* But we do need to remember to get our priorities straight.

There are of course plenty of times that a gift for gab is a real benefit, but every strength has its inherent reflective weakness. (e.g.; leadership can become pushiness, compassion can lead to over-sensitivity, etc.) A certain degree of eloquence helps in teaching; it's an asset if you find yourself in leadership positions where directing, encouraging, and admonishing might be necessary. I've been the speaker during seminars many times, both in my career as a math teacher and in my ministry commitments. Being good with words is essential in these scenarios, as in this present case – writing a book – though nothing is said aloud in this case so some of the rules don't apply. I have often told my students that they may have the most wonderful insights in all the world, but if they are unable to express themselves, to get their thoughts across to others, then their ideas will be lost or attributed to the next person to come up with them. But remember – the written word can be just as motivating as the spoken word, so you don't necessarily need to be a public speaker; you just need to be able to express yourself well in some form that captivates your audience's attention and gets your message across.

When engaged in speaking or conversation, we should have something that is both truthful and worthwhile to share, and present it in such a way that we show our respect for others by *actively listening* to them when they speak. Remind yourself often of these things and you will become a better listener, a better communicator, and a person whose ideas are valued. You will also become a better friend as you respect your friends' input into your conversations. And please pray for me because I still struggle with talking too much.

Bible Reading: There are two sides to the talking issue:
Having trouble talking: *Exodus 3:1-12, 4:10-14a*
How did God speak to Moses in *Exodus 3:1-12*?
Was Moses excited to do what God asked of him? Explain.
What was his excuse in *Exodus 4:10-14a*?
How did God react?
Having no trouble talking: *Ecclesiastes 5:1-3, I Corinthians 13:1-9, Psalm 19:14*
According to *Ecclesiastes 5:1-3*, what is the "sacrifice of fools"?
According to *I Corinthians 13:1-9*, how important *is* eloquence?
What is of the greatest importance?
According to *Psalm 19:14*, what we should strive for?

Challenge: *Always* try to stop and think before you speak.

> *"When words are many, sin is not absent. but he who holds his tongue is wise."*
> *Proverbs 10:19*

WEEK 47

"Exceptional pleasures"

I enjoyed singing with my trio for a few years even after high school because our soprano moved out East. She and our pianist were originally from North Dakota and Minnesota, respectively. Our second alto (lowest harmony) was from New York, and I (middle harmony) was from Connecticut. When our soprano moved to New York, the trio was able to do some regional singing. This is when our third record was made. The only awkward part was that our pianist was replaced by a local superstar. He was very good so that wasn't the problem, but somehow it didn't seem quite right. After all these years, and hours upon hours of practice, we were singing with a different accompanist. Then again, we had a mini- orchestra and a rock musician (or two?) backing us up on this record, so it was already noticeably different from the first two, and the piano was somewhat obscured by all of the other things going on instrumentally. (Somehow that made me feel better for the fourth member of our "trio.") We missed our regular pianist, but the new one was a great guy and was actually the force behind this record. Without him, I'm not sure it would have happened.

After a couple of years our soprano moved back to the Midwest and we contented ourselves with occasional reunions. No matter how long it had been, it always seemed like yesterday when we sang together again. We had gotten to the point where we even knew when the others would take a breath. During those years I was in several other groups, but nothing as tight in harmony and timing as this trio. The only thing that came close to it in enjoyment for me was singing with my cousin. I enjoyed all of the groups I was in, but there was something *different* about singing with the trio and with my cousin – exceptional pleasures.

Funny thing about singing with my cousin was that it was anything but tight. I don't think we ever did a song the same way twice. That may have been part of the fun for me. I liked the extemporaneous uncertainty of it all. And in spite of the shocking liberties we took with songs, we weren't too bad. First of all we had a great blend. Secondly, we always had fun … and it showed. He had a little bit of an Elvis thing going on with his voice, and he played a "mean" guitar. I would do most of the harmony jumping from higher to lower as needed. We kept it close and had a great time practicing and singing together. I would do a creative vocal imitation of one of the instruments in an original recording, and would often get him laughing at my heavy metal guitar, funky drums, or soulful horn. If he wasn't quite sure how something went, I would sing it for him, complete with all of the instrumental parts. (I was particularly effective on the musical interludes between vocals.) In the 70's we had about forty songs (secular and Christian) worked up that we performed at a coffee house in Massachusetts and wherever else they'd let us sing. We must have sung at 10-12 weddings and innumerable church services. Much as I loved it, at one point I was so tired of singing Noel Paul Stookey's *Wedding Song,* that I was glad to sing *anything* but that at the next nuptial event we were to grace.

What has been an exceptional pleasure in your life?
Is it still a part of your life?
Do you like things well-planned or spontaneous? Why?
Is one a better way to live? Discuss.
> But all things must be done properly and <u>in an orderly manner</u>.
> I Corinthians 14:40
> I will bless the Lord <u>at all times</u>; His praise shall <u>continually</u> be in my mouth. Psalm 34:1

As I began to write this book my cousin was very sick. (I told you about him in an earlier week.) The doctors said they could do no more and that it was just a matter of time before the brain cancer (glioblastoma multiforme) would take his life. I know that I have never prayed about anything like I did about this, except maybe my mother's cancer. But the problem remains: How do I know God's will? I've asked myself that question several times in my life, but especially when I find myself praying for life or health for someone I love.

I know the disciples were reprimanded by Jesus for not having enough faith when they failed to heal a man's son: *"Lord, have mercy on my son ... He is an epileptic and is suffering greatly ... I brought him to your disciples, but they could not heal him. 'O unbelieving and perverse generation,' Jesus replied, 'How long shall I stay with you? How long shall I put up with you? Bring the boy here to me.'"* (*Matthew 17:15-17*) I feel that he's calling me out too sometimes. Why don't the prayers of believing Christians seem to make any difference in some cases? Why can't we tell what his will is in certain situations? Or is the outcome his answer? I had asked God to heal my cousin in such a way that the doctors couldn't take the credit. Was that wrong?

Will God answer all of our questions? Why or why not?
"Before they call, I will answer; while they are still speaking, I will hear." Isaiah 65:24
This is the assurance we have in approaching God: that if we ask anything according to his will, he hears us. I John 5:14
Give ear to my words, O Lord, consider my sighing. Listen to my cry for help, my King and my God, for to you I pray. Morning by morning, O Lord, you hear my voice; morning by morning I lay my requests before you and wait in expectation. Psalm 5:1-3
O my God, I cry out by day, but you do not answer, by night and am not silent. Psalm 22:2
To you I call, O Lord my Rock; do not turn a deaf ear to me; for if you remain silent, I will be like those who have gone down to the pit. Psalm 28:1

Is it a problem for you that God may not always answer when we call? Explain.

What are some examples of unanswered prayer in the Bible?
You came back and wept before the Lord, but he paid no attention to your weeping and turned a deaf ear to you. Deuteronomy 1:45

So Saul asked of God ... But <u>God did not answer him that day.</u>
I Samuel 14:37b
Then <u>they will call to me but I will not answer;</u> they will look for me
but will not find me. Proverbs 1:28
<u>If I had cherished sin in my heart, the Lord would not have listened.</u>
Psalm 66:18

These verses seem to be all over the place: immediate answers, delayed answers, unheard requests, refused answers, etc.. What's going on? God is *always* the same in His righteousness, His love, and His omnipotence, so what else could it be? Us? Sometimes the answer is "no" or "it's not the right time"; other times the answer will not come because of something in the life of the one praying. Hardness of heart (*Proverbs 28:9*), cherished sin (*Psalm 66:18*), doubting (*James 1:6*), and poor motives (*James 4:3*) are a few of the problems that could have something to do with it. We need to have a healthy relationship with God to expect Him to hear us. This is not like sending our wish list to Santa because after all ... we've been pretty well-behaved this year so we must have made his "good" list. First of all, Santa is just a sweet legend (okay, one that has grown into a multi-million dollar business.). Secondly, it's got nothing to do with us deserving anything (because we don't) and everything to do with God's love for His people who talk with Him daily.

I know that healing is a gift of the Holy Spirit (*I Corinthians 12:9,28-29, James 5:14-16*), and that it can be used in mighty ways, but when we were encouraged to go to a healing service in southern Connecticut one evening to seek help for my cousin, I was sadly disappointed. My cousin, a man of faith and obedience, was told that all he had to do was to believe and he would be healed. He knew that God could heal him and he did believe. But at the end of the service my cousin remained unhealed. The speaker took time to meet with us in a small group and I asked the question most on my mind: "If faith will heal a true believer when he or she asks, why do Christians *ever* die here on earth? Wouldn't the most Godly live forever given enough faith (even just a mustard seed's worth)? I was concerned that my cousin was being persuaded to believe that maybe he just didn't have enough faith. The speaker/healer had to admit that there is a time when God calls each of us home. I asked how we were to know when that was? He never really answered that. In retrospect, after my cousin had finally gone to be with the Lord, I was comforted by the fact that God had now completely healed him … and I wondered if that may have been the answer to our prayers all along.

I do still believe that God heals miraculously today because I've seen it happen, but not in every case, even with His faithful children (e.g.; Paul's "thorn in the flesh" of *2 Corinthians 12:7*). Sometimes God answers even before we ask; sometimes He teaches us patience; sometimes, when we are not in a right relationship with Him, He does not listen. There are times I feel like David, the psalmist, when he cried out to God:

> *"How long, O Lord? Will you forget me forever? How long will you hide your face from me? How long must I wrestle with my thoughts and everyday have sorrow in my heart?"*
>
> *Psalm 15:1-2*

Bible Reading: *2 Samuel 12:15-23*

Who is this child for whom David is praying?

What else did David do besides pray?

What did David do when his child died? Does that seem backwards?

When they questioned his failure to mourn, what did David say?

So was there an answer to prayer here? What was it?

Challenge: Look for God's answer in requests made to Him, not for your own will. Even Jesus in Gethsemane left it all up to His Father. (*Matthew 26:39*)

> *"Ask and it will be given to you, seek and you will find, Knock and the door will be opened to you."*
>
> *Matthew 7:7*

WEEK 48

"You are a dangerous thinker!"

"You are a dangerous thinker!" I will never forget those words being spoken to me. I was always thinking outside the box. I couldn't help it. I sometimes had the most outrageous thoughts sprint through my mind. Ever had that happen? I had an overactive imagination. So, back to my story: I was attending an adult Bible study at my church. I was in college and was the youngest one there. We were talking about God's plan of salvation and my mind began to race, "Could there be life on other planets or in other galaxies?" I asked the leader of the class, my uncle and mentor, if God might have had a different plan somewhere else in the universe, or if He would have had to work out salvation there in the same way He did here. The room got very quiet before someone in the room pronounced the death knell for any other questions that I might have asked. "You are a dangerous thinker!" He wasn't smiling. I remember feeling warm and thinking that I must be an awful Christian to have asked such an obviously heretical question.

Well, I did what most young people would have done in my situation. I quit going to the class. Many would have quit because they were embarrassed or angry, but I had a different reason. I knew that my question had shaken up the people in the class. And their reaction had shaken me up. I loved these people and the last thing that I wanted to do was to shake their faith or to make them uncomfortable with my heresies. I knew if I stayed I would either do that again and again, or I would become frustrated withholding my questions. (Okay, I was a little embarrassed too.) The only trouble was … where *could* I ask my questions? My uncle was the one I had always gone to with spiritual questions, yet he had just become unavailable. I was still a strong believer, but I needed help to grow in my faith and in my ability to "give a reason for my faith." Now what was I to do?

> Do you ever think "outside the box"? Care to share?
> Have you ever felt like a heretic? Explain.
> Have you experienced the embarrassment of asking the *wrong* question at the wrong time?
> How did you react?
>> But as for you, <u>continue in what you have learned</u> and have become convinced of, because you know those from whom you learned it, and how from infancy you have known the holy Scriptures, which are able to make you wise for salvation through faith in Christ Jesus. All Scripture is God-breathed and is useful for teaching, rebuking, correcting and training in righteousness, so that the man of God may be thoroughly equipped for every good work. 2 Timothy 3:14-17
>> Don't let anyone look down on you because you are young, but <u>set an example</u> for the believers in speech, in life, in love, in faith and in purity. I Timothy 4:12
>> <u>If any of you lacks wisdom, he should ask God</u>, who gives generously to all without finding fault, and it will be given to him. But when he asks, he must <u>believe and not doubt</u>, because he who doubts is like a wave of the sea, blown and tossed by the wind. James 1:5-6

I was confused but I didn't "throw the baby out with the bath-water." Isn't that an outrageous cliché? It means to throw something valuable away with the worthless. If I had thrown my faith away because I had had doubts, I would have been doing that. Fortunately, I was smarter than that, though I admit that I was wandering in a fog for a while looking for a way out. The way out came through a most unexpected channel. I was majoring in English at UCONN at this time (the math major came a few years later), and I was taking a writing course. We were using an anthology that had many examples of different types of writing. When we began to look at argumentative literature we read an excerpt from *Mere Christianity* by C.S. Lewis. I was excited by his thinking. I looked at the footnote. (I never looked at footnotes.) I got the name of the author and the book, neither of which I had ever heard of before, and went to the bookstore to find it. So this was it then, my introduction to my Christian mentor … in a secular English class. For this I thank God.

God had seen me wandering in the mist and he had sent me a guide to show me the way forward. I was immediately intrigued by the works of C.S. Lewis. *Mere Christianity* was a stepping stone to other books of his and then on to works from which he quoted. A whole new world opened up to me. Lewis' "space trilogy" showed me that I was not the only one who had had outrageous thoughts of other planets with other means of salvation. Not that I believed in Martians, but what made them an impossibility? Maybe it was okay to have these ideas rattle around in my head. Maybe I wasn't a heretic after all. I had begun to question the very foundations of my beliefs and here was a way to study them at a deeper level and to come to a more mature understanding of what these beliefs really meant and the logical progression of thought that flowed from them. This was way beyond cool. My spiritual sanity was saved. Since then, I have discovered another great book that talks about doubt and confusion, and how these are not unusual for Christians with inquisitive minds, but how they also demand some type of reaction. (You can't just let them fester.) *In Two Minds – the dilemma of doubt and how to resolve it* by Os Guiness was a particularly good read. I felt as if the author had been inside my head and had read my very thoughts.

Who helps you with spiritual questions? your parents? your pastor?

Who is your favorite Christian author? Why?

Questioning things is good … as long as you remember the cardinal rule: "Don't throw the baby out with the bath water." So many new Christians fold at the first sign of a doubt. Doubts are actually growth opportunities if you sprinkle on a little wisdom. In *Mark 9:24* a man says, "I do believe, help me overcome my unbelief!" Smart guy. He recognized his doubts and asked for help. The deeper your questions, the more deeply you might understand your heavenly Father if you look to Him for the answers. It's so exciting to find the truth shining through the debris of doubt's destruction. The neat thing (or one of them anyway) about God is that He is strong enough to stand thorough examination. When we use our doubt or confusion to encourage us to dig deeper, we grow. It's like the "Parable of the Sower" in *Matthew 13*. When we first become Christians our roots don't go very deep. Through victory over adversity and resolution of doubts, looking to the Bible for the answers, we grow and our roots go deeper. But we need to be sure to plant ourselves in fertile soil, the rich soil within God's Word. So, don't be afraid of doubts; be afraid *not* to look for the truth when doubts come to give us another opportunity to grow. The worst thing you can do is to ignore them. "The truth is *in* there."

What does the Bible say about answers to questions?
> So <u>we fasted and petitioned our God</u> about this, and He answered our prayer. Ezra 8:23
> ... Ask and it will be given to you; <u>seek and you will find</u>; knock and the door will be opened to you. Luke 11:9
> Then Gideon said to God, 'Do not be angry with me. Let me make one more request. ...<u>This time make the fleece dry and the ground covered with dew.</u>' That night God did so. ... Judges 6:39-40

I love the story of Gideon and the fleece in *Judges 6*. In order to be sure of God's direction in his life, Gideon asks the Lord to have a fleece that he leaves out in the night air to be wet and the ground around it to be dry when morning comes. This God does. But then, Gideon asks the request in the Bible verse above – that God reverse the miracle and have the fleece dry and the ground wet in the morning. Again, God answers his prayer. I have used this miracle of the fleece often in my life. When seeking God's will, I lay out a fleece in a metaphorical sense. I ask God for something unusual but specific (something that wouldn't normally occur) to happen to assure me of His will. He has graciously answered my prayer each time. I have resorted to this only in decisions of real importance in my life – I guess I would feel out-of-line abusing God's faithfulness with trivial requests. But maybe I'm wrong there?

God welcomes our questions. Sometimes He answers them before we even ask, but at other times, the answers don't present themselves right away. Sometimes God wants us to learn to dig for them; sometimes He wants us to learn to wait patiently; sometimes we are not in a right relationship with Him and He will not listen. Sometimes the answer is "no," or "not now." He will often use others in our lives to resolve our questions, but our first line of offense against doubt is to understand the Bible better. We do that by reading it. Remember, *Ephesians* calls the Bible a sword, an offensive weapon. This could obviously come in handy in spiritual warfare. And it is Scripture that Jesus uses in *Matthew 4:1-11* to fight Satan in His own temptation. Answers to our questions come more quickly as our knowledge of God's Word grows. I remember an old saying from when I was a kid: "If you feel far from God, guess who moved." God calls us His friends in *John 15:15,* but in what kind of friendship does one person ignore the other all week long, acknowledging them only for an hour every seventh day? ... in spite of the fact that that friend has been right there next to her at every moment?

There is one parable that Jesus shares in the New Testament that deals with the need to dig deeply into God's Word to get a good root system of resources from which to grow. It shows four different types of people who respond to God's Word in different ways. Which type are you? Do you feed yourself daily on God's Word? Are you digging deeply to find answers to your questions? Or do questions cause you to doubt and walk away without a second thought?

Bible Reading: *Matthew 13:3-9, 18-23, 44-45*

> What is this parable talking about? (verses 3-9) Evangelism? Christian growth?
>
> How can you "listen" but not "hear"? Discuss.
>
> Who/what can interfere with our understanding of God's Word? (verses 18-23)
>
> Why is it important to go deep with our growth?

Why is it that troubles and worries, wealth and success can be so dangerous?

Try to go into each of these thoughtfully.

What might that pearl be that is talked of in the last two verses? (verses 44-45)

What do you do when you have doubts? Discuss.

Challenge: Make sure you have no unresolved issues with sin and that you actually have a close personal relationship with God. Then ask Him your questions. Talk to Him every day, all through the day.

"...I do believe; help me overcome my unbelief!"

Mark 9:24

"Random acts of nonsense"

I remember shopping with my boarding school friends in a mall on choir tour when one of them decided to *be* Norwegian. Hmmm. She was already of Norwegian descent, but she thought it would be fun to make-believe that she was actually visiting from Norway and unable to speak English. She began to use the little Norwegian she knew (mostly lines from a table prayer and assorted songs she knew) to talk to us, pretending to be discussing the dresses that she was looking at for the prom. The store clerk would look to the rest of us to translate and we got neatly drawn into the strange affair. Since none of us could actually converse in Norwegian, all of our talking was nonsense, and it took real effort to keep it sounding somewhat authentic. You just never knew what this friend would come up with next.

Then there was the time I was on the subway in New York City with another good friend during the second summer working at the college in Westchester county, New York. We had gone into the city to visit her grandmother and had stayed too late. (shades of *Little Red Riding Hood*?) We were alone on the subway one night when a group, no a *gang* of guys came into our car. One had a long knife with which he appeared to be cleaning his nails. They all looked at us menacingly. Who knows why? – probably just to scare us. Suddenly, my friend started to act as if she was intellectually challenged. You might be offended by this, but it worked. As she started to feign fear and difficulty in speech and thought, I feigned an attempt to help her. The gang began to talk amongst themselves, laughed a little, and moved to the next car deciding that we were not worth their time. Mission accomplished. Even some of the toughest seem to have difficulty giving a hard time to the mentally handicapped. (There is still hope for them.) My friend was from Long Island and a lot more city-wise than I was. I was impressed with how she pulled that off. She was always interesting, never boring.

My high school roommate (the second one) came out East to visit from Minnesota. We went down into New York City, where most visitors wanted to go, and had a great time checking out the sights. On the way home my '65 Mustang's tailpipe started to sound more like a Harley 1200 motorcycle (loud and rumbly). We stopped at a pull-over on the Westside Highway along the Hudson River and I got under the car to see what was wrong. The tailpipe was dangling and would certainly fall off soon if not adjusted. I opened the trunk to get a wire hanger for a temporary fix, when my friend began to talk very excitedly about a bunch of guys headed our way up through the nearby park. I said I just needed a couple more minutes when she yanked the tailpipe off of my car and threw it into the back seat. I was shocked. To this day I can't understand why she wasn't burned. We drove the rest of the way with the windows open to air out the fumes coming from under the car.

Nonsense abounded when I waitressed nights (10 pm – 6 am) at the local international airport the summer after my sophomore year of college. I dated a guy there whose best friend drove a food truck right into a jet out on the tarmac! Very memorable. I got invited into the airport radar tower one night (before modern security) to check out how they directed flights. Very interesting. Dean Martin (too young to remember this singer/actor?) came through another time. Very drunk. I served (and entertained) nearly one hundred Swedish women from a charter flight all by myself (plus one cook) once in the middle of the night and didn't get a dime for a tip. (I learned later that they include the tip in the bill over there.) That was discouraging. I met a late night disc jockey for the local classic rock station and got invited to visit the radio station in Hartford. He talked to me on the radio during my night shifts a few times. That was fun. One waitress (not me) got a $100 tip for a cup of coffee from a guy who had just won big in Vegas. ($100 was more like $1000 back then.) That was nice (for her). There was a farmer who thought he owned part of a runway so he cut the fence and let his cow out onto the field. They actually had to tranquilize the cow one night to clear the runway. That was exciting. Also cool was the huge transport that landed on its way to Chernobyl in Russia, and the needle-nosed SST from France that made an emergency landing one night. The airport was a great summer diversion – a lot of fun. Nonsense everywhere.

Two of my best friends were living with me at my mom's house that summer, my first high school roommate (the princess), and the lowest alto in my trio. They were both very pretty, very sweet, and very smart – triple threats. Sometimes it was a little discouraging hanging out with the alto because she was so *very* striking that every guy who met her was immediately enthralled by her. …but not really, because in spite of that, she was surprisingly humble – and an amazing friend. We took trips into New York City and Boston to visit museums, see the sights, and have fun. We did all that and more. Two of us worked nights, one worked days, and one (me) also took a summer college course. That made it tough to schedule things, but we worked it out – even having only two twin beds to sleep in, because rarely were we all sleeping at the same time. (Then I got the floor.) The beds were always warmed up for the next occupant. We did more than normal people would ever consider doing in seven or eight weeks, functioned on an average of *maybe* five hours of sleep a night. We will probably never forget the summer of '71.

Webster defines "fun" as "what provides amusement or enjoy-ment." The Bible doesn't say much about fun. It talks a lot about peace, joy and love, but fun sometimes seems as if it might even have a negative connotation in the Bible. Am I missing something? Is this why some people think that the Bible just throws cold water on their good times? Or … could it be that peace, joy and love are just so much more satisfying than fun that God doesn't waste time on the trivial? Fun may simply be overrated. The joy of the

Lord is so much deeper and more meaningful. Maybe we should focus more on joy? Joy does seem to have a more enduring quality, whereas fun seems to have short expiration limits. I can recount moments filled with fun in my life, but joy is a quality that seems to encompass huge amounts of time, including even tragic events, as odd as that seems.

Is there anything wrong with *having fun*?
> *"Everything is permissible for me" – but <u>not everything is beneficial</u>. "Everything is permissible for me" – but <u>I will not be mastered by anything</u>. I Corinthians 6:12*
> *Command those who are rich in this present world not to be arrogant nor to put their hope in wealth, which is so uncertain, but to put their hope in God, <u>who richly provides us with everything for our enjoyment</u> I Timothy 6:17*

What is it that is most important in the long run?
> *For what I received I passed on to you as <u>of first importance</u>: that <u>Christ died for our sins</u> according to the Scriptures, that <u>he was buried</u>, that <u>he was raised on the third day</u> according to the Scriptures ... I Corinthians 15:3-4*
> *The most important one, ... is this: "Hear, O Israel, the Lord our God, the Lord is one. <u>Love the Lord your God with all your heart and with all your soul and with all your strength</u>. The second is this: <u>Love your neighbor as yourself</u>. There is no commandment greater than these." Mark 12:29-31*

Are you a joyful person? Are you a loving person? Does it matter?
> *<u>Be joyful always</u>; ... I Thessalonians. 5:16*
> *... Do not grieve, for <u>the joy of the Lord is your strength</u>. Nehemiah 8:10*
> *But the fruit of the Spirit is <u>love, joy</u>, peace, patience, kindness, goodness, faithfulness, gentleness and self-control. Against such things there is no law. Galatians 5:22-23*
> *And now these three remain: faith, hope and love. But <u>the greatest of these is love</u>. I Corinthians 13:13*

C. S. Lewis' Book, *Surprised By Joy*, has always been a favorite of mine – especially as he describes "the pain of Joy and its foreshadowing of heaven." Is it pain because we long for it so deeply? Lewis calls Joy "an unsatisfied desire which is itself more desirable than any other satisfaction." He recounts his discovery of this fact as a young atheist: "As I stood beside a flowering currant bush on a summer day there suddenly arose in me without warning, and as if from a depth not of years but of centuries ...an 'enormous bliss.' It was a sensation of course, of desire; but desire for what? ...and before I knew what I desired, the desire itself was gone. ...That unsatisfied desire ... I call it Joy." Repeatedly in His life he would have glimpses of Joy: "That walk I now remembered. It seemed to me that I had tasted heaven then. If only such a moment could return!" In comparing pleasure with Joy he says, "I sometimes wonder whether all pleasures are not substitutes for Joy." Have you ever felt that "enormous bliss"? I have, and over the oddest things: a song, a child, a view. I have discovered tears rolling down my cheeks over what I recognized as that ultimate Joy yet to be fully experienced. I believe it's God revealing little glimpses of heaven and of Himself.

So, in Lewis' style, he digs deeper: "In reading Chesterton, as in reading MacDonald, I did not know what I was letting myself in for ... a sound atheist cannot be too careful of his reading. There are traps everywhere." Ultimately, "Joy itself ... turned out to be of no value at all. All the value lay in That of which Joy was the desiring." But he did not yet ask, "*Who* is the desired?" only "*What* is it?" He soon discovered through the writings of those quickly becoming his favorite authors (especially Chesterton) that "... Christianity itself was very sensible, 'apart from its Christianity.'" In other words: "mere" Christianity is simple, but it becomes difficult through the embellishments of the church's traditions and ponderous orthodoxy. He discovered that "God was Reason itself ... Total surrender, the absolute leap in the dark, were demanded." He was amazed that God would accept a convert on such terms. "But what, in conclusion, of Joy? ...To tell you the truth, the subject has lost nearly all interest for me since I became a Christian... It was valuable only as a pointer to Something other and outer." Only Lewis could boil it down so well: *Our search for joy is really a search for God!*

Random acts of nonsense occur every day as mankind dismisses the evidence for God all around him. We get caught up in the search for fun, pleasure, happiness and even Joy and ignore the signposts that continue to point to God, the Source of all true Joy. C.S. Lewis was a brilliant man, once an atheist, who was wise enough to lay down his pride and examine that evidence. He discovered Truth. I pray that you have also discovered Truth, which ultimately leads to Joy, which in reality is God.

Bible Reading: *Psalm 32:1-7, Isaiah 55:6, 2 Corinthians 6:2b*
> According to *Psalm 32:1-7* what is the true road to blessedness (Joy)?
> How does that happen exactly? (verses 5-6)
> *Isaiah 55:6* has a sense of urgency. Why?
> *2 Corinthians 6:2b* gives the best time to make a decision. When is that?
> Describe a time that you have been "stabbed" by Joy.
> Can you see the longing for God behind these moments of Joy? Explain.

Challenge: Examine Joy in your own life.
> Seek the Source and never be without Joy!

> *"May the God of hope fill you with all joy and peace as you trust in him, so that you may overflow with hope by the power of the Holy Spirit."*
> > *Romans 15:13*

WEEK 50

"College daze"

I hate to admit it, but my first two years of college, academically, were pathetic. I floundered. Many of my friends were still in Vietnam or just returning, tired and changed. I had no idea if college was worth the effort let alone the money; and I was mid-struggle with those unanswered spiritual questions with little help in sight. I jumped at any excuse to skip a class. I dropped one very easy introductory math class because I didn't care for the professor. I told the professor that I was dropping (not that I didn't like her) but neglected to tell the main office and wound up failing a class that I hadn't attended (first "F" in my life). But still I didn't seem to care! My German professor called me in to his office at the end of my first semester and told me I should drop out of college. I was shocked. He showed me his grade book. I was getting a "C" in his class – the hard way. I had a line of "F's" followed intermittently by "A's." When I went in unprepared and failed a test, I would study for the next one and get an "A." Thus, the "C". He said I should come back when I was ready to take school seriously. He was right. And I wish I could say that that changed my habits, but it took three more semesters for me to stop messin' around and get serious.

I bought a motorcycle before my sophomore year and took it to school as often as possible over the next three years. It was an inexpensive ride. I used it often for the sheer thrill of it also. If that certain something in the air was callin' me, I'd take my bike on a mini-holiday through the Granville, Massachusetts' apple orchards' or the Ellington, Connecticut back road farms instead of going to class. I remember stopping near a motorcycle shop once when I

266

was in need of repairs and slowly realizing that a group of guys was lining up in the front window watching me attempt to fix my bike myself. The pressure was on. It turned out to be an easy repair and as I got back on my bike to leave I noticed money changing hands in the window. Really? But I have to admit that I was feeling a little bit cocky as I drove away. Truth be known – that may have been the only repair I would have been capable of pulling off.

I worked twenty to twenty-five hours a week as a waitress while attending college full-time, and thus managed to pay my tuition, put gas in my motorcycle, and buy a few other things. Fortunately jeans were all the rage, which made my limited wardrobe a non-issue. Connecticut winters could be snowy and icy, so I bought a '65 Mustang for the bad weather. Sometimes I'd skip class to play cards (no gambling) with a group of Jewish guys/friends at the branch. We discussed the Old Testament and surprised each other with our common knowledge and interests. I learned a lot from them. In a way that was more of an education than my classes … but that's just an excuse. I had some good and some not-so-good professors. One showed up to class less often than I did! Like so many others of that era, I had a lot of questions: What exactly was I doing, right now? What did I hope for in my future? and … WHY? Did any of it make sense?

I liked either to experience things personally if they weren't *too* dangerous, or at least observe them up closely to see if what I had been told about them was true. This was not always the smartest thing. I went to a couple of college parties to check them out, watching as everyone got drunk or high and made fools of themselves. They were pretty much as rumored and I wasn't impressed. I tried a cigarette, once – that's all it took. Nasty thing. I tasted (sipped) alcohol in a few different forms but that didn't help me to understand its appeal. Drugs were something I would never even have considered checking out first-hand. They were one of those things that had the ability to kill you the first time you even tried them; and the possibility of addiction (no matter how remote) was too chilling a thought to ignore. No, I didn't have to experience drugs to know they were bad news. There was enough evidence of that all around me in the 70's. I was headed down a specific path in a definite direction, but I was mostly unaware of it.

Have you ever felt that you had *no* direction in life?
> *... he must believe and not doubt, because he who doubts is like a wave of the sea, blown and tossed by the wind. James 1:6*
> *My sheep wandered all over the mountains and on every high hill. They were scattered over the whole earth, and no one searched or looked for them. Ezekiel 34:6*
> *Teach me your way, O Lord, and I will walk in your truth... Psalm 86:11a*

Have you ever had a hard time hearing the truth?
> *... you will be ever hearing but never understanding; you will be ever seeing but never perceiving. Matthew 13:14*
> *Hear this, you foolish and senseless people, who have eyes but do not see, who have ears but do not hear. Jeremiah 5:21*

Have you seen others make fools of themselves? Explain.

Have *you* ever lost control?

What did you do about it (either situation)?
> *... But if you do warn the wicked man to turn from his ways and he does not do so, he will die for his sin, but you will have saved yourself. Ezekiel 33:9*
> *Blessed is the man who listens to me, watching daily at my doors, waiting at my doorway. Proverbs 8:34*
> *He who listens to a life-giving rebuke will be at home among the wise. Proverbs 15:31*

The Bible is more than prepared to anticipate our questions. You may think it out of date and archaic, but times haven't really changed that much. I was rereading "Saint" Augustine's *Confessions*, written about 1500 years ago, and was amazed at how timely his stories were. (By the way, the Bible says that all believers are saints. See *Revelation 14:12*.) This saint from early Christianity could have been a classmate of mine or yours. And he made some heavy duty mistakes as a young man, as his confessions reveal. People tend to make more of their poor decisions when they're young, especially in college. The incredible thing is that no matter how foolish we have been, there is *absolute* for-giveness available.

After two years at the Hartford branch of UCONN, working in an upscale restaurant from about 11:30 am to 2:30 each day, with morning and late afternoon classes, I managed to finish two years of college (sort of). I transferred to the main campus and was introduced to the big time. I was ready to get serious about school. The 1.8 average my first semester (ouch!) had become a "2-point-something" by the end of my sophomore year, but by the end of my senior year it had actually become a 3.2. (The 4.0's at the end helped.) I *did* get my act together eventually. Good thing too because though I was at times able to get by while neither attending class nor reading the assignments as I should have, things became much more difficult as I entered my major courses.

I had started out majoring in foreign languages intending to go to school in Europe for a year or two and then to become an interpreter at the UN (Hey! This was *my* dream. Don't mock it!), but my plans changed for a very good reason and I switched majors to English and education with no plans for either Europe or New York. Within English my emphases were in Medieval Literature and Mystery. This is where I developed a taste for the Arthurian tales and Agatha Christie mysteries. I enjoyed both and had a good time with my student teaching – Mythology and Media classes at a junior high school near my home. My math major came several years later.

I had a couple of shocks when I transferred to the main campus in Storrs for my last two years – like the time I sat down with some new friends (musicians) to find that little packets of drugs and money were being passed around under the table. I tried to get out of the booth I was in, but found myself blocked in by a pretty serious looking guy who wanted me to stay. I chose to keep him happy. I finally managed to escape when a couple of my friends came into the commons from across the room. I quickly got up and joined them. I could have just imagined my mother's reaction if I had been arrested in a drug bust. Hopefully you've never gotten caught up in the drug scene. It's so not worth it. If you have, *get some help!* It's hard to fight an addiction alone. There are people in your life who can help. I thank the Lord for watching over me during these years.

The next shock came fulfilling a drama course requirement. We had to attend three of five dramatic options and write a critique on each. I needed one more and only one was left – a college play. I managed to get one of the best seats in the house, toward the front in the middle, even though I was late. I then discovered why. The student actors were as close to nude as possible, including bare breasts. Yikes! And I was a pretty modest person. Somehow I got through it as I slumped way down in my seat, but I will never forget how uncomfortable I was through the whole thing. When my drama professor later discussed the class critiques of this play, he quoted a line from mine that he had enjoyed: "I thought the 'costumes' lacked imagination." The class had a good laugh.

Do you think your world is much different from your parents'? How?

What has been will be again, what has been done will be done again; there is nothing new under the sun. Ecclesiastes 1:9

As it was in the days of Noah, so it will be at the coming of the Son of Man. For in the days before the flood, people were eating and drinking, marrying and giving in marriage, up to the day Noah entered the ark. Matthew 24:37-38

My college education was over and I had learned a great deal – though not all in class. I had grown up (a little) and was ready for the next phase of my life, ready for something new. I had straightened myself out for the last half of my college years, was doing well in my classes, and was ready for whatever God had for me next. Have you ever turned things around? Do you need to? Let's take a look at how King Josiah turned Judah around for the Lord:

Bible Reading: *2 Kings 22:8-20*

What did the workers discover as they began to restore the temple?

What was King Josiah's reaction to the reading of God's Word?
Why was God going to bring disaster on them?
Was Josiah spared? Why/why not?
Was the nation spared? Why/why not?
Are you more like Josiah or the nation of Israel?

Challenge: If you find yourself in a daze at some point in your life, get into God's Word and start praying overtime for God's help. (See *Psalm 25:4-5*)

> *"Then we will no longer be infants, tossed back and forth by the waves, and blown here and there by every wind of teaching and by the cunning and craftiness of men in their deceitful scheming."*
> *Ephesians 4:14*

WEEK 51

"A hitchhikers' guide to the university"

I had never hitchhiked in my life and never imagined I would. But here I was stranded and it was getting late. A friend of mine was supposed to give me a ride home from a summer course I was taking at a college about 40 minutes from my home, but he had forgotten and had gone home. This was not the time of cell phones and easy access to communication. I used a pay phone to make a few calls but found no one home. I ran out of options. What could I do? It was still light out – which somehow made this all a bit less scary – so I decided that it might be okay to hitch a ride home just this once. What could go wrong just this once?

I started to examine potential candidates and was quite selective. The trucks seemed a bit intimidating so I avoided those. A nice little car would be my choice. I checked them out as they came toward me. I finally put out my thumb and a car stopped. Well, that was easy. But they were not headed my way. I had to try again. Another car stopped and offered to take me quite near my town. I jumped in without realizing that the back seat was occupied. There were two men in the front seat and one in the back. Could it get any worse? I started praying. It seems these men were professional picketers and were on their way to picket outside a business in the town next to mine. Professional picketers were not especially known for murder or mayhem against innocent girls, right? So far, so good, … I hoped.

As we neared *their* destination, they offered to take me all the way home. This did not seem like a good idea since I lived in a pretty remote spot and no one was home. I declined, but they remained adamant ... and they were in the driver's seat. Hmmm. Then, I believe God actually intervened. Ahead of us was my cousin's truck headed home. I asked them to beep and get him to pull over and they did. And he did. Thank You, Lord! I thanked them, jumped out of their car and ran over to my cousin's truck. He was surprised to see me and I quickly got in with him. All the way home I listened to his lecture on the dangers of hitchhiking. Funny thing is that I had actually just experienced all of those same dangers in my imagination and truly did not need a lecture for it to have struck home. He was "preaching to the choir." I would never be hitchhiking again.

Have you ever hitchhiked? Explain.
Were you at all scared? (I hope so.)
What does the Bible have to say about hitchhiking (or similar activities)?
He who trusts in himself is a fool, but he who walks in wisdom is kept safe. Proverbs 28:26
Pride goes before destruction, and a haughty spirit before a fall. Proverbs 16:18

The hitchhiking was, as you might have guessed from the verses above, just the tip of a large iceberg. I was trusting in myself, that I could handle whatever came along. Nothing bad had ever happened to me in my adventures. I was too smart to be a victim. We can be so arrogant in our decisions and in our confidence in our own wisdom and indestructibility. And sadly, there are more and more people out there who have few or no morals and would take advantage of others if it suited them. It's a broken world. And we do so many foolish things – at least I did. I'd like to think that I would do a better job now in thinking things through. But it is ultimately God's grace that brings us through every time and we don't even see His hand in it or stop to thank Him. If we were aware of all of His intercessions on our behalf I think we would be shocked. I thank God over and over for the protection He has continually given to me and for the protection He gives to my children. God has a host of angels looking out for us. Very little of my safety through the years was due to anything I did. God loved me *in spite of me* all along. I don't know how people can have any peace of mind without Him.

The Bible assures us of abundant help from God:
See that you do not look down on one of these little ones. For I tell you that their angels in heaven always see the face of my Father in heaven. Matthew 18:10
For He will command His angels concerning you to guard you in all your ways… Psalm 91:11

When we are young we tend to think that we are invincible, that nothing will ever go too terribly wrong. Though that may be the case so far, it isn't always true. Many tragedies happen to teenagers and young adults. But that is no reason to be fearful because God has "not given us the spirit of fear, but of power and of love, and of a sound mind." (*2 Timothy 1:7*, KJV) We are not to walk around in fear, but we are to tap into the power of the Holy Spirit through prayer, to do everything in love, and to use our heads (the "sound mind" part). Hitchhiking was a stupid thing to do and I regret it to this day.

God's angels are pretty cool and they really are here to help. They are "messengers of God" who bring news from God to the Old Testament heroes like Abraham (*Genesis 18*) and Daniel (*Daniel 10*), and to key figures in the New Testament like Joseph and Mary (*Luke 1:26-28*), Paul (*Acts 12:7*), and others. They guide us (*Exodus 14:19*). They go to war for God and for us (*Revelation 12:7-9, 20:1-2*). They watch over us and minister to us. (*Daniel 6:22a, Psalm 91:11*). They claim no honor for themselves (*Revelation 22:9*). Thank God for His angelic influence in our lives.

I have heard stories of missionaries who were miraculously saved when attackers saw an army of angels surrounding their compound, individuals who have been helped by a mysterious person who seemed to just appear and then disappear immediately afterward, conversations of people near death with angels, and so much more. Just before she died a dear woman in my

274

church described the scene she saw at heaven's gate – complete with angels and loved ones. (See *Acts 7:55.*)

I was leading a Bible study on the topic of heaven a while back. I had three unexpected women show up. All three of their young husbands had recently died. These women wanted to know all they could about heaven to help them to deal with their grief. I used several Christian books, besides the Bible, to try to give them all the insight that I could find. One of my favorites about angels was by Billy Graham and entitled simply: *Angels.* Randy Alcorn's book, *Heaven,* was helpful. And though I did not use it, he highly recommended Joni Eareckson Tada's book *Heaven ,Your Real Home* which he says is totally based on Scripture. *90 Minutes in Heaven* by Don Piper was a first-hand account in line with Scripture, that unlike others of this type, seemed plausible. We don't always know the extent of filler included to make a story like this readable, so a little skepticism is always in order. Bottom line? Because the Bible is the ultimate authority and it speaks often of heaven and of angels, we can be sure that heaven is a real place and that angels do exist and interact with us. However, anything that contradicts the Bible's clear teaching on angels or heaven should be disregarded. For instance: There is no Scripture to suggest that upon death, humans become angels. (as in the popular old Christmas movie, *It's a Wonderful Life!*) They are two separate creations. Both exist into eternity.

Have you ever felt that angels were protecting you? Explain.
We have several facts above about angels, but what do you know about heaven? Discuss.
Are you sure what you believe agrees with the Bible? Find verses to back you up.

Hitchhiking is like playing Russian Roulette where you take a chance on life or death by the spin of a gun's cylinder. Getting into the car of a stranger is putting your trust in them. Reality is that it could go either way, good or bad. It all boils down to the same basic idea. Our trust should be in Christ alone. When we focus on other gods like power, popularity, success, science, wealth, alcohol, drugs, the occult, relationships, or our own inde-structibility, we are putting something in the place of God – either ourselves or something else. It is a sin as old as time here on earth. "You will be like God." (*Genesis 3:5*) *But nothing is like God!* God is above all. He is omnipotent (all-powerful), omni-scient (all-knowing) and omni-present (everywhere present). And He loves us enough to send His Son to die in our place! What a blessing to know this God intimately.

Hezekiah was in a tough spot with the mighty Assyrian army who had invaded the land and were in command of most of the Middle East. They were now about to invade Jerusalem. In *2 Kings 18*, the commander of the incredible Assyrian forces threatens the people of God with complete annihilation and tells them that they are foolish to trust in the God of Israel. King Hezekiah sends his court officials to consult the prophet Isaiah. The response is encouraging, but after several more threats Hezekiah goes to the temple to pray to God. His humble prayer reaches the ear of God.

Bible Reading: *2 Kings 18:19b-25, 19:1-7, 14- 20, 32-36*
    What does the Assyrian king suggest in chapter18:19b-25?
    What does King Hezekiah do in chapter 19:1-7, 14-20?
    How does Isaiah encourage him?
    Did the King of Assyria have any power against God?
    How did the angel of God help in this situation (19:32-36)?
    If just one angel could do all this, what do we have to fear?

Challenge: Look for the work of angels in your own life. If you remember how "lucky" you once were, could it have been an angel?

"For he will command his angels concerning you to guard you in all your ways."
Psalm 91:11

WEEK 52

"You have chosen... wisely"

had changed majors suddenly at the start of my junior year of college. Why? *My* plans (let's call them, "Plan A") involved a degree in at least one foreign language, studying abroad, working at the UN as a translator, and possibly looking around for a husband when I was twenty-eight years old. *God's* plan brought the right guy into my life the summer between my sophomore and junior years of college. He was four years older than me, had already completed his bachelor's degree, and was halfway through his master's, with two years of army under his belt. He was very cute, smart, athletic, and even had a little savings account (huh? What's that?). It took me about eight seconds to decide to switch to "Plan B." I had never actually formulated a "Plan B," but that only took another eight seconds to come up with. I was smitten. Who would have guessed this could happen to me? I couldn't see this incredible guy waiting 5-10 years while I "discovered myself." I decided I was "discovered" enough and that he was well worth the change in plans. (He was ... and we made short work of that savings account.)

There was this party one evening down the road from my home at a friend's house. I usually stopped by at these briefly, but I wasn't all that comfortable in crowds, so I rarely stayed. I showed up late on my motorcycle to check it out, not expecting anything other than the usual. There he was – tall, tan and blonde, just home from the army driving a brand new '69 GTO convertible, baby blue, just like his eyes. (Yes, this is still me talking.) He was the hostess' cousin from New Jersey. I had seen him when I was younger but he had been too old for me then and I hadn't yet discovered the true magic of the opposite sex. He had also shown up at a couple of my trio's concerts in New Jersey two or three years earlier with a couple of his friends. A bunch of us had gone out for ice cream together. Since then it seemed that one of us had always been dating someone else or was at least rumored to be. At the time, I had been led to understand that he was practically engaged to a girl who had visited him in Germany where he had recently been stationed in the army. He wasn't, and we left together on my motorcycle.

I didn't want to embarrass him in front of everyone standing outside his cousin's house by suggesting he get on the back of my motorcycle, so I let him drive. This was a mistake. After we nearly hit a raccoon and wound up spilling the bike, we went to my sister's house to clean up before my mother saw me. It's amazing how superficial scrapes can bleed. Shakespeare's Lady Macbeth comes to mind from an excerpt I once had to act out in an English class: "Who would have thought the old man to have had so much blood in him?" There was blood everywhere. I have a scar on my knee to this day. I tease my husband that he branded me that night. We will *never* forget our first date.

Have you ever changed major plans in a big way? Why?
> *"Come, follow me," Jesus said ... At once they left their nets and followed him. Matthew 4:20*
> *God had planned something better for us ... Hebrews 11:40*

Would you have given up your plans for Europe and a career, for a guy?

Do you think God had anything to do with our first date? Explain.

Do you think He had anything to do with *any* of my stories?
> *"For I know the plans I have for you," declares the Lord, "plans to prosper you and not to harm you, plans to give you hope and a future." Jeremiah 29:11*
> *When you pass through the waters, I will be with you; they will not sweep over you. When you walk through the fire, you will not be burned; the flames will not set you ablaze. Isaiah 43:2*
> *Have I not commanded you? Be strong and courageous. Do not be terrified; do not be discouraged, for the Lord your God will be with you wherever you go. Joshua 1:9*

I'm not sure what to think of my life as I look back at it. I know I was blessed to be born into a Christian family with a heritage of faith over many generations. I was very fortunate to have the support of a great church and youth group, along with a big and loving extended family. I guess I had my share of tragedy along the way, but nothing God and I couldn't handle together … mostly God. God gave me certain talents and gifts that I wasted at times, but that I also used for Him. I was probably way too careless with the life He gave me as I drove too fast and put myself into harm's way again and again, but He lovingly brought me through it in spite of my foolishness. I was sometimes a pest and less than a stellar Christian. I wonder how people put up with me at times. In spite of that, I got to live out some of my wildest dreams as I toured the country singing. And fortunately, I was smart enough to set aside my dreams for God's when in wisdom I chose "Plan B." I'm not sure what kind of reputation I left behind me, probably a bit inconsistent and puzzling, and perhaps slightly too adventurous, but hopefully assuredly Christian in the final analysis. I do know that I always, *always*, loved the Lord and knew that God, my Father, would be the One I could look to (even if everyone else failed me) for the peace, joy, and love that He promised me in His Word. I saw glimpses of Him at times in the "enormous bliss" felt when unexpectedly "brushing up against Him" through the miracles of His creation.

When we met, my husband and I were both Christians who had asked God to direct us in our lives. We certainly weren't super-Christians with some special connection to God's ear, but we were doing our best to follow His lead in our lives. I honestly do believe that the Lord brought us together; not only that, but that He was with me through the joy and the sorrow all through my life. Remember what John Bradford, the Christian reformer, said? "There, but for the grace of God, go I." In other words, I was blessed to be born into my family and to make it through the weeks in my life relatively unscathed. Many people are not as fortunate. It is only by the grace of God that I am writing this today. But, you see, I've gotten smarter and smarter over the years as I've gotten older. I've learned to turn to God's wisdom rather than my own for direction in life. He is after all the First Cause of all the wonders that we see in our universe, and He is the One Source of all true Joy. Joy is simply a sign on the trail pointing to Him.

Have you gotten any smarter over the years? How?
Have you seen God's hand in your life? Explain.

As I think back on my life to date, one of my greatest pleasures has been climbing trees. "One could do worse." As a child I was apt to be found at the top of the tallest trees. I quickly discovered the best climbing trees in my world and made friends with them. I treasure the memories of the climb itself; the comfy niche for the lengthy visit that only the best trees afforded; and the painfully sweet solitude, the whispering breeze that had so many stories to tell, and the silent peek into the mystical world of the deer and other woodland creatures that would otherwise have been lost to me if I had visited in a more intrusive way. My eyes fill with tears as I remember those days. I watched my children enjoy the same pleasures that trees afford, and now wait expectantly to see my grandchildren do the same. The top of a tree is the very best place to find God and to seek His wisdom. I have learned so many lessons climbing trees! Robert Frost has a couple of great poems about trees that have always inspired me:

BIRCHES *(an excerpt)*
...
So was I once myself a swinger of birches.
And so I dream of going back to be.
It's when I'm weary of considerations,
And life is too much like a pathless wood
...
I'd like to go by climbing a birch tree,
And climb black branches up a snow-white trunk
Toward heaven, till the tree could bear no more,
But dipped its top and set me down again.
That would be good both going and coming back.
One could do worse than be a swinger of birches.

"You have chosen... wisely"

Is life ever like a "pathless wood" to you? God has the answer.

STOPPING BY WOODS ON A SNOWY EVENING

Whose woods these are I think I know
His house is in the village though;
He will not see me stopping here
To watch his woods fill up with snow.

My little horse must think it queer
To stop without a farmhouse near
Between the woods and frozen lake
The darkest evening of the year.

He gives his harness bells a shake
To ask if there is some mistake.
The only other sound's the sweep
Of easy wind and downy flake.

The woods are lovely, dark and deep.
But I have promises to keep,
And miles to go before I sleep.
And miles to go before I sleep.

How often I have quoted those last lines to my children over the years. We long to stay in those special times of Joy and we try to hold on to them like waves on the beach, but God calls us back to the task He has set before us. It is through quietness and trust in our Father's wisdom that we hear His will for our lives and obey. Even Jesus withdrew to pray and be alone with God.

"Your beauty should ... be that of your inner self, the unfading beauty of a gentle and quiet spirit, which is of great worth in God's sight."
I Peter 3:3-4
"... in quietness and in trust is your strength." Isaiah 30:15b
"but Jesus often withdrew to lonely places to pray." Luke 5:16

Bible Reading: *Galatians 5:16-26*
What are we to live by according to this epistle?
What two things are in conflict with each other?
Have you seen evidence of that in your own life? Explain.

What are the acts of the sinful nature?

What are the fruits of the Spirit?

Why do you think that last verse is in there?

Challenge: Set aside a regular quiet time with God to just listen.

"If any of you lacks wisdom, he should ask God, who gives generously to all without finding fault, and it will be given to him. But when he asks, he must believe and not doubt, because he who doubts is like a wave of the sea, blown and tossed about by the wind."
James 1:5-6

May God bless you with His wisdom and Joy in your life. ... that means you won't be tryin' most of the stuff I tried in my life that I've told you about in this book. Right? Right?

About the author

S haron Hansen was born and raised in Northwestern Connecticut. She graduated in 1969 from Hillcrest Lutheran Academy in Fergus Falls, Minnesota and received a BA in 1973 from the University of Connecticut (UCONN) with a degree in English and Education. She later earned certification in Mathematics at Westfield University in Massachusetts and taught in several high schools over the course of thirty years.

As a teenager she made three records with a Christian trio (the Harmonettes) and sang and toured with this group throughout the United States and Canada on and off for over three years including two long summer tours. She continued to sing in several other groups and individually throughout her life to date. She was for years the director of worship in her church in northwestern Connecticut.

For several years Sharon was involved with the youth board for the Eastern district of the CLBA (Church of the Lutheran Brethren of America). For twenty-three years she counseled and then directed a youth camp in Pennsylvania for nearly 500 teens and staff. She worked with some of the top national youth speakers in the country, and was encouraged by the teenage girls with whom she shared many of these stories to "write a book." She is still on the board of directors for the Tuscarora Inn and Conference Center, in Mount Bethel, PA.

Her greatest joy is the Lord. Her greatest accomplishment is her marriage to her husband, Art; and their three daughters, Debra, Kristina, and Beth, and their families. In 1986, together with her husband and a small group of other Christians, Art and Sharon had the privilege of helping to start Praise Christian Fellowship, a church in the northwest hills of Connecticut. She presently attends Bethany Lutheran Church in East Hartland, CT.

Here are three of the
only pictures of me
under the age of ten!

cousins

sisters

classmates

My trio (left and right)
and best friends (below)

friends

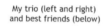

"Plan B" ! ☺

more on "Plan B" later...

285

CPSIA information can be obtained
at www.ICGtesting.com
Printed in the USA
FSHW021538161019

9 781545 672532